THE FORMATION
OF THE
CHRISTIAN
BIBLICAL CANON

THE FORMATION OF THE CHRISTIAN BIBLICAL CANON

Lee Martin McDonald

ABINGDON PRESS / NASHVILLE

THE FORMATION OF THE CHRISTIAN BIBLICAL CANON

Copyright © 1988 by Abingdon Press

This book is printed on acid-free paper.

Library of Congress Cataloging-in-Publication Data

McDonald, Lee Martin, 1942-
    The formation of the Christian biblical canon / Lee Martin
McDonald.
        p.   cm.
    Bibliography: p.
    Includes index.
    ISBN 0-687-13293-2 (pbk. : alk. paper)
    1. Bible—Canon.   I. Title.
BS465.M38   1988
220.1'2—dc19   88-14666
                                                                                    CIP

MANUFACTURED BY THE PARTHENON PRESS AT
NASHVILLE, TENNESSEE, UNITED STATES OF AMERICA

To Mary

Servant of Christ
Faithful Friend
Loving Wife
Mother of My Four Delightful Children

CONTENTS

The Bible of the Christians' religious tradition includes two books, the Old Testament and the New Testament. The first of these two books has always been a substantial part of the Christian scriptural authority. However, the exact definition of the writings that should be a part of the Old Testament canon never played a decisive role in the discussions about the Christian canon of Holy Scripture and its authority. While the so-called "Old Testament Apocrypha" are an undisputed part of the canon of the Greek church and a smaller corpus of apocryphal writings is included in the Bible of the Roman Catholic church, most Protestant churches have ascribed authority only to a smaller Old Testament canon, corresponding to the Hebrew Bible, from which the Apocrypha are excluded. But these differences are rarely considered to be divisive.

In contrast, the question of the exact extent of the New Testament canon has often been hotly debated among Christians. In recent decades, this issue has taken on new dimensions through the discovery of an increasing number of ancient Christian gospels, epistles, and books of revelation under apostolic names such as Peter, Thomas, Philip, and even Mary. At the same time, critical scholarship has questioned the "apostolic" authorship of writings of the New Testament canon itself. Matthew and John may not be the authors of the Gospels transmitted under their names, the apostle Paul was not the author of all letters of the Pauline corpus, and both Epistles of Peter were probably written half a century after Peter's death. Should we, therefore, revise the canon of the New Testament? Should we exclude the Second Epistle of Peter? Should we include the newly discovered *Gospel of Thomas?*

It is understandable that many Christians are disturbed by critical questions regarding the authority of writings of the New Testament canon, while others are excited about the discovery of new and hitherto unknown gospels, which claim to have been written by apostles. But what is happening to canonical authority, when there are apostolic writings outside of the canon and when the apostolic authorship of writings of the New Testament is questioned? The New Testament no longer seems to be the one and only collection of inspired writings from the hands of genuine apostles and disciples of Jesus. Its authority as Holy Scripture appears to be seriously questioned.

If there is an answer to this question, it will not come through abstract theological controversy but only through a reconsideration of the history that once created the canon of the New Testament. What did the Christians who established the canon mean when they spoke of "scripture," "inspiration," "tradition," and "apostolic authorship"? Why were these twenty-seven writings included and others excluded? How did these writings function in nourishing and building Christian communities, and why were other writings found lacking? What were the competing forces in the formation of the early Christian churches, and what roles did various writings claiming "apostolicity" play in these controversies?

Early Christianity appears to have been much less united and much more diversified than we have thought. The writings of the New Testament were not necessarily the only early Christian apostolic witnesses. Rather, from the beginning they had to compete with other books, produced by other followers of Jesus who were later considered to be heretics. The collection of the twenty-seven writings now comprising the New Testament canon was a long and arduous process, extending over many centuries. In order to understand this process, several generations of scholars have done most of the groundwork, have investigated the Greek and Latin sources from early Christian times, have tested, approved, and rejected various hypotheses, and have thus come to a much better understanding of the process. The literature on this topic is immense, often very technical and learned, and not always easily understood. But it is also very exciting, and it has opened up a much better understanding of the story of the formation of the canon. Holy books do not fall from heaven; rather, they are created in the historical experiences of religious communities. Scholars have learned much about this in an intense international debate.

But this story must also be told so that everyone can be informed by a better understanding of the developments that took place in the early centuries of the Christian communities. It is an exciting and enriching story, filled with the experiences and thoughts of Christian believers from the time of the apostles to the consolidation of the church three centuries later. The story must be told in terms easily comprehended by every reader, the interested layperson as well as the student in a theological school. The story must be told in such a way that everyone in the divided Christian churches of our day may share it and learn from it, evangelical Christians as well as those of a more liberal persuasion. The story must be told without apology and without zeal so that all may enter into the discourse with the history that created the foundations through which all Christians belong to the one Church universal and are bound to the same God whose word and witness are preserved in the book we call the New Testament.

I have spent countless hours with the author of this book, and I have been deeply impressed by his scholarship, his learning, his faith, and his commitment to Christian education. This book, the result of many years of research, has accomplished what few have ever achieved: telling a difficult story well. There are no shortcuts, no facile solutions, no easy reconciliations of problems. All the materials are there. All the relevant texts are quoted and interpreted. Everyone is treated fairly and judiciously. All scholarly hypotheses are presented and discussed. All that is required of the reader is the same fairness and the same patience that are evident in the author's effort of presenting both the ancient sources and the modern scholarly debate.

Helmut Koester

John H. Morrison Professor of New Testament Studies
and Winn Professor of Ecclesiastical History
Harvard University, The Divinity School

March 1988

PREFACE

Interest in the formation of the Christian biblical canon of scriptures* has been growing over the last few years. Whatever the causes, several important new questions have been raised about the normative status of the scriptures of both the Old and the New Testaments. Numerous articles, essays, and books on this subject have appeared in the last few years, which are challenging many of the traditional views about the biblical canon. Likewise, the growing interest in ancient nonbiblical religious literature, both "orthodox" and "heretical," has led many scholars to raise some very perplexing questions about what is referred to as "canonical criteria"—that is, the factors that led the Church to recognize the biblical literature and no other as sacred and authoritative. How do we know that these biblical books and no others are inspired and authoritative for the Church? What were the criteria that the early Church used to distinguish its sacred literature from the other ancient Christian literature? Why did it take the Church so long (centuries in fact) to recognize its canon of normative scriptures? Finally, why are a growing number of scholars asking whether the notion of a biblical canon is in fact Christian?

Although I will address these and other questions in the following study, my primary concern in this book is to provide a helpful guide to the origins of the Christian biblical canon for students, pastors, and informed laypersons who want to explore the often elusive historical processes of how we got our Bible.

Many of the standard introductions to OT and NT literature offer but a few pages of information on the origin of the Christian biblical canon and frequently only repeat older and no longer tenable positions. On the other hand, some authors refer their readers to some of the more technical works on the subject, such as Hans von Campenhausen's masterful, but highly technical (and consequently often neglected), opus on the canon. That work and a few others like it were written especially for the advanced scholar, and, unfortunately, not many students will take the time to work through it. For that reason, I have sought to provide a more readable and not too technical historical guide to the origins of the biblical canon as well as offer some understanding of the major issues involved in canonical research today. Although a number of Greek and Latin words are found in this book, all of them have been translated for the reader, using at times my own translations but most often some of the better known standard translations with a few of my own "modernizations" of those texts. Most of the canonical studies with which I am familiar have either presented ancient material in the original languages (which has great merit for critical scholarship, but not for most students in college or seminary) or worse, have only listed references to it in footnotes, which most readers would not have access to unless they were close to a theological library. As one who has taught for several years, I know the struggles professors have in trying to motivate their students to look up ancient references even when such resources are available in libraries! With that in mind, I have tended to add more of these primary sources in the body of the text so that the reader can see some of the context in which the more popular quotations are found. I have often been frustrated by writers who have included in their work only one or two lines of a crucial ancient text, a practice that allows the passage to be understood in more than one way. The sometimes lengthy quotations given here will, I hope, prove more helpful than burdensome to the reader. Also, numerous notes are provided throughout the book, especially for the reader who is interested in a more critical perspective and/or in knowing the sources that have informed my conclusions.

The book begins with a brief look at the recent focus on "canon criticism" and the problem of the Bible as canon. The essential study of the origins of the biblical canon, however, begins in chapter 2 with an understanding of the notion of "scripture" and its place in a religious community. It becomes clear that though there is an important overlap in meaning, one must distinguish between the notion of "scripture" and that of "canon." From there the focus is on the emergence of the notion of scripture and canon as they relate to both the OT and the NT.

A look at the table of contents will quickly show that the OT does not receive equal treatment with the NT in the discussions. This is certainly not because the development of the OT canon is easier to understand or that there is less controversy with it, but because many of the issues and arguments related to the study of the NT canon are equally applicable to the OT. I should also hasten to add that I am less knowledgeable in the OT than in the NT, and it is best that I do not extend myself further than the scope of my competence. In terms of the purpose of this study—to provide a readable text for students who wish to examine the formation of the Christian biblical canon—the chapter on the OT canon, though brief, has been added for the sake of completeness and is, therefore, more general both in detail and in scope. It is hoped, however, that it will offer important information, which will help the student's understanding of how we arrived at our present Christian OT canon of scriptures.

It is unfortunate that the recent publication of Bruce M. Metzger's significant new work *The Canon of the New Testament: Its Origins, Development, and Significance* (Oxford: The Clarendon Press, 1987) arrived in the States only as I was about to send the final form of this manuscript to Abingdon Press. Although I have made several references to Metzger's work, I did not have adequate time to review it completely. I have noticed that several of our conclusions are different, but I am impressed with the wealth of information as well as the helpful approach to the NT canon provided by Metzger.

This book is in part the product of a long theological pilgrimage that began years ago in a fairly narrow conservative context. Many individuals have been pivotal in the transitions of my pilgrimage, and it is only fitting that a few of their names be mentioned here. I have learned significantly from each of them, not only in the classroom but also by the way each has tried in his own way to make faith and thought both compatible and, indeed, complimentary. None of them is alike either in personality or in theological persuasion, but all have played important roles in my personal development and in the theological stance I have taken in the following pages. Each has been for me a gifted professor and a friend in my time of need. They include James Rosscup, whose biblical scholarship has always been beautifully combined with his love for Christ, his humility, and a strong dedication to Christian service. The late George Eldon Ladd, whose sometimes painfully honest inquiry into biblical literature was paralleled by his challenging his students to be prophetic witnesses in the Church, was the most instrumental person in challenging me to pursue my interest in theological education and in showing me that it was indeed a ministry. Hugh Anderson, my "doctor father," shared with me an invaluable historical-critical perspective as well as a genuine sense of responsible Christian mission and charity toward those who differ in theological stance. Douglas A. Templeton graciously offered many of his insightful observations about history, faith, and the resurrection as well as generous amounts of his time not only as my tutor but also as my friend. Finally, I must mention Helmut Koester, whose example of dedicated scholarship, as well as his love for the Church and its students of theology, is one from which I have personally profited greatly. His prophetic-like concern for truth both in his classes and in his writings has been a most significant challenge to me, and his many kindnesses both during and after my studies at Harvard have been especially meaningful. I am deeply grateful to God for all of these individuals, and I offer my heartfelt thanks for their time, patience, understanding, and guidance extended to me in my theological pilgrimage.

In terms of this book, I owe special thanks again to Professor Helmut Koester of the Harvard Divinity School for his guidance and encouragement throughout the various stages of my research on the biblical canon. There is no adequate way to express to him my sincere appreciation for all of his help. I would also like to offer my gratitude for the late Professor George MacRae, also of the Harvard Divinity School, for his many insightful suggestions, relevant observations that I had overlooked, and words of encouragement regarding the publication of this book. He and Helmut Koester were the original readers of my thesis on the canon, out of which this book has developed. Brian Daley of the Weston School of Theology was also encouraging to me in the initial stages of my research on this project and offered a number of helpful suggestions and corrections, which I have tried to incorporate.

I would be remiss if I did not mention several other persons by name who have given me their encouragement and practical help in bringing this manuscript to publication. My long time friend Craig Evans, whose many calls and letters of encouragement kept me from leaving this book in manuscript form on the top of a shelf, has drawn to my attention some important concerns that I have tried to address in the manuscript. My thanks are also in order to James A. Sanders, who not only expressed his pleasure with this work but also graciously took time out of a busy trip to the Graduate Theological Union at Berkeley to discuss with me the Christian biblical canon. He brought to my attention a number of significant essays and articles on the canon that I had overlooked, and I have sincerely appreciated his advice. In terms of practical help and astute observations, I must also mention Dr. Rex Matthews of Abingdon Press, whose numerous suggestions have not only improved the quality of this book but have also saved me some embarrassment! He has been most helpful and encouraging. Charles Hotchkiss, a computer engineer, a good friend, and a faithful member of the church I pastor was the first to introduce me to the world of computers and donated his valuable time putting this manuscript on the computer, which has made its revising infinitely easier. He also found a number of mistakes and inconsistencies. His was a labor of love for which I am deeply grateful. Finally, I want to say how much I have appreciated the invaluable typing and editorial assistance of my wife, Mary, whose love, patience, and understanding have been constant throughout the years of our marriage. Without her ministry in *word and deed* this book could not have been written. She has been an outstanding companion and source of strength during my career, and it is to her that this book is affectionately dedicated.

I approach the publication of my first book in the spirit and equal fear of Rufinus (ca. 401–404 C.E.) who introduced his *Expositio Symboli* with the words, "I am neither much inclined nor am I well-equipped for writing . . . for I know well the danger of exposing my poor talents to the criticisms of the many." The following study is offered, however, in the hope that it will add to our understanding not only of the origins of the Bible but also of the authority and role of the scriptures in the Church. At the very least, I sincerely hope that this book will promote an honest inquiry into how the Church got its Bible and what the implications of that inquiry might be for the Church today.

---

*The terms *scripture* and *scriptures* are put in the lower case throughout the book, not because of an attempt to depreciate the value of *the* "Scriptures," but because for the most part in this study, the notion of scripture is being discussed, not the Holy Scriptures themselves.

L I S T   O F
ABBREVIATIONS

ABBREVIATIONS OF ANCIENT LITERATURE

Ac. Pet.	The Acts of Peter and the Twelve Apostles
Adv. Apion	Josephus, *Adversus Apionem* (Against Apion)
Adv. Haer.	Irenaeus, *Adversus Haereses* (Against Heresies)
Adv. Marc.	Tertullian, *Adversus Marcionem* (Against Marcion)
Adv. Prax.	Tertullian, *Adversus Praxean* (Against Praxeas)
Apoc. Pet.	Apocalypse of Peter
Apoc. Mos.	Apocalypse of Moses
Ap. Jas.	Apocryphon of James
Ap. John	Apocryphon of John
I Apol.	Justin Martyr, I Apology
I Clem.	First Letter of Clement
II Clem.	Second Letter of Clement
De Prin.	Origen, *De Principiis* (On First Principles)
Did.	*Didache* (The Teaching of the Twelve Apostles)
Ep. Arist.	Epistle of Aristeas
Ep. Barn.	Epistle of Barnabas
Elench.	*Elenchus*
Gos. Eg.	Gospel of the Egyptians
Gos. Thom.	The Gospel of Thomas
Gos. Truth	Gospel of Truth

Herm.	The Shepherd of Hermas
Man.	Mandate
Sim.	*Similitude*
Vis.	*Vision*
Hist eccl.	Eusebius, *Historia Ecclesia* (Ecclesiastical History)
Phld.	Ignatius, *Letter to the Philadelphians*
Pol. Ep.	Polycarp, Letter to the Ephesians
Pol. Phil.	Polycarp, Letter to the Philippians
Praescript.	Tertullian, *De praescriptione* (The Prescriptions Against Heretics)
Strom.	Clement of Alexandria, *Stromata*, or *Miscellanies*
Trypho	Justin Martyr, Dialogue with Trypho

ABBREVIATIONS OF OLD TESTAMENT APOCRYPHAL LITERATURE

I Esd.	I Esdras
II Esd.	II Esdras
Tob.	Tobit
Jth.	Judith
Rest of Esther	Rest of Esther
Wisd. of Sol.	Wisdom of Solomon
Bar.	Baruch
Ep. Jer.	Epistle of Jeremiah
Ecclus.	Ecclesiasticus (or Ben Sirach)
Song of Three Children	Song of the Three Holy Children
Sus.	Susanna
Bel and Dragon	Bel and the Dragon
Pr. of Man.	Prayer of Manasseh
I Macc.	I Maccabees

ABBREVIATIONS OF OLD TESTAMENT PSEUDEPIGRAPHICAL LITERATURE

As. Mos.	The Assumption of Moses
I Enoch	The First Letter of Enoch
III–IV Macc.	III and IV Maccabees
T. 12 Patr.	Testament of Twelve Patriarchs

ABBREVIATIONS OF CLASSICAL AND RESOURCE MATERIALS

ANE	*A New Eusebius*
ANF	*The Ante-Nicene Fathers*
BB	*Background Books*
BJRL	*Bulletin of John Rylands Library*
BTB	*Biblical Theology Bulletin*
CBQ	*Catholic Biblical Quarterly*
CHB	*The Cambridge History of the Bible*
CTM	*Concordia Theological Monthly*
ECF	*Early Christian Fathers*
ET	*Expository Times*
GBS	*Guides to Biblical Studies*
HBT	*Horizons in Biblical Theology*
HTR	*Harvard Theological Review*
HTS	*Harvard Theological Studies*
IB	*Interpreter's Bible*
IDB	*Interpreter's Dictionary of the Bible*
IDBSup	*Supplementary Volume to IDB*
Int	*Interpretation*
JBC	*The Jerome Biblical Commentary*
JBR	*Journal of Bible and Religion*
LCL	*Loeb Classical Library*
NHLE	*Nag Hammadi Library in English*
NHS	*Nag Hammadi Studies*
NPNF	*Nicene and Post-Nicene Fathers*
OAA	*Oxford Annotated Apocrypha*, RSV edition
QR	*Quarterly Review*
SECT	*Sources of Early Christian Thought*
SJT	*Scottish Journal of Theology*
SR	*Studies in Religion*
StEv	*Studia Evangelica*
TDNT	*Theological Dictionary of the New Testament*
TSC	*The Second Century*
USQR	*Union Seminary Quarterly Review*
WDB	*Westminster Dictionary of the Bible*

OTHER ABBREVIATIONS

B.C.E.	Before the Common Era (before NT times)
ca.	around, approximately

C.E.   In the Common Era (in NT times and later)
D   Codex Claromontanus
LXX   Septuagint
MF   Muratorian Fragment
NT   New Testament
OT   Old Testament

FREQUENTLY USED SHORT TITLES

Aland, *Canon*	Aland, Kurt. *The Problem of the New Testament Canon* Oxford: A. R. Mowbray & Co., 1962.
Barr, *Scripture*	Barr, James. *Holy Scripture: Canon, Authority, Criticism* Philadelphia: Westminster Press, 1983.
Beckwith, *OT Canon*,	Beckwith, Roger T. *The Old Testament Canon of the New Testament Church* Grand Rapids: Wm. B. Eerdmans Co., 1985.
Brown, "Canonicity"	Brown, Raymond E. "Canonicity." In *JBC*. Englewood Cliffs: Prentice-Hall, 1968.
von Campenhausen, *Formation*	Von Campenhausen, Hans. *The Formation of the Christian Bible*. Translated by J. A. Baker. Philadelphia: Fortress Press, 1972.
Charles, *Apoc./Pseud.*	Charles, R. H., ed., *The Apocrypha and Pseudepigrapha of the Old Testament*. (Oxford: Clarendon Press, 1913).
Childs, *NT as Canon*	Childs, Brevard S. *The New Testament as Canon: An Introduction*. Philadelphia: Fortress Press, 1984.
Childs, *OT Theology*	Childs, Brevard S. *Old Testament Theology in a Canonical Context*. Philadelphia: Fortress Press, 1986.
Collins, *Introduction*	Collins, Raymond F. *Introduction to the New Testament*. Garden City, N.Y.: Doubleday & Company, Inc., 1983.
Dunn, *Unity*	Dunn, James D. G. *Unity and Diversity in the New Testament*. Philadelphia: Westminster Press, 1977.
Farmer, "NT Canon"	Farmer, William F. "A Study of the Development of the New Testament Canon." In *The For-*

	mation of the New Testament Canon. Edited by Harold W. Attridge. New York: Paulist Press, 1983.
Frend, *Rise*	Frend, W. H. C. *The Rise of Christianity.* Philadelphia: Fortress Press, 1984.
Gamble, *NT Canon*	Gamble, Harry Y. *The New Testament Canon: Its Making and Meaning* (GBS). Philadelphia: Fortress Press, 1985.
Georgi, *Opponents*	Georgi, Dieter. *The Opponents of Paul in Second Corinthians* Philadelphia: Fortress Press, 1986.
Grant, *Apost Fath*	Grant, Robert M. *The Apostolic Fathers: A New Translation and Commentary* (6 vols.; New York: Nelson, 1964–68).
Grant, *Formation*	Grant, Robert M. *The Formation of the New Testament* New York: Harper & Row, 1965.
Hennecke, *NT Apo*	Hennecke, Edgar. *New Testament Apocrypha.* Edited by Wilhelm Schneemelcher and translated by R. McL. Wilson, 2 vols. Philadelphia: Westminster Press, 1963–65.
Jurgens, *FEF*	Jurgens, W. A. *The Faith of the Early Fathers.* Collegeville: The Liturgical Press, 1979.
Kelly, *Doctrines*	Kelly, J. N. D. *Early Christian Doctrines.* New York: Harper, 1978.
Kelsey, *Uses*	Kelsey, David H. *The Uses of Scripture in Recent Theology.* Philadelphia: Fortress Press, 1975.
Koester, *Introduction*	Koester, Helmut. *Introduction to the New Testament.* 2 vols. Philadelphia: Fortress Press, 1982.
Koester, *Synoptische*	Koester, Helmut. *Synoptische Überlieferung bei den apostolischen Vätern.* Berlin: Akademie Verlag, 1957.
Kümmel, *Introduction*	Kümmel, Werner George, ed. *Introduction to the New Testament.* Translated by A. J. Mattill, Jr. New York: Abingdon Press, 1966.
Lasor, *et. al., OT Survey*	LaSor, William Sanfor, Hubbard, David Allen and Bush, Frederic William. *Old Testament Survey.* Grand Rapids: Wm. B. Eerdmans Co., 1983.
Layton, *Gnostic Scriptures*	Layton, Bentley. *The Gnostic Scriptures.* Garden City, N.Y.: Doubleday & Company, 1987.
Leaney, *Jewish and*	Leaney, A. R. C. *The Jewish and Christian*

Chr World	*World.* Cambridge, England: Cambridge University Press, 1984.
Metzger, "Canon"	Metzger, Bruce M. "Canon of the New Testament." In *Dictionary of the Bible.* Edited by James Hastings. Edinburgh: T. & T. Clark, 1963.
Metzger, *Canon*	Metzger, Bruce M. *The Canon of the New Testament: Its Origin, Development, and Significance.* Oxford: Clarendon Press, 1987.
Patterson, "Irenaeus"	Patterson, L. G. "Irenaeus and the Valentinians: The Emergence of a Christian Scripture." Unpublished article obtained from the author.
Perkins, *Dialogue*	Perkins, Pheme. *The Gnostic Dialogue.* New York: Paulist Press, 1980.
Richardson, *ECF*	Richardson, Cyril C. *Early Christian Fathers.* New York: Macmillan, 1970.
Sanders, *Self-Definition*	Sanders, E. P., ed. *Jewish and Christian Self-Definition.* Philadelphia: Fortress Press, 1980.
Sanders, *Canon*	Sanders, James A. *Canon and Community: A Guide to Canonical Criticism* (GBS). Philadelphia: Fortress Press, 1984.
Sanders, *Sacred Story*	Sanders, James A. *From Sacred Story to Sacred Text.* Philadelphia: Fortress Press, 1987.
Shires, *Finding*	Shires, Henry M. *Finding the Old Testament in the New.* Philadelphia: Westminster Press, 1974.
Stevenson, *ANE*	Stevenson, J., ed. *A New Eusebius.* London: SPCK, 1980.
Sundberg, *OT Early Ch*	Sundberg, A. C. *The Old Testament of the Early Church.* Cambridge, Mass.: Harvard University Press, 1964.
Theron, *Evidence*	Theron, Daniel J. *Evidence of Tradition.* Grand Rapids: Baker Book House, 1980.

THE BIBLE AS CANON

If our faith . . . is such that it is destroyed by force of argument,
then let it be destroyed; for it will have been proved that we
do not possess the truth. (Clement of Alexandria,
Stromata 6.10.80, *ANF*)

I. The Bible as Sacred Scripture

Because of its background in Judaism, the early Christian Church was accustomed to recognizing the authority of written documents as scripture—that is, the Christians believed that the revelation and will of God were located in a deposit of written materials that served both the cultic and moral needs of the community of faith. The notion of authority residing in what was later called the OT scriptures[1] was never doubted in the earliest Christian community, even though the normative status of the Law was held in question by many Christians. The example of Judaism in recognizing its own divinely inspired (and therefore authoritative) writings later became a model for the Church to recognize some of its own

27

literature as authoritative (prophetic and inspired) for faith and conduct, especially since it later became clear to many Christians that parts of the Old Testament—its legal codes and rites—were no longer relevant to their developing communities. The specific factors that led to this recognition, however, are somewhat obscure due to the lack of clear historical references that make the transitions from written text to scripture more understandable.

One traditional view holds that the early Church simply recognized (it did not decide) its own inspired NT scriptures and that this literature was believed by the Church at that time to be *apostolic* (either written by or "authorized" by an apostle), *early* (all of it was written in the first century), *unified* in its teaching about the gospel, and finally that it was *recognized* as such by the majority of the churches as being inspired by God. In regard to the OT, the traditional view holds that Jesus, the Church's final authority, cited or referred to a closed canon of Hebrew scriptures and that his authentication of them was the Church's mandate for accepting them as authoritative scripture; the Church simply adopted the canon of Jesus.

This traditional view has slowly eroded over the years largely as a result of the appearance of several important studies on the formation of the canon, especially those of Adolf von Harnack, Robert M. Grant, Hans von Campenhausen, A. C. Sundberg, and more recently James Barr. Their efforts have caused many biblical scholars to look again at the historical data related to the formation of the *Christian* biblical canon. Until recently, most (not all) introductions to both the OT and the NT allowed only a few pages of their research to be given over to this discussion, but more recent studies have given more serious attention to the major questions involved in canonical research, and by doing so have stimulated further research. Of course, not all of the more recent works on the formation of the biblical canon are of equal value. Some of them offer few advances and appear to repeat previously unjustified claims.[2]

II. Which Biblical Text Is Canon?

A relatively new approach to the biblical literature has been launched chiefly through the writings of James A. Sanders and

Brevard S. Childs. Their focus on "canonical criticism" has developed into an important new approach to the biblical literature and attempts to recover the Bible for Church use once again. Their approach asks, in part, which form of the biblical literature is authoritative for the Church today. Should the Church accept as its inspired and authoritative literature the earliest form of the writing, or the later, redacted form, which we presently possess? In other words, *is the Church's authoritative text the earliest form of a document or the final redacted form of it, which was passed on and developed in the Church?* Sanders asks the difficult question of whether it is the author or the biblical documents that we recognize as canonical and inspired.[3] Both he and Childs focus on the latter, but in clearly differing ways. Sanders emphasizes that the Bible is a product of history, and he examines how it functions as *canon*—that is as an authoritative book—in the life of the Church.

Brevard Childs,[4] though often with different conclusions from those of Sanders, also raises the question of whether it is not the final received (and redacted) text of scripture which is the proper authoritative text for the Church rather than its earliest form (without the redactor's additions) which the supposed author penned.[5] He stresses that "it is a basic tenet of the canonical approach that one reflects theologically on the text as it has been received and shaped."[6] It is precisely here, however, that a lot of confusion arises from Childs' work.

What is the value of the original *context* as well as the original *text* of scripture (so far as it can be determined) for the church today? Although Childs contends that his canonical approach is not opposed to historical criticism, it is difficult to see in his treatment of Matthew, John, Romans, or the Pastoral Epistles, for example, that he values its contributions to biblical studies. Childs clarifies his reservations about historical criticism when he unambiguously claims that his approach to the biblical text is threatened by the attempts of the critical scholars to "historicize the New Testament material by assuming that the sharper the historical focus, the better the interpretation."[7] Childs is correct in saying that the aim of both historical and textual criticism has been to arrive at the earliest form of a given text, assuming that that form is the authoritative text for the Church. His rejection of that aim, however, is most puzzling, since the very community that he believes gave us the canonical form of the text of the NT we use today—the second to the sixth centuries C.E., when most of the changes in the text occurred—is the same community of faith that strove to reach back to the apostolic community of faith of the first century to find its authoritative base. If anything can be termed an assured "find" of the patristic period, it must be the early Church's attempt to be apostolic in its understanding of Christian faith.

Indeed, books were rejected from the list of canonical NT literature (or the "received" list of NT documents, as Childs refers to them) precisely because they were not deemed apostolic. Tertullian even placed a lesser value on the Gospels of Mark and Luke because they were not apostolic.[8] Irenaeus before him is well known for his appeal to apostolic succession through the church's bishops as the means of securing the precise ecclesiastical tradition that formed the basis of the earliest church's faith.[9] From the very beginning of the Church, the appeal to apostolic authority—the earliest witnesses to the Christ event(s)—as the basis for a favorable hearing in the Church is evident. For example, what else is the basis for Paul's claim in I Corinthians and Galatians 1:1, 12 if not his apostleship, which came from the Lord? Does he not claim that his personal encounter with the Risen Lord is the basis of his authority to preach and of his right to be heard in the churches? What is the basis for the selection of Matthias to replace Judas Iscariot in Acts 1:21-26 if not Matthias' claim to be one of the earliest witnesses to the events that formed the basis for early Christian preaching? Even the much later Muratorian Fragment denies equal authority to the Shepherd of Hermas precisely because it was not considered to have been written in the earliest apostolic period.[10] It must also be noted that the gnostic Christian communities, who were the first to attribute apostolic authorship to their gospels (the Gospel of Thomas, for example, is the first to have an apostolic name attributed to it), were aware of the value of appealing to the earliest witnesses to the Christian faith to substantiate their positions. For the earliest churches, certainly, the author was considered to be the one who made the text authoritative, not a nameless later figure without close ties to the original events the document describes. What does the patristic church's focus on the apostolic origin of a document mean if it did not reveal a serious attempt by the Christian communities of the second through the sixth centuries to establish Christian faith on the earliest witnesses to the events and proclamation of their faith?

Childs does not face the question of why modern exegetes should ignore the earliest form of a text if they can with some assurance arrive at it. Clearly, the Christian communities of the patristic era did not accept themselves as the *canonical community*, but instead sought to build their faith on what was believed to have been tradition and writings from the earliest Christian community. Since the appeal to such witnesses was made by the very community that handed us our "received text,"[11] why should the Church not be interested in pursuing the earliest and most authentic (apostolic) witness to the Christ event, especially if we can come closer to it today than the churches of the fourth and fifth centuries did? In regard to that historical quest, Ernest Best rightly raises the question of whether the earliest Christian community, if it had had our modern expertise in determining date, authorship and setting, would have made other choices about the NT canon.[12]

With reference to the OT, for example, Childs opts for the final canonical form of Second Isaiah, which is placed by its final redactor in the eighth century B.C.E. as the Church's normative text, rather than its actual historical setting in the sixth century B.C.E.[13] This writer would counter, however, that it is precisely when the sixth century setting of Isaiah 40–55 is understood and made clear to the congregation that the text of Second Isaiah is most meaningful and relevant to today's community of faith. As a pastor who has taught the book of Isaiah in its "received" form and then later expressed its message in its original historical context (Second Isaiah from the sixth century B.C.E.), I would contend that the congregation has understood and appreciated Isaiah's message much more than before.[14] The same can be said with regard to the Pastoral Epistles, which when compared to the genuine Pauline epistles are clearly different in focus from what we have learned to expect from Paul. If it can be explained to the congregation that Paul did not write these books in their present form, even though they may contain some genuine reflections of the end of Paul's career, then the student or astute layperson will not be so confused by the seeming contradictions between the Pastorals and Paul's writings, especially in terms of eschatology, pneumatology, church organizational structure, and even vocabulary. Once it is shown that Paul did not write this literature, does it necessarily mean that the documents have no meaning for the church today? By no means! Clearly this literature shows how the second-century Church also considered itself inspired by the same Holy Spirit as did the followers of Jesus in the first century, and they struggled to meet the theological challenges of their day with the same determination and sense of the presence of God as did those Christians of the first century.

Peter Ackroyd suggests that a balance is needed in seeking an authoritative text of scripture.[15] He claims that the original text may not be possible to find, and the search for it may become unproductive, but the acceptance of the "finally agreed 'canonical' form" is also unacceptable. He contends that authority lies between the text and the reader and between the text and the expositor.[16] On the other hand, to ignore the original text when it may be possible to recover it in favor of a final ill-defined "received" text comes dangerously close to making Christianity less than a historical religion by removing it from its historical moorings. It comes close to favoring the *imagined* Christ, born out of the later Christian community, instead of the *historical* Christ—that is, the Christ of the earliest Christian community[17]—which the Church did its best to pass along to subsequent communities of faith. Christian faith, as is true of biblical criticism, is always interested in the primal history of the texts that help define the Church's faith as well as the earliest traditions about the events of Jesus' life. That has always been and must always continue to be the Church's guideline in its research of the biblical text.

Childs' view that canon consciousness "arose at the inception of the Christian Church and lies deep within the New Testament literature itself is also problematic" (*NT as Canon*, p. 21). If "canon consciousness" means that the Church was interested in shaping its written sources into authoritative documents to be used as scriptures or as other authoritative documents, it is difficult to find "canon consciousness" at an early date in the history of the Church at all. If "canon consciousness" means an authoritative guide in the Church, then it is true that from the very beginning the Church's canon consisted of the words and deeds of Jesus as well as the Church's acceptance of the authority of the still loosely defined OT scriptures. It is difficult otherwise to find canon consciousness related to a collection of Christian writings before the end of the second century, and then only in a most primitive stage. Also, there does not appear to be any concern about a closed collection of OT inspired literature in the earliest church either.

I am in sympathy with Brevard Childs' apparent attempt to provide a new methodology that will do justice to the significant new historical-critical finds of the post-Enlightenment age, and at the same time return to the Church the practical use of its Bible as canon, providing for us "a true and faithful vehicle for understanding the will of God" (*NT as Canon*, p. 37). However, I am not impressed with how well this vision has been realized in his own work. He is more convinced than I am that the fourth-century Church (evidently the Church he believes gave us our received text) was infallible in its decision as to what Christian literature was inspired and canonical. One could only guess why he does not accept the OT canon adopted by the earliest Christians (if it was a canonical community) who often appealed to the Deutero-canonical (Apocryphal) and Pseudepigraphal literature. At what point(s) do we accept the majority opinions of the ancient Church as normative for the Church today, especially if some of those opinions (as will be argued later) were based on faulty information? Further, if one does choose to accept these conclusions about the form of the text we have received, why not accept also the goal of trying to be as apostolic as possible, especially if we can be even closer to the witnesses of the earliest Christian community?

Childs' "descriptive task" is especially difficult to follow because he seems to presuppose the precise "canonical intentionality"[18] of the ancient Christian Church, which he sets out to establish. His aim of adopting the so called "received text" is a difficult if not impossible matter to demonstrate—as chapter 7, on canonical criteria, will show—but Childs does not make it clear just what that "received text" might be.

Many of the questions growing out of Childs' work will not be dealt with in the rest of this book, though many of the issues raised by Sanders on the development of the biblical literature as canon (or as an authoritative guide) for the Church will be studied in more

detail. The following study, however, will focus more on the historical development of the Christian Bible as well as some of the concerns the early Christian community faced as it defined the
parameters of its sacred literature. A few reflections at the conclusion of this study will address the significance of these matters for
the Church today. Before moving into the study, however, we should
be reminded that any examination of the origins of the Christian
biblical canon is loaded with problems from the beginning, due to
the scanty amount of information available, which also is often of
an inferential nature. For example, do the many patristic citations
of the NT literature necessarily mean that it was viewed as scripture? Or, again, is there any evidence that the early Church of the
first two centuries was significantly concerned about a canon of
scripture? What criteria were used by the Church to distinguish its
authoritative literature from other literature of the same era? Were
they the same criteria for all churches of the same period? We will
focus on these and other important matters related to the formation
of the Christian biblical canon, but the reader should be advised
that simple clear-cut answers to such questions are seldom possible.
Although the recognition and definition of the parameters of the
Church's scriptures was one of the most important developments in
the ancient Church, the Church has not left us any clear indicators
of how that process took place. As Metzger has remarked, "Nothing
is more amazing in the annals of the Christian Church than the
absense of detailed accounts of so significant a process."[19] Although
there are few brightly lit corridors leading to an understanding of
how the Church got its Bible, it is hoped that the following discussion will bring some light to what is often a complex and poorly
understood field of study.

SCRIPTURE AND CANON

I. The Notion of Scripture

For both Judaism and Christianity the final authority for faith is, of course, God. In the latter stages of Old Testament Judaism, the belief arose that the revelation and will of God were disclosed not only in mighty acts through which Yahweh invaded history—for example, the Exodus—but also in written materials. In the Pentateuch, the writing down of something was an important mark of revelation (Exod. 24:12; 31:8; 32:15, 32; 34:1; Deut. 4:13; 8:10; and so on). Just as Moses wrote down the commandments of the Lord in Exodus 24:4 and 34:27, so also do Joshua in Joshua 24:26 and Samuel in I Samuel 10:25. In the book of Deuteronomy, which was probably written toward the end of the OT times, the king is called upon to write down for himself a copy of the Law of God to read all the days of his life to remind himself of the statutes of God and to be humble in his dealings with his people (17:18-20). The people also were called upon to write the words of God on their doorposts (6:9; 11:20). In contrast, the Gospels of the New Testament do not indicate that Jesus wrote anything down or that he commanded others to write anything down. The only NT exception is found in the book of Revelation, where Jesus commanded the angels of the churches to *write* down his message (Rev. 2:1–1:14).[1]

Interestingly, however, as James Barr has observed, in the OT, "the writers do not reckon with a written 'scripture' as a totally dominant, known and acknowledged factor and force in the life of Israel."[2] He goes on to argue that even the prophets who say "thus says the Lord" are not speaking on the basis of an already existing text. Almost nothing in the OT before the time of Josiah suggests that there were sacred scriptures to turn to when guidance was needed.[3] Neither David, Solomon, nor Hezekiah had any focus or emphasis on any books that were normative in the life of Israel. Rather, as Barr has pointed out, the OT individuals related to God more through persons (priests, prophets) and institutions (tabernacle, temple).[4]

At what point was the religion of Israel governed by or built upon the Law? It was probably not much before the reforms of Josiah, but certainly no later than the reforms of Ezra (Neh. 8:1-8; 9:1-3). The Deuteronomic movement in Israel in the eighth to the seventh centuries B.C.E. no doubt had a major role in effecting that change. (See, for example, the admonition to obey the commandments of Yahweh and not to add to them or take away from them [Deut. 4:2].) At any rate, when that which was written down in Israel was later translated and explained to the people as having normative value in the life of their community (Neh. 8:8-11), the notion of scripture was clearly present in Judaism.

The belief in Judaism that the revelation and will of God had been preserved in written documents was also held in the earliest Christian community. The early Church, by and large, believed that God had acted decisively in the life, death, and resurrection of Jesus and that this revelation had also been foretold in the normative literature of Judaism—the Old Testament scriptures. It also held that the proclamation of and about Jesus was passed on faithfully through the oral tradition of the Church, much of which was written down and later (ca. 170 C.E.) also became recognized as normative literature in the churches; the New Testament writings began to function as sacred scripture. The recognition of the New Testament writings as scripture can only be described as a growing process, which was not unanimously or simultaneously acknowledged in the ancient churches. The Christian books that eventually received this normative status were not the same for all the churches, and even when there was agreement, the recognition of the authority of the literature was not acknowledged at the same time by all churches. This much can be seen in the differences in the "lists" of early Christian literature recommended or tabulated for church use in the fourth century and later.[5] Just how soon the *recognition* of the inspiration and authority of the New Testament literature—that is, the recognition of its *scriptural* status—took place is not possible to date with any precision, but it seems certain that with one possible exception no part of that body of literature was so recognized in the first century. Only the book of Revelation (ca. 90–95) claims such a lofty position that would come close to the notion of inspiration and scripture (Rev. 1:3, 10-11; 22:7-9, 18-19; Deut. 4:2). Indeed, Krister Stendahl has observed that this is the only book in the NT that claims to be a revelation from God.[6] Along with that, the author of II Peter 3:15-16 (written ca. 120–150 C.E. and possibly as late as 180 C.E.) apparently recognized Paul's letters as "scripture." However, nowhere does Paul or any other author of the NT claim this special recognition for his own writings. Even the Gospels, which tell the story of Jesus, do not in themselves claim final authority. Such divine authority appears to be reserved finally for Jesus Christ alone (Matt. 28:19-20), even though the many OT citations and allusions in the Gospels are evidence of their authoritative status in the early Christian communities. Although Paul was mindful that he was communicating the authoritative words of Jesus on occasion (I Cor. 7:10-11; 9:14; 11:23 ff.), he apparently was unaware of the divinely inspired status of his own advice (I Cor. 7:12, 25). He never wrote as if he himself were setting forth scripture, even though he did acknowledge the superior authority of the words of Jesus in settling matters of Christian ethics and of his own apostolic authority in resolving disputes in the churches he founded (I Cor. 4:14–5:5; 7:12-24; II Cor. 13:10, and so on). This is so in spite of the fact that Paul is the first New Testament writer to make a qualified claim to being inspired by the spirit in regard to what he himself has said. Paul concludes his advice on marriage relations with the words: "And I think that I have the Spirit of God" (I Cor. 7:40 RSV).

What makes it difficult to believe that the Gospels were viewed as scripture from the first is the liberty the evangelists took in changing their sources. Matthew and Luke took great liberty in using, changing, and smoothing out the Gospel of Mark[7] as well as a "Q" source,[8] which each made use of in his own way. At any rate, the kind of warning given in the Revelation 22:18-19 was certainly not heeded in reference to Mark. Also, as late as the last half of the second century, Tatian, who had a special interest in the Gospels and who was evidently concerned with the differences among them, showed a profound willingness to change them in order to set forth a unified gospel called the *Diatessaron*. Would he have taken such liberties with the Gospels if he had considered them to be sacred scripture? L. G. Patterson contends that even at the end of the second century Christian writings generally were not yet called "covenant" and in general not yet called "scriptures" either.[9] Although written Christian materials were in existence almost from the beginning of the Church,[10] there did not seem to be any early interest on the part of the Church in writing new scriptures. Von Campenhausen is right when he claims that early Christianity was not a "religion of the Book," but rather "the religion of the Spirit and the living Christ."[11] The Church had an oral tradition concerning Jesus that was taught and proclaimed in the early communities of faith (Acts 2:42; 4:33; 6:4) along with the scriptures of Judaism (the OT),[12] which they searched diligently in order to find witness (prophetic announcement) to the event of Jesus that they had experienced.[13]

The basic properties of "scriptures," both for ancient Judaism and Christianity, appear to have included at least four essential ingredients. According to Farley, scripture was: "(1) a written collection, (2) of divine origin (from Yahweh), (3) communicating his will and truth to his covenant people, (4) to function as an enduring source of regulations for the corporate and individual life of the people."[14]

Bentley Layton suggests that when a particular writing was recognized by a group of Christians as containing the presence of inspired authority, it was elevated to the status of scripture.[15] He correctly observes the limited agreement in the early Church at large on such matters, however, and finds only sporadic affirmation of Christian documents in the first three centuries. He defines *scripture* as a body of written religious literature that members of a religious group consider authoritative in matters such as belief, conduct, rhetoric, or the running of practical affairs. (See *Gnostic Scriptures*, p. 18.) Layton's understanding of the term *canon* is not clear, however, and he seems to suggest the presence of several early collections of closed canons of Christian literature before the year 200 C.E.[16] As will be argued throughout this book, I have not found such scripture canons prevalent in the church at that time.

The above descriptions of "scripture" are, however, only a part of an overall understanding of the matter for the early Church. An early Christian view of scripture, unlike that of Judaism, was also *eschatalogical* at its core—that is, there was the belief that the scriptures had their primary fulfillment in Jesus (see, for example, Matt. 2:5, 17, 23; 3:3; 4:14; Mark 14:49; 15:28; Luke 4:21; Acts 1:16; John 17:12; 19:24, 28). Although Paul adds that this fulfillment is also found in the Christian community (see, Rom. 4:23; 15:4; 16:26; I Cor. 9:10; 10:11), still Jesus the Christ was considered the primary norm for the understanding and use of the OT scriptures by the early Church (see especially II Cor. 3:12-16). However, the Church still held that the OT scriptures themselves were of unimpeachable authority (John 10:35; Matt. 5:18). Schrenk notes that for primitive Christianity, scripture is "the authoritative declaration of the divine will," but that it was "not valid apart from the 'I say unto you,'" of Jesus—that is, its christological fulfillment.[17] It is interesting to note in passing that the author of Acts (writing probably ca. 90–100 C.E.) relates that the community life of the early Church was focused on "the apostles' teaching" and *not* on the OT scriptures. None of its daily activities appears to have involved such a study (Acts 2:46-47). Although the book of Acts is sprinkled throughout with OT references, which were texts for preaching about Jesus (for example, 2:17-21, 25-28, 34, 35; 4:25-26; 8:32-33, *passim*), one does not find any particular devotion to OT study emphasized or commanded in most of the NT such as is found in the much later post-Pauline text of II Timothy 2:15.

Although there is no question that the OT scriptures (the limits of which in the time of Jesus were not yet precisely defined) were viewed as authoritative in the early Christian churches (for example, Matt. 21:42; 22:29; 26:56; Luke 24:32, 44; John 5:39; I Cor. 15:3-4), the matter of when the NT literature began to be given the same status as the OT writings in the ancient churches is difficult to determine and will be the primary subject of discussion in chapter 4. However, it can be said in advance that when the early churches began to place Christian writings alongside the Old Testament scriptures as authoritative documents for the Church, as some of the examples in chapter 4 appear to show, the transition to their recognition as sacred scripture had begun.

II. The Notion of Canon

The meaning of "canon" is not equal to that of "scripture," even though there is some overlap in definition. The Greek χανών is derived from χάνη, a loan word from the Semitic קָנֶה, which means "measuring rod" or "measuring stick." By a process that will not be dealt with in detail here, the word came to mean among the Greeks that which is a standard or norm by which all things are judged or evaluated, whether the perfect form to follow in architecture or the infallible criterion (χριτήριον) by which things are to be measured.[18] The term was used in several areas with a similar meaning. It was a concept found in sculpture and architecture as the perfect frame to be copied as well as in music where the monochord was the canon by which all other tonal relationships were controlled. The term was also used in regard to grammar by the Alexandrians, who set forth a canon of writers whose Greek was used as a model. It was even employed in philosophy as the criterion, or canon, by which one discovers what is true and false. Beyer has shown that Epicurus himself argued that logic and method in thought stem from a canon (χανών) or basis by which one could know what was true or false and what was worth investigating or not. (See Beyer, pp. 596-98). This is not unlike the way scriptures were understood and employed in both Jewish and Christian communities of faith.

The ancient world was filled with canons (guides, models, regulations) for almost every sphere of activity. The Roman grammarians by 25 B.C.E., for example, were following not only the model of Virgil's *The Aeneid* in their writing, but also the models of Cicero and Sallust. These Latin grammarians, in the tradition of the Greeks, deemed it very important to follow certain models in their writing and, according to Suetonius, they were also actively involved in training the rhetoricians of the day in the best principles of grammar. The importance of strict adherence to these rules of grammar can be illustrated with three examples from Suetonius' *Lives of Illustrious Men*. One writer by the name of Marcus Pompilius Andronicus was more interested in his Epicurean sect than in giving special attention to matters of grammar in his writing. The result of the grammatical criticisms of his work forced him to leave Rome. Suetonius writes:

> Marcus Pompilius Andronicus, a native of Syria . . . was considered somewhat indolent in his work as a grammarian and not qualified to conduct a school. Therefore, realizing that he was held in less esteem at Rome, not only than Antonius Gnipho, but than others of even less ability, he moved to Cumae, where he led a quiet life and wrote many books. (*The Lives of Illustrious Men: On Grammarians*, VIII, *LCL*.)

Similarly, one of the worst insults of the day was to be accused of ignorance of proper grammar. In the story of Lenaeus' response to Sallust's criticism of Pompey, Lenaeus, the freedman of Pompey, criticized Sallust with biting satire and several debasing adjectives. He concluded with a final salvo, claiming that Sallust "was besides an ignorant pilferer of the language of the ancients" (Suetonius, *Lives*, XV, *LCL*).

The high authority attributed to the canons of grammar around the time of the birth of Christ can be seen in the well-known account of Marcellus' attack on the grammar of leading Roman officials, including that of the Tiberius Caesar himself!

> Marcus Pomponius Marcellus, a most pedantic critic of the Latin language, in one of his cases (for he sometimes acted as an advocate) was so persistent in criticizing an error in diction made by his opponent, that Cassius Severus appealed to the judges and asked for a postponement, to enable his client to employ a grammarian in his stead: "For," said he, "he thinks that the contest with his opponent will not be on points of law, but of diction." When this same Marcellus had criticized a word in one of Tiberius's speeches, and Ateius Capito declared that it was good Latin, or if not, that it would surely

be so from that time on, Marcellus answered: "Capito lies; for you, Caesar, can confer citizenship upon men, but not upon a word." (Suetonius, *Lives* XXII, *LCL*)

In the Roman world the works of Virgil especially were considered a canon or model to be followed in various forms of writing. Even Tacitus, perhaps "the most individualistic and most psychological of ancient historians,"[19] who wrote between 78–115 C.E., was still guided by the model of Virgil's *The Aeneid* as well as by Cicero and Sallust.

Among the Greeks, Plato especially, and later also Aristotle, were the canons for philosophers. The Egyptians much earlier had canons of art by which the artisans were guided in their craft. The *cartouche*, for example, an almost rectangular closed circle with the Pharaoh's name written in hieroglyphics inside, is uniform in almost all paintings and statuary of the ancient dynasties of Egypt. In a recent tour of the Egyptian Museum in Cairo, I discovered numerous canons of art dating from the time of the Old Kingdom (ca. 2700–2060 B.C.E.) and the Middle Kingdom (2060–1580 B.C.E.). Some of these common patterns included the uniform shapes of the human figures, the color of the skin (women were almost always given a lighter skin than men), the arms crossed over the chest to indicate a person's death, and the foot extended forward with the hands at the side, indicating that the person being portrayed was still alive at the time of the object's creation. Again, one constantly finds the symbols of the cobra and/or of the falcon god, Horus (a deity later associated with kingship), on the headdress of the kings or within the design of the art objects related to kingship. It appears that only in the New Kingdom in Egypt (1580 B.C.E. and following) was there a loosening of some of the more rigid patterns of art, which allowed for more realistic depictions of the actual torsos of the Pharaohs.

⊦Law, regulations, and patterns (canons) were commonplace in the ancient world long before the time that both Jews and Christians began to take interest in closed canons (precise patterns) of scriptures. The question that requires further exploration is whether and to what extent these and other cultural influences had any conscious or unconscious effect on the decisions of Jews and Christians in the common era, leading them to establish canons of sacred scriptures.[20]

At the end of the first century C.E., Clement of Rome called the Corinthians away from strife to the "glorious and venerable *rule* (κανόνα) of our tradition" (I Clem. 7:2).[21] As will be shown later, Irenaeus used the term in reference to the rule of faith that governed orthodox Christianity at the end of the second century in Rome. In the late second century, Clement of Alexandria spoke of the *rule* (κανών) of faith that was the *truth* of the Church, even though he did not apply the term specifically to the biblical literature.[22] From around the middle of the fourth century of the common era and onward, κανών was also increasingly used in reference to the collection of sacred writings of both the OT and NT.[23] The first writer known with certainty to have used the term in reference to Christian writings is Athanasius in his *Festal Letter* of C.E. 367.[24] Amphilochius (ca. 394 C.E.), provides us with the second clear use of the term in reference to a body of sacred literature.

With such a delay in the Church's using the term *canon* to describe a closed body of Christian scriptures, one can only ask why there was such an emergence of "canon consciousness" in the fourth century and not before. The answer may, in part, lie with a better understanding of the socio-historical conditions present in the fourth century C.E. Again, we must ask about the extent to which the Hellenistic understanding of the notion of canon influenced the Christian and Jewish communities in their establishment of closed biblical canons. To what extent was the Hellenistic idea of following that which is a perfect guide taken over into the religious thought of Judaism, Christianity, and later of Islam (the three major ancient religions with a canon of sacred scriptures)? It may well be that in the historical climate of the developing Church the many interactions with "heretical" teachings and other factors (chapter 5) led the Church to propose a standard by which it could define authentic Christianity. This was done at first by the "rule of faith," which appears to have embodied the oral tradition about Jesus, but eventually also by the rule of certain writings.

This proposal of a standard eventually led to the formation of a closed canon of authoritative writings (scriptures) that, as A. C. Sundberg has argued, was unique in the Christian Church since it had not received a closed canon of scriptures from Judaism.[25] There appear to have been no rigid guidelines on what could or could not be regarded as Christian scripture, though apostolicity and tradition (long use in the churches) were certainly prominent features.[26] The Church, then, inherited from Judaism the notion of sacred scripture, but not a closed canon of scriptures, which, as will be argued in chapter 5, was a much later development. According to Sundberg, there were three stages in the history of the development of New Testament canon: (1) the rise of the New Testament writings to the status of scripture; (2) the conscious groupings of such literature into closed collections—for example, the four gospels and the epistles of Paul; and (3) the formation of a closed list of authoritative literature.[27] In some of the early discussions of the Christian writings—in Origen and Eusebius—a threefold classification of literature was made, indicating at least a category between authoritative and heretical for literature that was deemed profitable for teaching but not considered normative in the Church. According to Eusebius, Origen's three categories were: (1) ὁμολογούμενα, meaning those writings recognized by all; (2) ψευδῆ or νόθα, referring to those writings that were forged by heretics; and (3) ἀμφιβαλλόμενα or ἀντιλεγομένα, referring to writings whose apostolic origins are doubtful.[28] Eusebius, who probably invented this classification that he attributes to Origen, also adopted it for himself, though not precisely the same terms, to express a similar classification of ancient literature.[29] That final grouping of both Origen and Eusebius—the questionable category—gradually fell away in the church, and the ancient literature became either canonical or apocryphal.

Before moving on to a discussion of the recognition of the OT as canon, some observations by James Sanders about the nature of the biblical canon should be noted. Sanders emphasizes two essential characteristics of canon: *adaptability* and *survivability*.[30] He claims that a key factor in a document's becoming canonical in a particular community was its ability to be adapted to the historical circumstances and life setting, or *Sitz im Leben*, of the people and also its ability both to survive and to give life to that community. In regard to Israel, Sanders contends that what was first canonical was not a document or writing, but a story that gave Israel its identity and also gave the nation life. Written documents as canon came later in the canonical process, but still functioned in the same way in the community (see *Sacred Story*, pp. 18-19). What that story was for Israel, he says, had two primary themes—Moses and David—and only those two themes survived. Sanders claims that throughout the history of the Israelites in the OT little focus was put on a written word, but much on a story that gave Israel its identity and that was adaptable to the Israelites historical situation, giving them life as a people.

In trying to explain why the northern tribes lost their identity and the southern ones maintained theirs, even during deportation, he shows that the answer does not lie with either their Temple (which was destroyed in 587 B.C.E.) or with their cult (which was interrupted), but with a story that alone was an indestructible element in the society as well as a commonly available, highly adaptable, and, when necessary, portable element.

What Sanders says of the OT people of God has several close parallels in the early Christian community. It was clearly not the OT or the NT literature that gave the church its identity, but a story about a person, Jesus the Christ. This was true well before the writings of the NT either came into existence or came to be accepted as scripture. The story of Jesus gave identity to his followers. Later, as in the case of the OT literature, that story became stabilized in a written text and was received by a community that clarified its identity by that literature.

Sanders makes another point about the stabilization of that story in the OT period in written form between the time of the Persian domination of Israel until near the end of the first century C.E. He contends that during this time the written text was in a state of relative textual fluidity marked by two distinct ideas about the Word. These included "the idea of the living Word of God ever dynamically new and fresh, and the idea of traditions that were becoming stabilized into certain forms but were generation after generation in need of being adapted to and heard afresh in new historical contexts" (*Sacred Story*, p. 140). He cites examples of how scribal changes of the sacred text actually continued until the end of that period and were dramatically reduced after that time. He also links this cessation of alterations of the text to the development of the notion of the demise of prophecy in Israel and the emergence of the notion of verbal inspiration (see *Sacred Story*, p. 140). There is evidence for Sanders' argument in the NT itself, in which the NT writers quote or cite the OT text with great freedom, sometimes even changing or adapting the wording of the OT texts to suit their own needs.[31]

Again, there seems to be almost an exact parallel to this development in the case of the NT writings. At first the Church existed with a story and without its own "sacred text"—"Christian" scriptures. Even though the earliest Christian communities acknowledged the OT writings as their scriptures, those writings could not in themselves explain the Church's identity or give it its peculiar life. That was wrapped up in a story about Jesus the Christ. The earliest canon of the Christian community was the story of Jesus, which was later written down and subsequently stabilized in a sacred text. For quite some time, however, that Christian text (primarily the Gospels, but also Paul's letters) was highly adaptable and changeable in the Christian community, as is evidenced by the many textual variants in the NT documents.[32] The sacred text was adaptable to the life circumstances of the community of faith, its *Sitz im Leben*, but it is also clear that the community adapted the text to make it more relevant to its needs. This is especially so in the Church of the first two centuries when, unlike in parts of Judaism, it is believed that the age of the Spirit (and consequently prophecy) was still in operation. In the beginnings of the Church, there is much change and adaptability in the biblical text.[33] In the fourth to the sixth centuries, there is a movement toward a stabilized NT text and the formalization of that text as canon in the Christian community. During the first century and even later, however, it will be argued that the story of Jesus (however differently it was told, adapted, or changed) continued to be the canon of the earliest Christians.

In the broadest definition of the term *canon*, neither the Israelites nor the Christians were ever without a canon or authoritative guide. They always had a story that enabled them to establish their identity and that gave life to their community, even though a stabilized text of scriptures was not with them in their earliest development. It will be argued in the remaining parts of this book that the existence of a closed collection of sacred scriptures was a later development for Israel and for the Church as well. It will be shown in chapter 4 that the basic outlines of the NT canon began to emerge with Irenaeus in a polemic against heretical teachings in which he lists the writings of the four canonical Gospels, which he believes are free from such errors and which faithfully reflect the Christian message (the "rule" κανών of faith). Before that, chapter 3 will focus on questions related to the emergence of a Christian OT canon.

THE CHRISTIAN OLD TESTAMENT

I. The OT as Scripture

It has long been argued by many biblical scholars that the earliest Christians received from Judaism a closed canon of scriptures. In fact, it has even been argued by more conservative scholars that Jesus endorsed the current Protestant OT literature comprising the Law, the Prophets, and the Writings. LaSor, Hubbard, and Bush begin their discussion of the OT canon with the traditional view that "the Christian church was born with a canon in its hands."[1] They propose that the threefold OT (Law, Prophets, and Writings) existed prior to 150 B.C.E., and they go on to state unequivocally that "the New Testament authors never cite apocryphal writings directly, and it is probably safe to assume that the Old Testament they used was identical with that known today."[2] Such statements, however, are overly optimistic and do not help to clarify the actual development of the OT canon.

In his recent book on the origins of the OT canon, Beckwith also argues unconvincingly that the OT had reached its final form in the

time of Judas Maccabaeus, around 164 B.C.E.[3] He tries to show that
there was essentially no difference among the canons of the Pharisees, Sadducees, Essenes, and the early Christians. Although Beckwith acknowledges the fact that at a later time a distinction can be
found between the Christian OT canon and that of Judaism, he
stresses that only after the breach between the Christians and the
synagogue did the Christians try to expand the OT canon, "when
their knowledge of the original Christian canon was becoming
blurred."[4] He has no evidence to support this claim, however, and
the likelihood of the early Church's forgetting the boundaries of its
own holy scripture, if it were known, is incredibly remote! The following study will argue that the OT scriptures of the late first-
century Christian community and subsequent generations of the
Church were the same widely diverse body of scriptures that were
also recognized as scripture by Pharisaic Judaism, or the major Jewish sects that existed *before* the separation of the Church from the
synagogue. Further, I will try to show that the final fixing of the
canon of scriptures in Judaism or in the surviving Jewish sects is a
rather late development—not before the second century C.E.

Although Beckwith's substantial and highly researched work on
the OT canon of the earliest Christian community is a treasure of
valuable information, it is quite clear that he has not given adequate
consideration to the wide body of authoritative literature appealed
to by the early Christian community. It appears that his conclusions
about Jude's use of two pseudonymous writings give evidence of
Beckwith's having made his conclusions prior to his exegesis of the
texts. His claim that Jude saw this literature as edifying but not as
history is not a careful examination of Jude's use of I Enoch. The
author of Jude bases his argument on the facticity of a statement in
I Enoch. Is there any example of a writing that was classified as
prophetic (Jude 14 says that much), but was not considered true and
inspired? Especially suspect is his conclusion that "if Jude had selected two such edifying stories from books which he may even have
regarded as otherwise unedifying, this would neither have im-
pugned his own authority nor have conferred authority upon the
pseudonymous apocalypses from which he drew."[5]

It is generally agreed that Israel had acknowledged the authoritative nature of some sacred writings at least by the time of Josiah's

reforms (II Kings 22:8-13), which probably emerged as a result of the finding of the book of Deuteronomy. Although many OT scholars acknowledge that the Law (Torah) was in existence long before the time of Josiah—indeed, some parts of it probably preceded Moses[6]—it is not at all clear that the Law was the moving force behind the religion of Israel in its early formative period. Barr argues that it was "the Deuteronomic movement, around the eighth and seventh centuries, that began to make something like a 'scripture' central to the life of Israel" (*Scripture*, p. 7). He claims that only with this movement and Josiah's reforms did any religion built around a book (or sacred scripture) begin to emerge. It was especially after the exile of the Jews in Babylon during the reforms of Ezra and Nehemiah (notice especially Neh. 8:1–9:5) that the most significant move took place which led the religion of Israel to develop or recognize a body of sacred scriptures. It is widely acknowledged, then that the Law was recognized in Israel as its sacred scripture no later than ca. 400 B.C.E. and probably sooner. However, the "Law" for Ezra was not necessarily the same as our Pentateuch, which contains far more than laws and regulations. At that time there was still no notion of a closed canon of scriptures, even though the Law was "scripture" for the post-exilic Jews. The Pentateuch, at that time, was still in the process of change.

There also seems to be little doubt that by ca. 200 B.C.E. most of the Jewish people had also adopted a collection of writings called the "Prophets" (*nebi'im*), the bulk of which existed earlier than 400 B.C.E. but had not yet generally been included as "scripture" in the life of Israel. It is possible that some parts of the prophetic literature, as well as the Law, were an exilic canon for the Jews in Babylon,[7] though that view is difficult to substantiate. This "prophetic" collection of writings included what was called the "Former Prophets" (Joshua-Ezra/Nehemiah, but not including the Chronicles), and the "Latter Prophets" (Isaiah, Jeremiah, Ezekiel, and the book of the Twelve, or the "Minor Prophets"). Pfeiffer is probably correct when he claims that these books were adopted into Israel's canon not only because of growing public interest in them, but also because of their recognized value "for enhancing the national pride and the hopes for a better future."[8]

There is no indication in ancient Israel during that period that inspired literature had ceased to be written, although there is later evidence that claims that the prophetic voice in Israel had ceased. The author of I Maccabees (ca. 100 B.C.E.), for example, in writing about the difficult times in Israel following the death of Judas Maccabee, acknowledged that the prophets as well as the spirit of prophecy were gone in Israel and, therefore, inspired writing had ceased. Speaking about the chaos caused by the Syrian military in Israel, he concludes, "Thus there was great distress in Israel, such as had not been since the time that the prophets ceased to appear among them" (I Macc. 9:27 *OAA*). Later in the same book when the author is describing the election of Simon Maccabee to be high priest as well as ruler, he writes, "And the Jews and their priests decided that Simon should be their leader and high priest forever, until a trustworthy prophet should arise" (14:41 *OAA*). (See also 4:45-46, in which the author makes it clear that the time of the prophets had ceased, at least temporarily.) Much later, near the end of the first century C.E., Josephus claimed that the role of the prophet, and thereby the inspired and authoritative literature written by the prophet, had ceased with the time of Artaxerxes.[9]

From Artaxerxes to our own time the complete history has been written but has not been deemed worthy of equal credit with the earlier records, because of the failure of the exact succession of the prophets.

We have given practical proof of the reverence for our Scriptures. For, although such long ages have now passed, no one has ventured either to add, or to remove, or to alter a syllable; and it is an instinct with every Jew, from the day of his birth, to regard them as the decrees of God, to abide by them, and if need be, cheerfully to die for them. (*Against Apion*, 1.8.41, trans, by A. C. Sundberg in *OT Early Ch*, p. 115)

However, in spite of a number of later Jewish writings that indicate that the prophetic movement had ceased in Israel following the time of Ezra,[10] other literature continued to be written long after the time of Ezra and was highly regarded in Israel both before and after the time of the Jamnia council in 90 C.E.[11] Ecclesiasticus, or the Wisdom of Jesus the Son of Sirach (written ca. 200–180 B.C.E.), was considered by many Jews to be inspired literature and worthy of being read not only by the Hebrew speaking Jews but also by those Jews who spoke Greek in Alexandria, Egypt. The book, in fact, appears to have almost made it into the Jewish canon of scriptures. The Prologue to the book (written by the author's grandson ca. 130 B.C.E.) argues that since its author, Jesus the son of Sirach, was "led to write something pertaining to instruction and wisdom," the people were therefore urged "to read [it] with good will and attention." The promise in reading the book was that one might "gain learning, being prepared in character to live according to the law." In short, he does not hesitate to commend his grandfather's written work along with that of the Law and the Prophets. At least he does not distinguish Sirach from the other sacred writings.

Along with Ecclesiasticus, a large body of literature, some of which was written well before 200 B.C.E. and some even later, circulated in Palestine and was later translated from Hebrew into Greek not only for the Jews in Egypt but also for the other Jews of the Diaspora. The name given to this literature by the Jews was simply the Kethubim, or "Writings."[12] The precise boundaries of this body of literature were not defined until sometime after the Jamnia council,[13] when the Writings also became a closed canon of authoritative scriptures for the surviving elements of Judaism (primarily the Pharisaic Jews). Israel's tripartite canon was only beginning to close when the evangelists were writing their Gospel literature; at a time when Christianity had essentially ceased to be another Jewish sect heavily influenced by Judaism, the boundaries of the third part of that canon were not yet fixed. Notice, for example, in Luke 24:44 that Jesus, after his resurrection, reminds the disciples: "These are my words which I spoke to you, while I was still with you, that everything written about me in the law of Moses and the prophets and the psalms must be fulfilled."[14]

This is the closest reference in the NT for a tripartite canon of scriptures, but it manifestly does not include all of the literature that makes up that third part. Normally in the NT, only the Law and the Prophets are mentioned in reference to the Jewish scriptures. In Matthew 5:17, Luke 24:27, and Acts 28:23, for example, the Law and the Prophets appear to comprise all of the sacred scriptures. James Barr concludes from this and from other NT references that perhaps the Prophets, as a collection, included more than we have previously thought, that it includes all authoritative writings, not just the Former and Latter prophets noted above. He claims that such references in the NT "strongly suggests that the category of 'Prophet' was not a closed one: any non-Torah book that was holy scripture was a 'Prophet'" (*Scripture*, p. 55). This is further supported by Melito's reference to the Jewish scriptures in 180 C.E. as simply "the Law and the Prophets" (see sect. IV, below). Although Barr agrees that the Law was a separate and distinct part of the Jewish canon, he maintains that the boundaries among the Prophets and the other books were still imprecise even in the first century C.E.[15] His point, however, does not negate the fact that for some Jews well before the first century C.E. the category of "Prophets" appears to have been more precise. See again, for example, the Prologue of Ecclesiasticus (Sirach), written ca. 130 B.C.E. The author indicates that his grandfather (Jesus son of Sirach) was led to write wisdom only "after devoting himself especially to the reading of the law and the prophets and the other books of our fathers." Later in the same Prologue, while explaining some of the difficulty he had in translating his grandfather's work into Greek, he adds, "Not only this work, but even the law itself, the prophecies, and the rest of the books differ not a little as originally expressed." Barr, however, raises a good point regarding how precisely Josephus himself, who acknowledged a tripartite canon, was able to distinguish the three parts. He has observed that even if the number of books found in Josephus' list is the same as it is in the present Jewish canon, the division of books in the Prophets and Writings differs, possibly indicating that Josephus did *not* have a tripartite canon, but rather a two-stage canon.[16] His reasoning should probably lead us to a conclusion that will be argued in more detail in the next section: that Judaism in the last two centuries B.C.E. and in the first century C.E. was by no means uniform in its understanding of which of its writings were considered sacred. There were many views both inside and outside of Israel in the first centuries B.C.E. and C.E. on which writings were deemed sacred.

II. The Greek OT

Following the decree of Cyrus, king of Persia, allowing the Jews to resettle in their homeland (Ezra 1, 2) many, but not all, Jews did so. The rest either remained in Babylon or in that region or, as occurred in great numbers, many resettled in major cities all over the Mediterranean world. Those Jews who lived outside of Palestine were called Diaspora Jews or the Jews of the Dispersion (James 1:1). It was not long before many of those Jews had forgotten their native Hebrew and could communicate only in the language of the lands to which they had migrated. By the middle to late fourth century B.C.E., a leader from Greece emerged whose actions had a significant impact not only on the future of the Jews of the Dispersion but also on the Jews in Palestine and even on the later developing Christian communities. It was Alexander the Great's plan in his conquests to create a universal empire, dominated by the Greek culture and by the Greek language. Following his conquest of a people, he immediately instituted the reforms that made the Greek language and culture a dominant influence in the lives of the subjugated peoples. The author of I Maccabees wrote perhaps one of the most succinct histories of this period.

> After Alexander son of Philip, the Macedonian, who came from the land of Kittim, had defeated Darius, king of the Persians and the Medes, he succeeded him as king. (He had previously become king of Greece.) He fought many battles, conquered strongholds, and put to death the kings of the earth. He advanced to the ends of the earth, and plundered many nations. When the earth became quiet before him, he was exalted, and his heart was lifted up. He gathered a very strong army and ruled over countries, nations, and princes, and they became tributary to him. (I Macc. 1:1-4, DAA)

The Hellenization of the ancient world was quite successful in spite of the resistance offered by the Jews of Palestine and others in different parts of Alexander's empire. The Hellenization that he promoted was not completed in his lifetime, but was carried on with varying degrees of intensity by his generals who ruled after him. This Hellenization—which was in fact an amalgamation of the Greek culture, language, and religious heritage with other cultures—led to a universal language and culture shared throughout the Mediterranean world and even beyond. Although most Jews in Palestine resisted the Hellenization of their homeland,[17] many Diaspora Jews were much more receptive to it, even though they continued to be loyal to their own religious heritage from Palestine. Philo (ca. 15 B.C.E.–45 C.E.), for example, tried to address the Hellenistic community of Alexandria with the Law of Moses, though he interpreted it allegorically in numerous places in order to make it more acceptable to the Hellenistic world.

Following the changes instituted by Alexander, most of the Jews of the Dispersion could no longer speak Hebrew and communicated only in Greek. This situation led to the need in these Jewish religious communities for a translation of the Hebrew scriptures into the Greek language. A major undertaking to translate the Law of Moses took place in Alexandria, Egypt, sometime during the reign of Ptolemy II Philadelphus (ca. 283–246 B.C.E.). According to the *Letter of Aristeas* (ca. 130–70 B.C.E.), a legendary account of this event, King Ptolemy II not only wanted to have a copy of the Law of Moses for his library, but he also took remarkable steps to ensure the integrity of the translation itself. Although no one today seriously believes everything in this composite and anachronistic account,[18] it is probably fair to say that the translation of the Law of Moses began during the Ptolemy II reign, when Palestine was under the rule of Egypt.[19] Relations were also very good between Alexandria and Jerusalem at that time, and good Hebrew manuscripts as well as capable Jewish scholarship were easily accessible from Palestine to help with the project.[20]

The traditional name given to the Greek translation of the Palestinian sacred scriptures is the *Septuagint,* or the more frequent designation *LXX.* It is commonly believed that the term derives from the tradition passed on in the *Letter of Aristeas* that seventy-two translators (six from each of the twelve tribes of Israel) worked on the translation.[21] The Aristeas letter also claims that exactly seventy-two days were spent on the project. "And it so chanced that the work of translation was completed in seventy-two days, just as if this had been arranged of set purpose."[22] That this translation was considered sacred and unchangeable is seen in the following conclusions Aristeas makes regarding the *LXX.*

After the books had been read, the priests and the elders of the translators and the Jewish community and the leaders of the people stood up and said, that since so excellent and sacred and accurate a translation had been made, it was only right that it should remain as it was and no alteration should be made in it. And when the whole company expressed their approval, they bade them pronounce a curse in accordance with their custom upon any one who should make any alteration either by adding anything or changing in anyway whatever any of the words which had been written or making any omission. This was a very wise precaution to ensure that the book might be preserved for all the future time unchanged. (*Ep. Arist.*, p. 311, trans. by R. H. Charles)

The belief that this translation was sacred and therefore the only one that could be used is made clear from Aristeas' further telling about the visitation of divine judgment upon one historian named Theopomus, who was "driven out of his mind for more than thirty days" because he had attempted to make use of other faulty translations of the Law in writing his history. It was only after a prolonged illness and much prayer that God finally restored his health to him (*Ep. Arist.*, pp. 314-16).

Some scholars have suggested that the term *LXX* comes from the rounding off of the number "seventy-two" to "seventy," hence Septuagint,[23] but it is also quite possible that the number derives from the tradition of the seventy elders of Exodus 24:1, 9 who accompanied Moses to Mount Sinai, where he received the Law from Yahweh on tablets of stone.[24] If this is the case, then the use of the term *Septuagint* by the Jews could well be in itself an acknowledgment of the early belief in the divinely inspired status of the translation—that it authentically and faithfully conveyed the full intent of the Law given to Moses. That is certainly in keeping with Aristeas' clear purpose of establishing the sacredness of the translation with his well-known letter.

It should also be noted that the term technically should be applied only to the Pentateuch and not to the rest of the OT scriptures, though it later came to be used in reference to these other books as well. By no later than ca. 130 B.C.E. the Prophets and other sacred Jewish writings were likewise translated from the Hebrew into the Greek language.[25]

At any rate, this translation helped to meet the religious needs of the Jews in Alexandria, but very soon thereafter it began to serve the religious needs of the rest of the Diaspora Jews as well. It was also well known and circulated throughout Palestine in the first century C.E.[26] The Aristeas tradition that this translation was miraculously accomplished with the help of God, which is another way of acknowledging its inspired status, was passed on not only by the Jews (Philo and Josephus) but also by such Christian writers as Justin, Irenaeus, Tertullian, Clement of Alexandria, and Eusebius as well as others. See, for example, the following passage from Eusebius who claims to be reporting a tradition from Irenaeus regarding the origins and recognition of the inspired status of the *LXX*.

> For before the Romans established their government, while the Macedonians still possessed Asia, Ptolemy, the son of Lagus, being very anxious to adorn the library, which he had founded in Alexandria, with all the best extant writings of all men, asked from the inhabitants of Jerusalem to have their Scriptures translated into Greek. They, for they were at that time still subject to the Macedonians, sent to Ptolemy seventy elders, the most experienced they had in the Scriptures and in both languages, and God thus wrought what he willed. But Ptolemy, wishing to make trial of them in his own way, and being afraid lest they should have made some agreement to conceal by their translation the truth in the Scriptures, separated them from one another and commanded them all to write the same translation. And this he did in the case of all the books. But when they came together to Ptolemy, and compared each his own translation, God was glorified and the Scriptures were recognized as truly divine, for they all rendered the same things in the same words and the same names, from beginning to end, so that even the heathen who were present knew that the Scriptures had been translated by the inspiration of God. (*Hist. eccl.* 5.8.11-14, LCL)

One of the most amazing facts about the *LXX* was the rapidity of its adoption within the Christian community. This appears to be so even in Palestine where the Hebrew scriptures were also in circulation. Because it was a Greek document, it was an especially useful tool in the Christian evangelization of the Roman world. The NT writings themselves appeal to the *LXX* over the Hebrew scriptures more than 80 percent of the time. Matthew, who uses the *LXX* the least, still freely makes use of it when it furthers his argument. Shires has noted one famous example of this in Matthew's quotation of Isaiah 7:14 where Matthew refers to the prophecy of the virgin birth of Jesus (Matt. 1:23). Although the Hebrew text indicates that a young woman (in Hebrew, *ʿlmah*) shall conceive and bear a son, the *LXX*, on the other hand, states that a virgin (in Greek, *parthenos*) shall conceive and bear a son.[27] Shires adds that "every part of the New Testament shows some knowledge and use of the Septuagint, and no book depends solely upon the original Hebrew form of the Old Testament."[28]

This very heavy use of the *LXX* by the Christian community no doubt was a major factor in the Jewish reaction against the *LXX* at the end of the first century C.E. and their rejection of it altogether in the second century C.E. This rejection could also have stemmed from the fact that some Christians had based some of their criticisms against Judaism upon faulty *LXX* texts.[29] In the second century, the *LXX* became identified as the Bible of the Christians, and another version was deemed necessary for the Jewish community. The task of a new Greek translation of the OT was undertaken first by Aquila, a Jewish proselyte from Pontus (ca. 128 C.E.), who produced a text slavishly literal and loyal to the Hebrew text. Wevers, commenting on this translation, concludes that it could only be understood by one familiar with the Hebrew.[30] Two other Greek translations of the Hebrew scriptures were made by Theodotion, of whom little is known including the precise time of writing, and by Symmachus somewhat later than Aquila. Other Greek versions of the OT were also around by the time of Origen in the early third century, though little is known of them.

III. The Alexandrian Canon of the OT Scriptures

A comparison of the *LXX* to the Hebrew canon of scriptures shows not only significant differences in the text, but also a different collection of books. The *LXX* has a much larger collection of writings than does the Hebrew canon. Also, as was indicated above, the NT has many allusions to some of the noncanonical literature found in the *LXX*, and, as one would suspect, the oldest Christian collections of OT scriptures contain much of that literature.[31] These findings have led many scholars to postulate that the earliest Christian churches adopted an Alexandrian canon of Jewish scriptures that was larger in the number of writings it contained than the Hebrew canon of scriptures. The late R. H. Pfeiffer argued for the existence of an Alexandrian Jewish canon. He distinguished it from the canon of the Palestinian Jews, which he claimed was a conservative group who "made a sharp distinction between inspired scripture and human writings."[32] He further argued that the Alexandrians "tended to accept as scripture any writing in Hebrew or Aramaic which came from Palestine."[33] He held that the same was true of the rest of the Jews of the Dispersion who, unlike the Palestinian Jews, did not believe that prophecy had ceased with Ezra, but instead had continued on.

The biggest problem with this theory is that there are no Alexandrian canons that one can point to and say that these books and no others comprised it. Pfeiffer himself acknowledged that no one knows what the canon of the Alexandrian and other Diaspora Jews was before the LXX was condemned (ca. 130 C.E.) in Palestine. What is more, it has not been shown conclusively that the Alexandrian Jews or the other Jews of the Dispersion were any more likely to adopt other writings as sacred scriptures than were the Jews of Palestine in the two centuries B.C.E. and the first century C.E. Further, there is no evidence as yet to show the existence of a different canon of scriptures in Alexandria in this period than the one in Palestine. Although there were many differences between Philo and the rabbis in Palestine in their interpretation of the scriptures, it must be conceded that most of Philo's references to scripture are from the Law, and only a few from other Jewish books.[34] *Philo appears to have had an even more conservative canon than the Jews of Palestine!* Moreover, since the communications between Jerusalem and Alexandria were considered quite good during the first century B.C.E. and C.E., it is not likely that either the notion or the extent of divine scripture would vary significantly between the two locations during the period before 70 C.E. This does not necessarily mean, however, that there could have been no differences between the Jews in the Diaspora and those in Palestine. There were, indeed, many differences among the Jews in Palestine alone regarding what was in fact scripture (for example, the Sadducees, Essenes, and Pharisees all had differing beliefs about what was believed to be authoritative scriptures). It has already been said that the Jews of the Dispersion were more affected by Hellenism than were the Jews of Palestine, but there is little evidence to show that these differences also affected their notion of scripture or the boundaries of their scriptures.

A more likely explanation for the larger collection of sacred writings in the *LXX* and later in the Christian canons of OT scriptures is that the process of limiting the number of sacred scriptures in Palestine began after the time Judaism had a significant effect on the Christian community. When the Christians left Jerusalem in 62–66 C.E., following the death of James the brother of Jesus, they moved to Pella, east of the Jordan River. After that the influence of Judaism on the Christians, and especially its understanding and limits of authoritative scriptures, significantly diminished. When the Jews of a Pharisaic bent met as a college in Jamnia (ca. 90 C.E.) and discussed sacred literature, the Christians had already determined at an earlier time the wider collection of sacred Jewish writings that they inherited from Judaism. George Anderson is no doubt correct when he concludes that the third part of the Jewish canon, the Writings, was still imprecise before the meeting in Jamnia and that it was, therefore, left up to the churches to carry out the further definition of their Christian canon, the third part of the OT scriptures.[35]

IV. Jamnia and the Christian OT

It is unlikely that the Jewish religious leaders who gathered together (there was no council as such) at Jamnia (or Jabneh) ca. 90 C.E. made final or binding decisions about their canon of scriptures since the lists of books acknowledged to "defile the hands" continued to vary within Judaism itself up through the fourth century C.E. Also, there does not appear to have been any recognized group of individuals speaking on behalf of all Jews regarding religious matters near the end of the first century C.E. The significance of the "college" of individuals at Jamnia after the destruction in 70 C.E. is that they apparently helped to clarify how a religious faith that had once been centered around a temple and a sacrificial cult could survive without these institutions.[36] During this time and later, however, it also became necessary for the Jews to clarify what their scriptures were since they, as well as the Christians, appealed to the same scriptures to justify their doctrinal beliefs. The rapid growth of the Christian movement within Judaism, with its strong focus on apocalyptic and messianic literature, no doubt had an effect on the Jewish religious community in Palestine after 70 C.E., when the Jews were trying to work through their new and significantly changed role as the people of God. There was a rapid decline in the influence of messianic literature in Judaism, especially after the tragic events surrounding the Bar Cochba rebellion, which had its roots in messianism (132–135 C.E.). During the period of self-definition and reassessment after 135 C.E., a more conservative canon of Hebrew scriptures emerged with a minimal apocalyptic focus (the book of Daniel and Isa. 24–26) began to emerge in the surviving elements of Judaism.

It appears that before the destruction of Jerusalem in 70 C.E. the Law and Prophets were generally recognized by most Jews (except the Sadducees), as well as by the Christians, as sacred scriptures. The third part of the Jewish sacred writings, however, was not yet precisely fixed for the Jews in Palestine at that time. Among the various sects in Palestine in the first century C.E., at least three other religious groups adopted differing bodies of sacred literature in the Yahwistic tradition—viz., the Samaritans, who only accepted a slightly modified form of the Pentateuch; the Sadducees, who acknowledged as scripture only the Law of Moses; and the Essenes at Qumran, who appear to have adopted an even wider body of sacred literature than did the Pharisees.

What criteria were used to establish the Jewish canon of scriptures? To this question there are more possible answers for Judaism than for early Christianity. According to the passages cited from Josephus, the time of inspiration in Israel was considered over by the time of Artaxerxes (ca. 465–424 B.C.E.). Hence, any book believed to have been written after that time was not considered inspired. It does not appear that all rabbis agreed with Josephus' dating of the cessation of prophecy, but probably most agreed that by the time of the writing of I Maccabees that the time had come.[37] Leiman suggests that if a book were composed in Greek it was automatically eliminated from inclusion in the biblical canon, and, if a book written in Hebrew originally challenged the halaḥic teachings of the rabbis it was also rejected. Finally he notes that those books whose status was uncertain but that were highly esteemed by sectarian groups—Ben Sirach was so esteemed by the Christians—were sometimes excluded. He notes that Ben Sirach was excluded from canonical status but continued to be used by the rabbis long after the Jewish canon had been determined.[38]

Whatever the criteria of Judaism, which doubtless excluded most apocalyptic literature from consideration for canonization, the Christian OT canon was not contracting as it was in Judaism, but indeed appears to have been expanding. The early Christian OT canon probably better represents the canon of Jesus than that of second-century Judaism. The canon of Jesus, or books considered by his earliest followers to be sacred and, therefore, authoritative, was much more broad and included much of the apocryphal and pseudepigraphal literature. Unlike many of the adherents of Judaism at the end of the first century C.E., they did not believe that the age of prophecy—or of the Spirit—was over, but indeed had just begun. This belief, as will be argued later, made it easier for the Christians to acknowledge not only books from the apocryphal and pseudepigraphal literature as inspired scripture but also, at a later, time Christian writings, too.

At any rate, the final limits of the Old Testament canon for Judaism may to some extent have been determined in the context of the Jewish-Christian conflicts in which those in Judaism sought to keep the Christian literature from being read by the Jews. George Foot Moore insists from his study of ancient Jewish literature that a decision about the extent of the Jewish canon was made due to the rise of Christian "heresy" and the circulation of Christian writings in the Jewish community in Palestine.[39] He claims that the polemic against the Christians and their writings continued vigorously by the Jews until around the mid-second century, when Christianity was much less a threat to Judaism and the Jewish concern about the influence of the Gospels on their people had subsided due to the effective separation of the Jewish Christians from the synagogue.[40] The influence of the Jewish Christians ceased to be a threat, in part, as a result of their failure to join in the Bar Cochba rebellion, since in doing so they would have denied in principle their own Messiah, Jesus. This lack of participation in the rebellion was viewed as treason by many of the Jews, and the influence of the Jewish Christians among their fellow countrymen declined rapidly after that. Moore boldly concludes his study with the assertion that "the attempt authoritatively to define the Jewish canon of the Hagiographa [the Writings] begins with the exclusion by name of Christian Scriptures" ("Definition," p. 125).

The process of OT canonization by the Jews may have been largely completed sometime before 180 C.E. when Melito of Sardis traveled to the East (Palestine) and brought back a list of twenty-two books of the OT. Eusebius writes about this visit and also passes on the following letter from Melito.

> "Melito to Onesimus his brother, greeting. Since you often desired, in your zeal for the true word, to have extracts from the Law and the Prophets concerning the Saviour, and concerning all our faith, and moreover, since you wished to know the accurate facts about the ancient writings, how many they are in number, and what is their order, I have taken pains to do thus, for I know your zeal for the faith and interest in the word, and that in your struggle for eternal salvation you esteem these things more highly than all else in your love towards God. Accordingly when I came to the east and reached the place where these things were preached and done, and learnt accurately the books of the Old Testament, I set down the facts and sent them to you. These are their names: five books of Moses, Genesis, Exodus, Numbers, Leviticus, Deuteronomy, Joshua the son of Nun, Judges, Ruth, four books of Kingdoms, two books of Chronicles, the Psalms of David, the Proverbs of Solomon and his Wisdom, Ecclesiastes, the Song of Songs, Job, the prophets Isaiah, Jeremiah, the Twelve in a single book, Daniel, Ezekiel, Ezra. From these I have made extracts and compiled them in six books." Such are the facts about Melito. *(Hist. eccl.* 4.26.13, 14, *LCL.)*

In spite of Melito's letter, however, it is not clear what the boundaries of the OT canon were since some disagreement still persisted in Judaism. Melito's list, for instance, does not contain Esther. Among a number of conclusions one is drawn to from Melito's letter is that the contents of the OT canon were by no means clear to at least one leader of the Christian Church near the end of the second century C.E. This uncertainty is difficult to understand if the matter had already been settled long before the origins of the Church (by ca. 150 B.C.E.).

Melito's discovery of a Jewish canon, as Sundberg has shown, made a significant impact on the Christian Church after the third century C.E. and especially later, when Jerome wrongly considered it to be the canon of Jesus and of the Apostles.[41] It appears from this that it was only at the end of the second century C.E. that the question of fixing the limits of the OT canon in Christian communities began to emerge and that this development probably came primarily as a result of the Marcionite and gnostic rejection of the OT literature as sacred scripture.[42] Jerome's preference for the Jewish OT canon was a minority position in the Church of his day and, that view did not prevail until later in the Protestant OT canon.[43]

That the Jewish canon (which eventually became the Protestant canon) was not the complete canon of scriptures for Jesus and the Apostles can be argued fairly convincingly by the listing of the more than 150 references or allusions to the deuterocanonical (apocryphal) and pseudepigraphal literature in the New Testament in *Appendix A* on pages 172-77. Albert C. Sundberg collected these references from the marginal references in the *Novum Testamentum Graece*, edited by Eberhard Nestle, and grouped them together with a list of the New Testament texts that allude to them.[44] The allusions to or reflections of the apocryphal writings in the NT are especially from the Wisdom of Solomon, Ecclesiasticus, Baruch, II Esdras, and I Maccabees. Those texts reflecting or alluding to the pseudepigrapha primarily cite or allude to the Psalms of Solomon, I Enoch (which is also directly quoted as inspired literature— prophetic literature—in Jude 14), the Assumption of Moses and III and IV Maccabees.

Along with the above, as Shires has suggested, Paul may have used the Testament of the Twelve Patriarchs and Jude may have alluded to the Assumption of Moses.[45] To this may be added the quotations of the Greek authors Aratus, Menander, and Epimenides in Acts 17:28, I Corinthians 15:33; and Titus 1:12. The statement by LaSor, Hubbard, and Bush, then, that "Christ and the Apostles, by not quoting the deuterocanonical works, likewise seemed to consider them of lesser authority"[46] appears either to dismiss these references or to ignore them.

It is clear from the survey of the references and allusions listed in *Appendix A* that the least one could say is that *the theology of the first-century Christians was informed by more than the literature of*

our current Protestant OT canon, even though the New Testament
writers never specifically call any extra-canonical literature "scripture." Jude 14, however, certainly comes close to this when it refers
to I Enoch 1:9 as inspired authoritative literature. In the earliest
writings of the Apostolic Fathers[47]—that is, those closest to the time
of the writing of the NT literature, along with their references to the
OT literature, we also find quotations, references and allusions to
II Maccabees, Judith, Tobit, Sirach, the Wisdom of Solomon,
II Esdras (IV Ezra), and I Enoch. On the other hand, there are no
references to the canonical books of Ruth, Ezra-Nehemiah, Lamen-
tations, Obadiah, Micah, or Haggai.[48] It is obvious from this that
the second-century churches were likewise informed by more than
the current OT literature.

Kurt Aland, referring to the practice of the early churches' use of
a larger collection of ancient sacred texts, rightly concludes:

> If the Old Testament Pseudepigrapha are quoted in Jude, if Paul
> according to the reliable testimony of Origen does the same, if the
> Apostolic Fathers likewise call on the Pseudepigrapha, that is already
> the clearest indication that the Holy Scriptures of the Old Testament
> did not yet exist as a fixed Canon in the days of the primitive church.
> (Aland, *Canon,* p. 4)

All of this, of course, raises the question of whether the parameters of the Christian OT canon ought to be reexamined, especially
since the current Protestant OT canon not only appears to have been
fixed by the Jews during a polemic against the Christian community, but also because it appears that the "Writings" of the Protestant canon and the "Writings" referred to in the early Christian
community are not the same.[49] Sundberg has included in his study
an impressive table based on ancient documents that list the OT
books and their order in both the Eastern and Western churches of
the patristic period (see *OT Early Ch,* pp. 58-59). The various collections of lists of OT canons in the ancient churches (see *Appendix
B*) is strong evidence that the church fathers overwhelmingly acknowledged a broader OT canon than did Jerome, whose collection
of OT scriptures has prevailed only in Protestantism. None of these
canonical lists is precisely the same as another. This evidence also
points to the broad diversity of opinion about such matters in the

early Christian communities. If a precise list of authoritative and inspired OT books was handed on by the apostles stemming from Jesus, then incredibly the early Church must either have lost it or it never existed. Avery Dulles believes that the latter option is, in fact, the case when he explains that "if the apostles ever certified a list of biblical books (a most unlikely hypothesis), their testimony was not appealed to or apparently not remembered during the disputes about the canon in subsequent centuries."[50] It is much easier to believe that such a tradition was *not* passed on in the Church because none existed from the first century like the second century Melito Jewish canon than it is to believe such a canon was lost.

V. The Authority of the OT

Although the acknowledgment of the OT as authoritative scriptures was never seriously doubted in the Church before the time of Marcion, there is little evidence from the NT writers that they were much interested in the original *contextual* message of the OT itself. Rather, as is clear from an examination of many of the NT writings, the early Christians were far more interested in finding prophecies of the life, death, and resurrection of Jesus in their Jewish scriptures.[51] The primary authority of the early Church was not so much the message of the OT, but rather the proclaimed words and deeds of Jesus, which the OT scriptures, it was believed, foretold.[52] Greer concludes from his study of the early Church fathers that "while the Hebrew Scriptures were the Bible of the church, their authority was secondary to that of the Christian preaching."[53] He is also correct in concluding that the Christian people as a whole were less a "people of the book" than were the Jews because, for the Christians, the revelation of God was primarily located in Christ and only secondarily in the OT scriptures that bore witness to him.[54]

The Christians believed that the whole story of God's plans and purposes for Israel, as developed in the OT scriptures, had reached its completion in the life and work of Jesus.[55] The NT writers saw continuity in what they were describing, presenting, or advocating with the ancient Jewish scriptures, which they accepted as the authoritative Word of God. However, they also took many liberties in citing the OT, sometimes even altering the passages cited. An example of this is Paul's use of Psalm 94:11 in I Corinthians 3:19-20, which he modifies to fit his purposes. Other examples of this are Ephesians 4:8 (compare with Ps. 68:18) and Hebrews 2:6-8 (compare with Ps. 8:4-6). A study of the NT's use of the OT clearly shows that the driving force behind the NT writers is not the OT, but rather the word of and about the risen Lord.[56] Paul, for example, in II Corinthians 3:12-18 sets forward a commonly held view in the early Church that the OT could only be understood through Christ. James Barr has observed that though the OT had the status of the Word of God in the early Church, this "did not alter the fact that, for the men of the New Testament, though authoritative, [it] was no longer the communication of salvation. . . . Only the preaching of Jesus Christ as crucified and risen communicated salvation in the Christian sense" (*Scripture*, p. 14). Later Barr adds that Jesus' teachings likewise do not result from an exegesis of OT texts, but rather Jesus uses the OT to support *his* claims, not so much to elucidate meanings of the OT texts. Seldom, Barr notes, do the NT writers interpret whole passages, for example Genesis 1–3. This is so, he claims, because the NT writers never set out to interpret the OT itself, but rather the new substance of the gospel. (See *Scripture*, pp. 68-70.)

The Christian use of the OT was highly selective and designed especially to clarify or to confirm Christian beliefs. The real moving force of the NT, then, is not the OT, as Shires correctly asserts, but it is, rather, the experiences of Jesus.[57] Using the OT primarily, though not exclusively, as a predictive book was the most common way it was appealed to by the earliest Christian community in their first hundred years. The difficulty the OT itself raised for the Christian faith in the first and second centuries, however, will be discussed in more detail in chapter 4 when we look more closely at the issues raised by Marcion and Justin.

The above not withstanding, there can be no question that the OT scriptures were viewed by the earliest Church as an authoritative source of Christian faith and life, even though the limitations of the canon had not yet been fully decided. Almost every point of faith, order, and morals in I Clement is driven home with the aid of OT citations or quotations. For Polycarp, "Prophets" (or the OT) were inseparable from the authority of Christ and the apostles. In an admonition, he declared, "So then 'let us serve him with fear and all reverence,' as he himself commanded us, and as did the Apostles, who brought us the Gospel, and the Prophets who foretold the coming of our Lord" (Pol. *Phil.* 6:3, *LCL*). Tertullian combined the "Law and Prophets" with the writings of the evangelists and the apostles when he wrote:

> One Lord God does she [the Church] acknowledge, the Creator of the universe, and Christ Jesus (born) of the Virgin Mary, the Son of God the Creator; and the Resurrection of the flesh; *the law and the prophets she unites in one volume with the writings of evangelists and apostles*, from which she drinks in her faith. (*Praescript.* 36, *ANF*, italics added)

The early Church received from its Jewish heritage the notion of sacred scriptures (though not that of a closed "canon") in which it was believed that the revelation of God was disclosed and also in which the Church believed that the prediction of the Christ event had been foretold. Even though that collection of scriptures was used in the Christian communities to argue for church order and discipline (Rom. 14:10-13; I Cor. 6:12-16; 9:7-10; 14:20-22, and so on) as well as for mission (Rom. 10:14-17), payment of church leaders for services rendered (I Tim. 5:17-18), and many other functions relevant to the life of the early Christian community, the most important function of those scriptures for the early Church appears to have been their predictive witness to the Christ event (Luke 24:44; John 5:39; II Tim. 3:15).

The next chapter will shift focus to the developments and factors that led the second- and third-century churches to recognize many of the NT writings as having the same authoritative value (scriptural status) as the OT scriptures.

CHAPTER FOUR

THE RECOGNITION OF
CHRISTIAN WRITINGS
AS SCRIPTURE

The earliest Christian community did not possess a canon of *Christian* scriptures, even though it freely and most naturally adopted the OT scriptures as its Bible. As was noted earlier, however, the very selective use of the OT scriptures shows that the interpretation of the OT was not the driving force behind the early Church, but rather their interpretation of the significance of the Christ event—the life and teachings of Jesus of Nazareth, but especially his death and resurrection. This message, which focused on Jesus, called the community of faith into existence. Indeed, the complete and literal adoption of the OT scriptures, the heart of which lies in the Mosaic Law, is at variance with much of the teaching of the NT, especially that of Jesus and Paul. The recognition of this fact helps to explain why the NT's use of the OT is quite narrow, even though citations are from all three major sections of the Hebrew scriptures.

The problem of how to be free in Christ and yet subject to the legal codes of the Law was critical for the Christian community. It dealt with this problem in a number of ways: (1) by ignoring or denying vast portions of the Law; (2) by allegorizing such portions of the OT to bring them into harmony with the teachings of Jesus; (3) by emphasizing the faith principle that preceded the Law (as did Paul in Gal. 3 and Rom. 4, which in effect created a "canon within the canon"); (4) by rejecting the whole of the OT, as did Marcion [ca. 140 C.E.]; or (5) by redefining the meaning of the Law, as did Justin and others after him. However one chose to do it, it did not appear possible to have complete loyalty to a literal understanding of the OT and at the same time loyalty to the essentials of Christian faith. Some interpretative steps had to be taken in order to make the OT a Christian book, and the variety of ways the ancient Christians sought to make the OT at one with the Christian faith attests to the Church's great desire to have continuity with the faith of its Jewish ancestors.

The earliest *regula*, or canon of faith, for the Christian community was Jesus himself, whose words and deeds were interpreted afresh in numerous sociological contexts in which the early Christians lived. The prophetic voice, which was believed by many Jews to have ceased in Israel, was believed to be very much alive in the community of the followers of Jesus. In the earliest Christian preaching, it is clear that the followers of Jesus believed that the age of prophecy—that is, the age of the Spirit, which was believed to be manifested at the end of the age—that had once ceased in Israel was now alive in the power of the Church's preaching (Acts 2:16 ff.). The power of God was to be found in the Church's witness to the Risen Lord (Acts 1:8).[1]

I. From Oral Tradition to Written Documents

Jesus himself never wrote a book or, with the exception of the command of the Risen Lord to the angels of the seven churches of Asia Minor reported in Revelation, is he ever said to have commanded any of his followers to write a book. Written Christian documents in the final decades(s) of the first century were beginning to have a much more significant role in the life of the churches of Asia Minor than they did at first. See, for example, the comments of the only writer in the NT who unequivocally claims an inspired status for his own writing in Revelation 22:18-19 (see I Cor. 7:40 for a possible parallel), but also such passages as John 20:30, 31 and I John 1:4; 2:1, 7, 12-14; 26; and 5:13, which point to the value of a *written* message. It is clear that what Jesus said, whether it existed in written or oral form, was authoritative and was held in highest regard in the Church.[2]

From the beginning, however, the teaching of Jesus as well as the proclamation about his death and resurrection circulated among the Christian churches in oral form. Some of this tradition was written down quite early (ca. 35-65),[3] but much of it remained in oral form for a considerable period of time. Papias could still say ca. 120-140 that he preferred these oral communications to that of books—that is, the Gospels of Matthew and Mark.[4] Papias' well-known sentence in question is quoted by Eusebius: "For I did not suppose that information from books would help me so much as the word of a living and surviving voice."[5] Although he did not reject the written traditions about Jesus, it is clear that he preferred the oral communication of that tradition. According to F. C. Baur, Papias appears to have wanted "to keep the immediacy of the original revelation as a present reality by clinging to the living word, not to the dead, transient written text."[6]

James Barr has made the interesting observation that both from Plato and from the Pharisees a "cultural presupposition" suggested that the writing down of profound truth was an "*unworthy* mode of transmission."[7] His more important conclusion from this observation, based in part on the fact that Jesus neither wrote nor commanded his disciples to write anything down, is that the "idea of a Christian faith governed by Christian written holy scriptures was not an essential part of the foundation plan of Christianity" (*Scripture*, p. 12).

The living witness of Jesus the Christ was carried on in the early Church first by the apostolic community and later by the prophets and teachers who continued to have a significant role in the Christian community well into the second century. Even in the late second century, Clement of Alexandria had a great deal of appreciation for the oral tradition of the Church, even though the tradition to which he referred consisted primarily of the exegesis of scripture.[8]

Pheme Perkins has tried to show in her study of the orthodox and gnostic Christians of the second century that their relationship to their past before the time of Irenaeus, and to some extent after-wards, was still largely oral.[9] She, following von Campenhausen's lead,[10] maintains that the only authoritative text for Christians (or-thodox and gnostic) in this period was the OT writings, which were perceived as witnesses to the tradition embodied in the community at large.[11] She refers to Irenaeus, who, though strongly committed to a fixed written tradition, believed that the Christian community would have preserved its message accurately even if there had been no written Gospels.[12] The well-known statement by Irenaeus to which Perkins refers is as follows:

> Since therefore we have such proofs [of the truth], which is easily obtained from the Church, it is not necessary to seek the truth among others [the heretics]. [This is so] because the apostles, like a rich man who [deposited his money] in a bank, placed in her [the church's] hands an abundance of things pertaining to the truth: so that every man, whosoever will, can draw from her the water of life. For she is the entrance to life and all others are thieves and robbers. Because of this we are obligated to avoid them [the heretics], and to choose of the things pertaining to the Church with the utmost diligence laying hold of the tradition of the truth. Now how do we decide the issue? Sup-pose there arose a dispute relative to some important question among us. Should we not be obliged to turn to the most ancient Churches with which the apostles had dialogue and learn from them what is certain and clear in regard to the present question? And what should we do if the apostles themselves had not left us writings? Would it not be necessary, [in that case,] to follow the course of the tradition which they handed down to those to whom they entrusted the leadership of the Churches? (adapted from *Adv. Haer.* 3.4.1, *ANF*)

Although Perkins is correct in perceiving that, generally speak-ing, there were no authoritative Christian texts at that time and that the only texts reckoned to be binding on the Christian community were the OT scriptures (hence hermeneutical reflection at this time was largely on OT writings and *not* on the NT), examples will be shown presently that point to a growing awareness of the value of the fixed text of Christian writings in the mid-second century and following.[13] It is largely with Irenaeus, however, that the move of the center of authority away from oral tradition to a fixed normative text began to take place, even though the promptings for such a move in the "orthodox" community probably came from Marcion. At this point, we must raise the question of why the literature of the NT was written down at all, since we know that the earliest Church's message existed for a considerable time in oral form and was transmitted in that form. Why was the written tradition later preserved and given priority in the Church? Many motives are possible. First, it is a well-recognized fact that memory has been known to fail, especially over a long period of time. R. M. Grant cites three such examples of poorly kept oral tradition in the early Church Fathers that illustrate the difficulty of certifying oral tradition, but he further argues that as Christianity spread into the big cities the only tradition that could have survived was preserved in books.[14]

Second, although there was a fairly reliable means of communicating significant amounts of information through Jewish oral traditions, which form critical scholars have shown were used by the early Christians,[15] the deaths of some of the first witnesses to the Christ event (the apostles) and also the delay of the parousia must have had some effect on the writing down and preservation of those oral traditions.

Third, it should not be forgotten that apologetic motives are also likely to stand behind several of the NT writings; for example, Acts was written to point to certain catholicizing tendencies in both Judaistic Christianity (the primitive form represented by Peter) and the later Hellenistic Christianity (represented especially by Paul) to come together as one unified Church (Acts 15). The pastoral epistles may have been written in the name of Paul especially to meet the practical and organizational needs as well as the doctrinal needs of a post-Marcionite Christian community.[16]

Fourth, although most of the literature of the NT was written prior to the turn of the first century,[17] the need for such literature for community worship and instruction as well as the recognition of its value for apologetic purposes became more apparent to the Church in the second century. One could also add that to some extent it was also recognized by its own authors in the first century (for example, Rom. 15:15; the whole of Gal.; II Cor. 1:13; John 20:30, 31; I John 2:1, 7, 8, *passim*).

Finally, the epistles especially, but possibly the Gospels, were in part written as matters of policy for an expanding Church that was becoming more difficult to communicate with in person. Paul's letters often indicate that they were sent in lieu of a visit or to prepare the community for his visits.[18]

All of these reasons, and perhaps others, influenced the various writers of the NT to produce Christian literature, but, with the exception of the author of the book of Revelation, no conscious or clear effort was made by these authors to produce Christian scriptures. It is only at a later stage in the second century, when the literature they produced began to take on the function of scripture within the Christian community, that its status as scripture began to be acknowledged. That development is the focus of the next section.

II. From Written Documents to Scripture

When the New Testament writings were placed alongside the scriptures of the OT and appealed to authoritatively in the life and worship of the early Church, they functioned as scripture in the Church.[19] This function occurred, as one would expect, earlier than the time when the term *scripture* was actually employed to designate those writings. There are numerous references, citations, quotations, and allusions to the NT writings in the apostolic fathers of the second century.[20] But do these references necessarily mean that the NT writings were considered scripture? More specifically, when were they actually called "scripture" (γραφαί) and introduced with the words "the scripture says" (ἡ γραφὴ λέγει), "it is written" (γέγραπται), or any comparable formulae that were used in reference to the OT? Scholars of the second century do not agree on the answer, but the following information may be helpful in finding one.

It is clear that the sayings of Jesus had a scriptural status from the very beginning of the Church. See for example the high regard given to Jesus' words in I Corinthians 7:10, 17, and by implication 7:12, 25; I Thessalonians 4:15; Matthew 28:18; and elsewhere. Clement of Rome (ca. 95) likewise acknowledged the authority of the teaching of Jesus for the Church when he wrote

> *Let us, therefore, be humble-minded,* brethren, putting aside all arrogance and conceit and foolishness and wrath, and let us do that which is written (for the Holy Spirit says, "Let not the wise man boast himself in his wisdom, nor the strong man in his strength, nor the rich

man in his riches, but he that boasteth let him boast in the Lord, to seek him out and to do judgment and righteousness"), *especially remembering the words of the Lord Jesus* which he spoke when he was teaching gentleness and longsuffering. For he spoke thus: "Be merciful, that ye may obtain mercy. Forgive, that ye may be forgiven. As ye do, so shall it be done unto you. As ye give, so shall it be given unto you. As ye judge, so shall ye be judged. As ye are kind, so shall kindness be shown you. With what measure ye mete, it shall be measured to you." *With this commandment and with these injunctions let us strengthen ourselves to walk in obedience to his hallowed words* and let us be humble-minded, for the holy word says, "On whom shall I look, but on the meek and gentle and him who trembles at my oracles." (*I Clem.* 13:1-4, *LCL,* italics added)

Ptolemy, also, in his well-known *Letter to Flora* (ca. 160 C.E.) frequently referred to the "words of the Savior" (3:5, 8; 4:1, 4; and also 7:5, 10) as authority for his instruction. See for instance the devotion to the teaching of Jesus in Ptolemy's explanation of the proper way to understand the Law of Moses and his reference to those who have misunderstood it.

> That is what happens to people who do not see what follows from the words of the Saviour. For a house or city divided against itself cannot stand, our Saviour declared. Furthermore the apostle says that the creation of the world was peculiar to Him and that all things were made through him, and apart from him nothing was made, refuting the flimsy wisdom of these liars; not the creation of a god who corrupts, but of a just God who hates evil. That is the opinion of heedless men who do not understand the cause of the providence of the Demiurge, who are blind not only in the eye of the soul but also in that of the body.
> How they have strayed from the truth is clear to you from what has been said. Two groups have gone astray each in their peculiar fashion, the one through ignorance of the God of justice, the other through ignorance of the Father of All, whom only he who alone knew him revealed at his coming. Now it remains for us who have been granted the knowledge of both of these, to explain the Law to you with accuracy, what its nature is and the one by whom it has been given, the Lawgiver, *proving our demonstrations from the words of our Saviour, through which alone it is possible without error to travel toward the comprehension of reality.*

First one must learn that the whole Law which is contained in the Pentateuch of Moses has not been decreed by some one person, I mean by God alone; but there are also some commandments in it given by men; *and that it is tripartite the words of the Saviour teach us.* For one part is ascribed to God himself and his legislation; another is ascribed to Moses, not meaning that God gave the law through him, but that Moses legislated starting from his own understanding; and the third is ascribed to the elders of the people, who are themselves found from the beginning introducing ordinances of their own. *How this came about you may learn from the words of the Saviour.* When the Saviour was talking somewhere to those arguing with him about divorce, which was allowed by the Law, he said to them, Moses because of the hardness of your hearts permitted a man to put away his wife; from the beginning it was not so. For God joined them together, and what God has joined, let not a man, he said, put asunder. Here he shows that the law of God is one thing—it forbids a woman to be divorced by her husband—and the law of Moses is another—it permits this bond to be sundered because of hardness of heart. So in this way Moses ordains a law contrary to God, for divorce is contrary to no divorce. (Stevenson, *ANE*, pp. 92-93, italics added)

For both Clement of Rome and Ptolemy the words of Jesus undoubtedly functioned as sacred scripture even though the specific formulae are not used in the above passages.

In terms of the NT literature itself, citations of or allusions to the Gospels (mostly Matthew) and to a lesser extent to the NT epistles was commonplace in the second century. This practice indicates some recognition at least of the esteem and authority (though not necessarily its scriptural status) that this literature had in the Christian community. Hans von Campenhausen adds an important qualification to these references by drawing a distinction between the authoritative words or commands of Jesus and the Gospels that contained *some* of them. He claims that it was the words of Jesus in the written and oral tradition that had a scriptural-like status in the Church, but not the whole Gospel text itself. It was a word from Jesus that, when written down, became scripture-like. (See *Formation*, pp. 118-21.) He further notes that in the first one and a half centuries of the Church's history no prominence was given to a Gospel writer or to a Gospel writing. (See *Formation*, p. 121.) The sayings of Jesus located in these documents were given prominence.

Also, although the Gospels may have been intended at the outset to be used (or read) in the Church alongside the OT literature, von Campenhausen contends that the earlier gospels did not claim exclusive authority, "nor did they acquire it" (*Formation*, p. 123) as the history of the redaction of these gospels indicates. Several of the references to the NT literature in the second century are rather explicit with regard to the authority of the writings, while other references are more veiled or subdued.

The following examples of ancient texts focus on some of the second-century attitudes about the NT writings.

1. The unknown author of *II Clement* (ca. 120–140, but no later than 170) acknowledges as the authoritative basis for his comments the "scripture" (no doubt the Jewish scriptures) and subsequently both the "Books and the Apostles."

> Now I imagine that you are not ignorant that the living "Church is the body of Christ." For the scripture says, "God made man male and female;" the male is Christ, the female is the church. *And moreover the books and the Apostles* (τὰ βιβλία καὶ οἱ ἀπόστολοι) declare that the Church belongs not to the present, but has existed from the beginning; for she was spiritual, as was also our Jesus, but he was made manifest in the last days that he might save us. (14:2, *LCL*, italics added)

In this passage, it is almost certain that the appeal to "the Books" (τὰ βιβλία) is a reference to the OT scriptures (see also II Tim. 4:13), and "the Apostles" (οἱ ἀπόστολοι) is probably a reference to the NT tradition common in the churches in both oral and written form.[21] If this is so, then this text is an early indication that the NT tradition was placed in a parallel relationship to the OT scriptures in that both are appealed to in an authoritative manner for support of the author's teaching about the pre-existent Church. The apostles appear at this early date to function as the "guarantors" of the NT tradition.[22]

Again, in II Clement 2:4, the author quotes Mark 2:17 (or Matt. 9:13*b*), introduced by the words, "and another Scripture also says" (καὶ ἑτερά δὲ γραφὴ λέγει). Here, as in 14:2 above, it appears that the sayings of Jesus, which had not yet found a universally acknowledged fixed form, came to be recognized early as on a par with or closely related to the authority of the OT scriptures in support of theological arguments and moral behavior in the early Church.[23]

2. The *Epistle of Barnabas* (ca. 90–130) introduced one of its two Gospel quotations (Matt. 22:14) in the following manner: "Let us take heed lest *as it is written* (ὡς γέγραπται) we be found 'many called but few chosen'" (*Barn.* 4:14, *LCL*, italics added). This suggests that the words of Jesus were equal in authority to the OT—that is, the words of Jesus, when written down, became scripture. Kümmel goes a step further, however, and contends that this text is evidence that an individual gospel writing—the whole text itself—was becoming valued as equal in authority to the OT scriptures.[24] More proof appears necessary, however, before making such a claim.

3. Ignatius (ca. 110–117), in an often quoted passage from his *Letter to the Philadelphians*, shows his preference for the "Gospel" (probably the kerygma about Jesus, found in the oral and/or written tradition of the Church) over the authority of the OT scriptures. He writes:

> But I beseech you to do nothing in factiousness, but after the teaching of Christ. For I heard some men saying, "If I find it not in the charters, I do not believe in the Gospel." And when I said to them that it is in the Scripture, they answered me, "That is exactly the question." But to me the charters are Jesus Christ, the inviolable charter is his cross, and death, and resurrection, and the faith which is through him; —in these I desire to be justified by your prayers. (*Ign. Phld.* 8:2, *LCL*)[25]

This text strongly indicates that Ignatius viewed the Jesus' teaching as on par with or superior to the authority of the OT scriptures. More especially it shows that the primary locus of authority for Ignatius was in the *event* of Jesus Christ, and more specifically, in the early Christian kerygma about "his cross, and death, and resurrection." The full extent of that tradition is not clear in Ignatius, but it appears that the oral and/or written traditions concerning Jesus the Christ were more important to him than were the OT scriptures.[26]

4. Polycarp, in his *Letter to the Philippians* (ca. 140–155), cites portions of both Psalm 4:5 and Ephesians 4:26 and calls them "Scriptures." Although the original Greek portion of this passage has been lost, the Latin is still quite instructive. Polycarp writes:

> For I am confident that you are well versed *in the Scriptures (in sacris literis)*, and from you nothing is hid; but to me this is not granted. *Only, as it is said in these Scriptures (Mondo, ut his scripturis dictum est)*, "Be ye angry and sin not," and "Let not the sun go down upon your wrath." Blessed is the man who remembers this, and I believe that it is so with you. (*Pol. Phil.* 12:1, *LCL*, italics added)

Polycarp appears to have consciously placed an OT scripture and a Christian writing on an equal authoritative footing.[27] The least one could say about this conjunction of the two texts is that we find an authoritative appeal to texts found in both the OT and the NT with the promise that persons following their advice will be blessed. That is certainly close to a description of inspired literature in any religious community. Also relevant here is the recognition of the authority of Jesus' teaching and example which Polycarp admonished his hearers to obey and imitate. Notice the following examples.

> Now "he who raised him" from the dead "will also raise us up" if we do his will, and *walk in his commandments* and love the things which he loved, refraining from all unrighteousness, covetousness, love of money, evil speaking, false witness, "rendering not evil for evil, or railing for railing," or blow for blow, or curse for curse, *but remembering what the Lord taught when he said*, "Judge not that ye be not judged, forgive and it shall be forgiven unto you, be merciful that ye may obtain mercy, with what measure ye mete, it shall be measured to you again," and, "Blessed are the poor, and they who are persecuted for righteousness' sake, for theirs is the Kingdom of God." (*Pol. Phil.* 2:2, 3, *LCL*, italics added)

The following example shows both the authority of the words of Jesus in the early Christian communities in which Polycarp was ministering and the danger of tampering with them. This is close to the warning given in Revelation 22:18-19 (compare to Deut. 4:2).

> For everyone who does not confess that Jesus Christ has come in the flesh is an anti-Christ"; and whosoever does not confess the testimony of the Cross is of the devil: *and whosoever perverts the oracles of the Lord for his own lusts*, and says that there is neither resurrection nor judgment,—this man is the first-born of Satan. Wherefore, leaving the foolishness of the crowd, and their false teaching, let us turn back

to the word which was delivered to us in the beginning, "watching unto prayer" and persevering in fasting, beseeching the all-seeing God in our supplications "to lead us not into temptation," *even as the Lord said*, "The spirit is willing, but the flesh is weak." (*Pol. Phil.* 7:1, 2, *LCL*, italics added)

In terms of the importance of the example of Jesus as a rule or guide to the Christian community, Polycarp's following example is also instructive: "*Let us then be imitators of his endurance*, and if we suffer for his name's sake let us glorify him. *For this is the example which he gave us in himself*, and this is what we have believed" (Pol. *Phil.* 8:2, *LCL*, italics added).

The preceding passages clearly indicate the scriptural-like status of the words and example of Jesus for Polycarp, and he assumes the same for his readers. Another equally interesting passage in Polycarp is 6:3, in which he gives evidence of a "triptych" focus of authority in the Church: "So then 'let us serve *him* with fear and all reverence,' as he himself commanded us, and as did the *Apostles*, who brought us the Gospel, and the *Prophets* who foretold the coming of our Lord" (*Pol. Phil.* 6:3, *LCL*, italics added). In this passage, Polycarp acknowledges an awareness of the three canons of authority for mainstream second-century Christianity—Jesus, the apostles, and the OT ("Prophets"). Evidently, the words of Jesus, when written down as in this case, took on the significance of scripture even if they were not specifically called scripture. In I Clement 13:1-3, we find a possible parallel to this scriptural-like authority attributed to the words of Jesus, even though what is cited there may be extra-canonical tradition and not necessarily traditions in Matthew's Gospel.[28] Regardless, what is abundantly clear from these examples is that *Jesus himself was the authoritative canon of the Church* for Polycarp.

5. The author of II Peter (ca. 150, but possibly as late as ca. 180) referred to Paul's writings as being twisted by the "ignorant and unstable [that is, the heretics—Marcionites or Gnostics?] *as they do the other scriptures* [ὡς καὶ τὰς λοιπὰς γραφὰς]" (3:15-16). This author apparently placed Paul's epistles on a par with the OT scriptures, or, less likely perhaps, on a par with other Christian writings that were recognized as authoritative or normative at that time. He

is also aware of the "heretical" use of Paul's letters, a possible veiled reference to Marcion.

6. In his Letter of Ptolemy to Flora (ca. 160), Ptolemy, while seeking in 3:6 to establish the integrity of the Jewish scriptures (the OT) and also their correct interpretation, appealed throughout his letter to the "words of the Savior" (3:5, 8; 4:1, 4) as well as to the command of the Savior (5:9) and his teachings (7:9) as his primary authority. However, he also cites "the apostle" (John, in 3:6) as one would quote scripture.[29] These references are especially meaningful since Ptolemy comes from outside of what was later known as mainstream Christianity. Nonetheless, they show quite clearly his acceptance of the authority of the words of Jesus, some of which he took from the Gospel of Matthew and some from John. Along with the authority of a properly interpreted OT, Ptolemy also completes his triptych of authority with an acknowledgment of the authority of the words of the Savior and of the apostles (at least John and probably also Matthew).

7. Justin Martyr (ca. 150–160) gives two strands of evidence of the recognition of the scriptural status of the gospel writings. First, he refers to Jesus' words in Matthew 11:27 with a scripture-like designation.

> In the Gospel *it is written* (γέγραπται) that He said: "All things are delivered unto me by My Father;" and, "no man knoweth the Father but the Son; nor the Son but the Father, and they to whom the Son will reveal Him." (*Trypho* 100:1 ff., also 101:3, *ANF*, italics added)

Second, Justin shows that the Gospels, or the "memoirs of the Apostles" (ἀπομνημονεύατα τῶν ἀποστόλων) as he calls them, were used to establish doctrine (*Trypho* 100:1), and also to relate the story of Jesus' passion. For instance, when introducing quotations from Luke 22:44 and 42, Justin writes: "For in the memoirs which I say were drawn up by His apostles and those who followed them, [it is recorded] His sweat fell down like drops of blood." (*Trypho* 103:8, *ANF*). He also appeals to the canonical gospels when explaining the apostolic testimony regarding the Eucharist, acknowledging that "the Apostles commanded them: that Jesus, taking bread and hav-

ing given thanks he said" (I *Apol.* 66:3, *ECF*). After these opening
words, Justin cites Mark 14:22-24 and I Corinthians 11:23-25 as
descriptions of what was said in the Eucharist. He also describes the
use of the Gospels as reading materials in Church worship, either
read alongside of or used alternatively with the OT writings. In his
account of a typical worship service in the Christian community, he
explains that "on the day called Sunday there is a meeting in one
place of those who live in cities or the country, and *the memoirs of
the apostles or the writings of the prophets are read as long as time
permits* (I *Apol.* 67:3, *ECF,* italics added).

For Justin, the canonical gospels functioned as scripture on a par
with the OT scriptures. Strangely, however, he makes no clear reference to Paul's writings, which were surely known in Rome well before Justin's time. On the other hand, Justin does refer to the book of
Revelation (*Trypho* 81:4) with favor, giving us one of the earliest
expositions of a text from that document, which was finally wel-
comed in the Western churches in the fourth century. In I *Apol.*
28:1, he calls Revelation one of "our writings" (ἡμέτερα συγγράμματα).

8. In the letter known as The Martyrs of Lyons and Vienna
(ca. 175–177)—found in Eusebius (*Hist. eccl.* 5.1.3-63)—many references, allusions, and quotations from the NT literature are found,
including references to noncanonical literature. One of the most interesting references for our purposes is the one to Revelation 22:11,
which is preceded by the words "that the Scripture might be fulfilled" (5.1.58, *LCL*). Again, not only does this text show us the
high regard for the book of Revelation in the Western churches, but
it is also one of the earliest references to the book as "scripture."

9. Irenaeus (ca. 170–180) also expresses the triptych of the early
Church—that is, the threefold source of authority in the church—
when he writes, "the *Lord* doth testify, as the *apostles* confess, and
as the *prophets* announce" *(Adv. Haer.* 3.17.4, *ANF).* It is interesting that he put these three in the order he did (prophets last). However, his ordering is still very much like the triptych of authority
found elsewhere in second-century writers, who acknowledged the
authority of the Lord (sayings of Jesus, and especially the Gospels,
after 150 C.E.), the OT (Prophets), and the Apostles (primarily
Paul).[30] We will return to Irenaeus later.

A few other observations of the second century should be mentioned before summarizing the significance of the above references
for our present study. Tatian (ca. 160–170) did not consider the four
canonical gospels inviolable. His creation of the Church's first harmony of the four evangelists and other gospel traditions into one
account known as the *Diatessaron* was used in the Syrian churches
up to the fifth century. Eusebius, speaking of what he considered
heretical groups originating with Tatian, claimed concerning him:

> Their former leader Tatian composed in some way a combination
> and collection of the gospels, and gave this the name of *The Diates-*
> *saron*, and this is still extant in some words of the apostles, *as though*
> *correcting their style.* He has left a great number of writings, of
> which the most famous, quoted by many, is his discourse *Against the*
> *Greeks.* In it he deals with primitive history, and all those who are
> celebrated among the Greeks. This seems to be the best and most
> helpful of all his writings. Such are the facts of this period. (*Hist.*
> *eccl.* 4.20.6-7, *ANF*, italics added)

Tatian's willingness to change the four canonical gospels is important to us in many regards, not the least is his perception about their
inspired status. Although he valued them sufficiently that they
served as his primary sources for compiling his *Diatessaron*, he was
not afraid to change the texts in order to make a unified gospel text.
In the above passage, Eusebius indicates that Tatian not only made
use of the four Gospels in his *Diatessaron*, but also that he "para-
phrased some words of the apostle," a reference probably to the
apostle Paul. After Tatian, both Athanagoras (ca. 180) and
Theophilus of Antioch (ca. 190–200) made use of Paul's writings
alongside the canonical gospels as normative Christian literature.
Athanagoras, for instance, appeals to Paul to argue his case about
life after death.

> The result of all of this is very plain to everyone, —namely, that, in
> the language of the apostle (κατὰ τὸν ἀπόστολον), "This corruptible
> (and dissoluble) must put on incorruption, in order that those who
> were dead . . . may, in accordance with justice, receive what he has
> done by the body, whether it be good or bad." (*The Resurrection of*
> *the Dead* 18, *ANF*; compare with I Cor. 15:54)

Theophilus also shows heavy dependence on the writings of Paul, especially Romans 2:7-9 and I Corinthians 2:9, in calling on Autolycus to hear and reverence the Word of God.

> But you also, please give reverential attention to the *prophetic Scriptures*, for they will make it plain to you how to escape the eternal punishments and obtain the eternal prizes of God. For He who gave the mouth for speech and formed the ear to hear and made the eye to see will examine all things and will judge [with] righteous judgment. [He will also] render merited awards to seek immortality, and He will give life everlasting, joy, peace, rest, and abundance of good things, which neither has the eye seen nor the ear heard nor has it entered into the heart of man to conceive. But to the unbelieving and despisers, who do not obey the truth but are obedient to adulteries and fornications, filthiness, covetousness, and unlawful idolatries, there shall be anger and wrath, tribulation and anguish, and at the last everlasting fire shall possess them. (adapted from Theophilus *Ad Autolycum* 1:14, ANF)

The significance of the preceding references is that they show a growing tendency on the part of the Church to transfer the recognized authoritative teaching of Jesus found in the Gospels to a recognition of the authority of the documents themselves. This is especially seen for the first time in the writings of Justin. After the time of Justin, Paul's epistles also seem to appear with a scriptural-like authority in the churches, especially in the writings of Irenaeus, Theophilus of Antioch, and Athenagoras. By the year 200, it is almost certain that the collection of Christian writings that had achieved the status of scripture in the Church at large had as its core the Gospels and the writings of Paul. This was by no means a closed canon of NT writings, however, even though for Irenaeus only the four canonical gospels among the literature of that genre had obtained a widely recognized scriptural status in the Church. The authority of Jesus was still the most important authority in the Church at the end of the second century, even though most of his teachings that survived by that time were found only in the written Gospels. The growth of authoritative writings for the Church now included the OT scriptures; the teachings of Jesus, located primarily in the canonical gospels; and the epistles of Paul. However, a number of other NT writings circulated in the churches with growing appreciation and, in the case of some (Revelation), a scripture-like status gradually became accepted in many churches.

One is tempted to venture guesses as to why literature that was not recognized as scripture in the first century Church took on that distinction in the churches of the second century. One historical example of this exists in the case of the OT canon in Judaism, though not with complete parallels. Only the Law had scriptural importance to the Jews in the reforms of Josiah. After the time of Ezra, the whole Pentateuch became important. Subsequently, the Prophets also obtained that position, though no later than 200 B.C.E. When many of the religious leaders believed that the prophetic presence had ceased, there was a tendency to "inscripturate" the writings of the generation when that prophetic-spiritual presence of the Lord was believed to have resided in Israel. In the case of the second-century Church, however, there are no examples of a time when the Church believed that the age of the Spirit and prophecy itself had ceased, even though the office of prophet had already begun to diminish in favor of a more stable local bishop-presbyter. Chronological distance from the primary events that called the Church into existence no doubt played some role in the recognition of the value of the testimony of the first generation Christians. The further removed the Church was from the eyewitnesses of the events primary to the Church's confession of faith, so it seems, the more venerated those early documents became. This is, of course, only "informed guess work," and it is safer to return to what historically can be shown to have led to the emergence of a closed Christian canon.

The primary significance of the above references is that they are helpful in finding already in second-century Christianity seeds of the later recognition of the authority and scriptural status of the NT writings. This conclusion, however, calls for three important cautions. First, any acknowledgment of the authority of one part of the NT literature at this time does not imply that all of it was so recognized everywhere. Second, because one writer may have referred to a part of the NT as scripture or its equivalent does not mean that all Christians of the same era came to the same conclusion. Finally, even if some of the NT writings were recognized as having the status of scripture in the second century, this is still not the same as a closed canon of scriptures, even though it is clear that with the recognition of the authority of certain Christian writings the canonical process was in motion.

III. Marcion and an Early Canon

Although the mid-second-century Church was gradually recognizing the usefulness of a body of Christian literature for its life and worship, there were as yet no fixed normative collections to which one could appeal. It was Marcion (ca. 140–150), a native of Sinope in Pontus and a wealthy ship owner, who first saw the importance of a fixed list of authoritative Christian writings, a *Christian* canon. However, his design appears to have been not so much an insight into the normative value of NT writings (an edited Paul and an abbreviated Luke) as it was a rejection of the value of the OT scriptures and the Jewish influence on the Christian community. Marcion believed that the Christian gospel of absolute love was completely contrary to the Law. This belief led him to write his *Antitheses*, which rejected the OT altogether. Along with the Judaistic influence on Christianity, Marcion also rejected the dissatisfying typological and allegorical hermeneutical approaches to the OT, which the Church commonly employed to make the OT relevant to the Christian faith. He believed that Christianity was something completely new, and he stressed that the God of the Law was a *Demiurge*,[31] or the creator god according to gnostic belief. He argued that the god of the OT was not the same as the unknown God of the gospel and of Jesus; therefore, he turned his attention toward effecting a total separation of Christianity from its Jewish roots and influences. Although he has often been considered one of the Gnostics, or believed to have been heavily influenced by them, he would have had little sympathy with their mythological speculations.[32]

Tertullian's criticisms of Marcion, which included five lengthy books some fifty years later (190–200), show not only the importance of the arguments of Marcion, but also tell of his significant impact on the greater Church for a considerable period of time. Reflecting Marcion's two most significant teachings, Tertullian writes:

Marcion's special and principal work is the separation of the law and the gospel, and his disciples will not deny that in this point they have their very best pretext for initiating and confirming themselves in his heresy. These are Marcion's *Antitheses,* or contradictory propositions, which aim at distinguishing the gospel from the Law in order that from the diversity of the two documents [OT and NT ?] that contain them, they may contend for a diversity of gods also. Since, therefore, it is this very contrast between the Law and the gospel that has suggested [to the Marcionites] that the *God of the gospel is different from the God of the Law,* it is clear then that, before the said separation [before the gospel came], that the God of the Christians (the God of the gospel) could not have been known [before] the argument of the separation itself. He therefore could not have been revealed by Christ who came before the separation, but must have been devised by Marcion who is the author of the breach of peace between the gospel and the law. Now this peace, which had remained unhurt and unshaken from Christ's appearance to the time of Marcion's audacious doctrine, was no doubt maintained by that way of thinking which firmly held that the God of both law and gospel was none other than the Creator. It was against this God that the heretic from Pontus [Marcion] introduced a separation [or division] after such a long time of there being a unity. (adapted from *Adv. Marc.* 1, 19, *ANF*)[33]

Marcion recognized perhaps more clearly than others of his day the embarrassment the OT posed for the early Church. The God of the OT seemed to him to be quite harsh, even cruel at times, and especially both vengeful and changeable. The moral standards of an "eye for an eye" were hard for Marcion to reconcile with Jesus' call to "turn the other cheek." Equally difficult was the task of ascribing a normative value to the OT, which he saw as no longer binding for the Christian. This was especially true of the legal and moral codes and traditions associated with keeping the Law. Taking his cue from Paul, Marcion argued that the Christian is free from the Law and, therefore, has no reason to give token allegiance to that which has been rendered obsolete by faith in Christ. It was only by the most arbitrary means of interpreting (using allegory and typology—or *pesher* exegesis), he claimed, that the OT could have the slightest meaning at all.[34] Marcion's rejection of the OT, together with the most common hermeneutical approach for interpreting it, stripped

the Church not only of its scriptures but also of its prized claim to
the heritage of antiquity and to being the religion of historical fulfillment.[35] Marcion's primary aim was the task of separating the
Christian tradition from the influence of the OT and Judaism. He,
therefore, created this tradition by selecting as authoritative literature[36] only the Gospel of Luke, from which he eliminated all OT
influences and traces,[37] and a freely edited collection of ten Pauline
epistles,[38] which he used as the basis for his teaching. He apparently
added nothing new to these documents except his introduction, or
antitheses.[39] His bible was composed of a Gospel (Luke)[40] and Epistles (ten of Paul's), or, in keeping somewhat with an earlier tradition, the sayings of Jesus and the writings of the apostles.[41] His
triptych was now two-fold, with a conscious effort to reject the
Prophets (OT).[42]

For the sake of canonical studies, Marcion undoubtedly was a
major catalyst in forcing the Church to come to grips with the question of which literature best conveyed its true identity. ("Heretics"
have always had that kind of positive effect on the Church![43]) Both
Irenaeus and Tertullian reacted against Marcion's rejection of the
OT and his rejection of all the Gospel literature except Luke,[44] but
with Marcion one finds the first clear reference to Luke and to a
fixed collection of Pauline writings.[45] More complete collections of
NT writings began to appear only later in the time of Irenaeus—
that is, the four Gospel canon[46]—probably as a response to the
teachings of Marcion.[47] Marcion's rejection of all Jewish influences
on the gospel and his exclusive opting for an edited Luke has an
interesting counter parallel in the Ebionites, who, according to Irenaeus, also had a one-Gospel canon—Matthew—and they rejected
Paul. He writes:

> Those who are called Ebionites agree that the world was made by
> God; but their opinions with respect to the Lord are similar to those
> of Cerinthus and Carpocrates. They use the Gospel according to Mat-
> thew only, and repudiate the Apostle Paul, maintaining that he was
> an apostate from the Law. (*Adv. Haer.*, 1:26.2, ANF)

It may be too strong to suggest, as Harnack and later von Campenhausen did, that Marcion was the "creator of the Christian holy
scripture" (*Formation*, p. 163) since it has already been shown that

there were tendencies in that direction before Marcion, but it is generally conceded that Marcion was the first to set forth a well-defined collection of Christian writings. In spite of his motive of effecting a separation of Christianity from the influences of Judaism,[48] Marcion had the effect of spurring the Church into rethinking its understanding of its scriptures. The Church eventually may have recognized the need for a canon of Christian scriptures without the aid of Marcion, as Blackman maintains,[49] but there is little doubt that the evidence points toward Marcion as the source of the earliest Christian canon—that is, a closed collection of sacred Christian writings—and also as one of the primary influences that caused the Church to focus more clearly on the scope of its authoritative literature. The notion of canonicity was not in itself unique to Marcion, since, as was shown earlier, such ideas were common in the contemporary Hellenistic world and were beginning to emerge in Judaism. However, so far as our present knowledge goes, his was the first closed canon of Christian writings to appear in the ancient Church, even though the establishment of a closed canon was not his primary goal.[50]

IV. Justin and the Roots of a Christian Bible

The years following Marcion were mixed and troubled as a result of the impact of his challenge to the emerging "orthodox" Church, especially with regard to the Church's use of the OT. Justin Martyr, who appears to have given implicit scriptural status to Christian writings,[51] tried to make it clear that, in spite of Marcion's objections, the OT was a *Christian* book. In his defense of the OT, he became the first orthodox writer to set forth a doctrine of holy scripture. He specifically answered the questions of how the Christians could reject the normative status of the Law (a common practice by that time) and yet still accept the OT as scripture. This problem was first addressed by Paul.[52] Later, and in more detail, Justin tried to rescue the OT as a Christian book in two important ways. First, he appealed to a historical scheme of prophecy and fulfillment—that is, that the truthfulness of *all* scripture is proved by the OT prophecies that were fulfilled in Christ. His unwillingness to subject the OT to careful assessment and his blind appeal to its infallibility, whether or not he could respond to critical questions related to it, however, were not his best defense. Notice, for instance, his insistance on the infallibility of scripture in his *Dialogue with Trypho*, when he remarks:

> If you spoke these words, Trypho, and then kept silence in simplicity and with no ill intent, neither repeating what goes before nor adding what comes after, you must be forgiven; but if you have done so because you imagined that you could throw doubt on the passage, in order that I might say the scriptures contradicted one another, you have erred. But I shall not venture to suppose or to say such a thing, and if a scripture that appears to be of such a kind be brought forward, and if there be a pretext for saying that it is contrary to some other, since I am entirely convinced that no scripture contradicts another, I shall admit rather that I do not understand what is recorded and shall strive to persuade those who imagine that the scriptures are contradictory to be rather of the same opinion as myself. (adapted from *Trypho* 65:2, ANF)

More important, in defending the Christian use of the OT, Justin made little use of the readily available allegorical or typological exegesis of the Law, which at any rate would have been understandable only to those who were Christian and also would not have satisfied the Marcionite Christians, who rejected that kind of exegesis.[53]

Second, Justin uniquely interpreted the Law as *divine ordinances* given by God because of Israelite disobedience. He argued that the Law was intended solely for the Jews as punishment for their sins. Although he argues that circumcision preceded Moses' giving of the Law, he adds that the other ordinances came as a result of Israel's failure. Trypho apparently agrees with some of this argument.

> Then I answered [Trypho the Jew], "you perceive that God by Moses laid all such ordinances upon you on account of the hardness of your people's hearts, so that, by the large number of them, you might keep [obey] God continually in every action before your eyes and never begin to act unjustly or impiously." (adapted from *Trypho* 46:5, ANF; see also 27:2-4)

Even the imposition of the Sabbath, circumcision, temple sacrifices, dietary laws, ritual washings, Justin claimed, were God's punishments for a disobedient people. In a clear reference to the recent edict of Hadrian the emperor (135 C.E.) to expel the Jews from Jerusalem *(Aelia Capitolina),* Justin argues that God gave circumcision to the Jews as a sign of identification so they could be punished!

> For the circumcision according to the flesh, which is Abraham, was given for a sign that you may be separated from other nations and from us, in order that you alone may suffer and your land be made desolate and your cities burned with fire, and so that strangers may eat your fruit in your presence and not one of you may go up to Jerusalem. *(Trypho 16:2, ECF)*[54]

Justin concluded that the OT laws were harmless in themselves and that it would not be wrong to keep them, even though they would not be beneficial to those who kept them *(Trypho 27:2-4; 46:5).* His attempt to rescue the OT in this way appears to have been both successful and influential since the same argument was picked up later by both Irenaeus *(Adv. Haer.* 4:15; 16:3-5; 2:1, 28) and Tertullian *(Adv. Marc.* 2:18 ff.; 22).

Justin did not specifically call for a new collection of Christian scriptures, even though he unquestionably recognized the authority of the "memoirs of the Apostles" for Christian faith and claims that they were used in Rome in liturgical readings along with the OT scriptures (I *Apol.* 66, 67).[55] The "memoirs" were an authoritative guide to the teaching of Jesus on church matters,[56] and they appear to have been restricted to the Synoptic Gospels.[57]

Justin, in the earliest description of Christian worship, indicated that these "memoirs" (or Gospels) were read along with the Prophets as time allowed.

> After these [services] we constantly remind each other of these things. Those who have more come to the aid of those who lack, and we are constantly together. Over all that we receive we bless the Maker of all things through his Son Jesus Christ and through the Holy Spirit. And on the day called Sunday there is a meeting in one place of those who live in cities or the country, and the *memoirs of the apostles* or the writings of the prophets are read as long as time permits. When the reader has finished, the president in a discourse urges and invites [us] to *the imitation of these noble things.* Then we all stand up together and offer prayers. And, as said before, when we have finished

the prayer, bread is brought, and wine and water, and the president similarly sends up prayers and thanksgivings to the best of his ability, and the congregation assents, saying the Amen; the distribution, and reception of the consecrated [elements] by each one, takes place and they are sent to the absent by the deacons. Those who prosper, and who so wish, contribute, each one as much as he chooses to. What is collected is deposited with the president, and he takes care of orphans and widows, and those who are in want on account of sickness or any other cause, and those who are in bonds, and the strangers who are sojourners among [us], and, briefly, he is the protector of all those in need. We all hold this common gathering on Sunday, since it is the first day, on which God transforming darkness and matter made the universe, and Jesus Christ our Saviour rose from the dead on the same day. For they crucified him on the day before Saturday, and on the day after Saturday, he appeared to his apostles and disciples and taught them these things which I have passed on to you also for your serious consideration. (I *Apol.* 67, *ECF,* italics added)

Notice that the above text shows that immediately after these documents were read, "the president in a discourse urges and invites [us] to the imitation of the noble things." This, of course, implies that the "imitation" of the "noble things" in these documents also called for a recognition of their value in the life of the Christian community. This practice eventually led the Christians to recognize the gospel literature as scripture; because this literature served the cultic needs of the community of faith and was viewed as normative, it was shortly thereafter called "scripture" in the Church.[58] Justin's practice, as well as that of the church he attended in Rome, of placing Christian literature alongside the OT for reading during Christian worship services no doubt made Irenaeus' recognition of the Christian writings as scripture easier.[59] Justin's arguments for the authority of the OT writings and his use of the Gospels helped to pave the way for Irenaeus' designation of those two bodies of sacred literature not only as "scriptures" but also as "OT" and "NT."

V. Irenaeus and the Principle of "Canon"

Irenaeus of Lyons (writing ca. 170–180), according to von Campenhausen, marked "the transition from the earlier period of belief in tradition [primitive Christianity] to the new age of deliberate canonical standardization" (*Formation*, p. 182). Unlike Justin, he did not defend just the OT scriptures alone, but he also explicitly named and defended the scriptural authority of the Christian writings. His point, however, was not so much to establish a canon as it was to defend the truth of the Christian message.[60] In fact, *the "canon" of Irenaeus was not a list of inspired books, but rather the faith of and about Christ*, which he believed had been passed on in the Church from the apostles—that is, the apostolic tradition (see *Adv. Haer.* 3.2.2). Irenaeus' summary of "the faith" or "the canon" on which the Church depended for its life and witness is summarized in one major text that merits our attention since the major tenets of this passage became the foundation stones of "orthodoxy" in the Church and were a major part of most of the significant ancient creedal formulations.

> The Church, though dispersed throughout the whole world, even to the ends of the earth, has received from the apostles and their disciples this faith: It believes in one God, the Father Almighty, Maker of heaven and earth and the sea and all things that are in them and in one Christ Jesus, the Son of God, who became incarnate for our salvation and in the Holy Spirit, who proclaimed through the prophets the dispensations of God, the advents, the birth from a virgin, the passion, the resurrection from the dead, and the ascension into heaven in the flesh of the beloved Christ Jesus, our Lord. He also proclaimed through the prophets his future manifestation from heaven in the glory of the Father "to gather all things in one" and to raise up anew all flesh of the whole human race in order that to Christ Jesus, our Lord, God, Savior, and King, according to the will of the invisible Father, "every knee should bow, of things in heaven, and things in earth, and things under the earth, and that every tongue should confess" to him, and that he should execute just judgment toward all sending into everlasting fire "spiritual wickednesses," and the angels who transgressed and became apostates, together with the ungodly, and unrighteous, and wicked, and profane among men. But that he may, in the exercise of his grace, confer immortality on the righteous and holy, and those who have kept his commandments and have persevered in his love, some from the beginning of their Christian course and others from the date of their repentance. He will surround them with everlasting glory. (adapted from *Adv. Haer.*, 1:10.1, *ANF*; compare with 3.4.2)

Irenaeus began to use both the OT scriptures and selected Christian writings as a basis for demonstrating the authenticity of his teachings. Also, he was the first, so far as our present knowledge allows, to use the terms *Old Testament* and *New Testament*, and he claimed that both testaments were scripture and, therefore, authoritative for Christian faith. See, for example, how Irenaeus introduces a premise for his line of argument with the words, "Inasmuch, then, as in both testaments there is the same righteousness of God [displayed]" *(Adv. Haer.* 4.28.1, *ANF).* Also illustrative of Irenaeus' view is the brief comment at the end of Book II in which he claims that

> the preaching of the apostles, the authoritative teaching of the Lord, the announcements of the prophets, the dictated utterances of the apostles, and the ministration of the law—all of which praise one and the same Being, the God and Father of all, and not many diverse beings . . . are all in harmony with our statements." *(Adv. Haer.* 2:35.4, *ANF)*

In another place he writes:

> If, therefore, even in the New Testament the apostles are found granting certain precepts in consideration of human infirmity . . . it ought not to be wondered at, if also in the Old Testament the same God permitted similar indulgences for the benefit of His people . . . so that they might obtain the gift of salvation through them." *(Adv. Haer.* 4.15.2, *ANF)*[61]

Hans von Campenhausen, referring to Irenaeus' larger list of authoritative writings, explains that he was "the first catholic theologian who dared to adopt the Marcionite principle of a new 'scripture' in order to use it in his turn against Marcion and all heretics" *(Formation,* p. 186).

It should be stressed before moving on that the establishing of a closed canon of inspired scriptures was not Irenaeus' primary concern. He wanted to defend the Christian message with all the tools at his disposal; he sought the guarantee of apostolic preaching by the argument of the succession of bishops as well as by the authority of the scriptures of both the OT and the NT.

Irenaeus' strongest argument that the rule of faith or tradition that he proclaimed was the correct one was his belief in apostolic succession. He emphasized this again and again, but nowhere more clearly than in the following well-known text.

> The blessed apostles, then, having founded and built up the Church, committed into the hands of Linus the office of episcopate. Paul makes mention of this Linus in the Epistles to Timothy. Anacletus succeeded him, and Clement was allotted the bishopric. Clement, since he had seen the blessed apostles and had been conversant with them, might be said to have the preaching of the apostles still echoing in his ears, and their traditions before his eyes. . . . Evaristus succeeded this Clement, and he was succeeded by Sixtus, the sixth from the apostles. After him came Telephorus, who was gloriously martyred, then Hyginus, after him Pius, and then after him Anicetus was appointed. Anicetus was succeeded by Soter and Eleutherius, who is the twelfth from the apostles and now holds the inheritance of the episcopate. In this order and *by this succession, the ecclesiastical tradition from the apostles and the preaching of the truth have come down to us. And this is the most abundant proof that there is one and the same vivifying faith, which has been preserved in the Church from the apostles until now, and handed down in truth.* (adapted from *Adv. Haer.* 3.3.3, ANF)[62]

If questions are not clearly dealt with in the "apostolic deposit," or if no deposit had been left, where does one turn for the answer? For Irenaeus, the obvious answer lies with those to whom the apostolic deposit was given: the bishops of the churches.

> For how should it be if the apostles themselves had not left us writings? Would it not be necessary in that case to follow the course of the tradition they handed down to those to whom they handed over the leadership of the churches? (adapted from *Adv. Haer.* 3.4.1, *ANF*)

The effect of Irenaeus' concern to preserve the truth of the gospel was that the Church began to recognize a collection of authoritative NT writings (the Gospels especially, but also Paul), which, as Koester notes, was later followed—though not uniformly—by the churches in Asia Minor and Greece as well as by the churches in Antioch, Carthage, and Rome.[63] This collection was not yet closed in Irenaeus' time, even though with reference to gospel literature, he only acknowledged the four canonical Gospels.

In Irenaeus' writings, the boundaries of the Christian faith became more precise than before relative to the catholic dimensions of the Church. For him the Church was much broader in scope than Marcion would allow, though not yet broad enough to include Marcion or the Gnostic Christians. Nonetheless, it should be observed that this recognition of the normative status of the Christian writings emerged during a period when the definition of what it meant to be a Christian was being framed. What grew out of his polemic against heresy was a Church that was clarifying its identity along with its Bible within a broad and often conflicting tradition that was partially oral in form. Again, Irenaeus' *primary* concern was to defend the Christian message, which was his "canon." In that process, however, he also set forth the limits of that message in terms of the apostolic tradition resident in the Church and by setting forth the primary literature (the four NT Gospels) that he believed was reflective of that tradition. His defense of the four-fold gospel "canon" that he employed in his argument against the heretics is certainly strange by today's standards. Indeed, the manner in which he tried to limit the authoritative gospel literature to the four canonical Gospels was not the most convincing line of reasoning even in the ancient world!

> It is not possible that the Gospels can be either more or fewer in number than they are. For, since there are four zones of the world in which we live and four principal winds, while the Church is scattered throughout all the world and while the "pillar and ground" of the Church is the Gospel and the spirit of life, it is fitting, therefore, that the Church should have four pillars, breathing out immortality on every side, and vivifying men afresh. . . .
>
> But that these Gospels [the four canonical Gospels] alone are true and reliable and admit neither an increase nor a diminution of the aforesaid number, I have proved by so many such arguments. (adapted from *Adv. Haer.* 3.11.8, 9, *ANF.* See also 3.1.1.)

Irenaeus believed that the four gospels and other NT literature, along with the OT writings, were normative for the Church, and he clearly called these writings "scripture" (1.9.4; 2.26.1, 2; 3.1.1, and so on). However, although it is evident that Irenaeus intended to acknowledge the necessity of the four canonical evangelists, he also unwittingly did something that no canonical Gospel writer ever intended to do—namely, to suggest that somehow the Christian message was incomplete if only one Gospel (or less than four) were used by the Church. Luke seems either to have ignored or to have rejected the Gospels that preceded him (Mark?), apparently writing to correct them with a "more orderly account" (Luke 1:1-4). John, who must surely have known of Mark, offers a significantly differ- ent picture of Jesus' life, message, death, and resurrection. John also does not suggest that his Gospel needs the others to support his claims or even to supplement them.[64] Although Irenaeus may have seen the need for four "pillars" of gospels for the Church, it is diffi- cult to establish that the four evangelists themselves or anyone be- fore Irenaeus saw such a need.[65]

Irenaeus' notion of canon—the *faith* that was delivered over to the Church by the apostles—was not unique to himself, but appears fairly widespread as the criterion of truth, which defined the pa- rameters of acceptable behavior in the Church. For example, Bishop Serapion of Antioch (ca. 200), when asked by the Christians in Rhossus for permission to read the Gospel of Peter in the Church, agreed at first to let it be read. However, after reading it himself at a later time and seeing that it denied the humanity of Jesus, Serapion reversed himself. Eusebius preserves this letter of reversal.

> For our part, brethren, we receive both Peter and the other apos- tles as Christ, but the writings which falsely bear their names we reject, as men of experience, knowing that such were not handed down to us. For I myself, when I came among you, imagined that all of you clung to the true faith, and, without going through the Gospel put forward by them in the name of Peter, I said: If this is the only thing that seemingly causes captious feelings among you, let it be read. But since I have now learned from what has been told me that their mind was lurking in some hold of heresy, I shall give diligence to come again to you. Wherefore, brethren, expect me quickly. . . . For we have discovered that the Gospel of Peter was, for the most part, *in accordance with the true teaching of the Saviour,* but that some things were added, which also we place below for your benefit. (adapted from Esuebius, *Hist. eccl.* 12.3-6, *LCL*)

This concern for the truth—the widespread understanding of the truth of and about Jesus—was the primary emphasis of the churches in the last half of the second century. Irenaeus, however, also signaled the primary transition in the Church to a focus on the NT writings as scriptures. This focus eventually became the dominant concern in the Church by the fourth century, when the term *canon* came to mean a fairly precise collection of sacred writings. The factors leading to this development will be the focus of the next chapter.

CHAPTER
F I V E

FACTORS LIMITING THE SCOPE OF THE NEW TESTAMENT CANON

I. The Canon of Irenaeus

According to Irenaeus, his "canon of faith" *(regula fidei)* did not originate with him, but he received it through the succession of bishops of the Church from the apostles. Although not all scholars today would agree that Irenaeus' canon originated with the apostles, many would agree that for the most part he reflects beliefs of long standing in the Church. Not only were there earlier creedal formulations (some quite well known) in the first and early second centuries of the Church—I Corinthians 15:3-4; Philippians 2:5-11; Romans 10:9-10; I Timothy 3:16[1]—but also there was a high regard for what later became the canonical Gospels (especially Matthew in Syria and the West, but John in Asia Minor) and for Paul.[2] Such precedents were not new in the time of Irenaeus, but the recognition and actual referral of such literature as "scripture" were rather recent, even though it appears that the Church was headed in that direction for some time.

The literature that was or became normative in the second century churches no doubt included that which was most relevant to their own needs. This is a logical inference, evidenced by the many differing collections of Christian scriptures in the fourth-century churches. Most Christian churches at the turn of the second century were or appear to have been in basic agreement with the core of Irenaeus' collection of NT scriptures, even though no precise limitations were imposed on that collection. What becomes apparent is that this wide (but not exclusive) agreement emerged from the local churches themselves and not from any church council. There were, in fact, no council decisions regarding the scope of the NT scriptures before the last half of the fourth century.

What this also evidences is the wide popularity of "the faith" or a set of creedal beliefs similar to those set forth by Irenaeus. In this sense, the literature that found wide acceptance was that which was in basic agreement with this tradition of faith. The objections of the "orthodox" against the Gnostic "heresies" were not based on some new idea of what was true but on what had earlier roots within the Church itself. Among all the diversity that existed in the early Church, the broad parameters of the Christian message were not in serious doubt. For example, though the person of Jesus was difficult to describe for the early Christians, and the trinitarian formulations of his person are for the most part of late date, developing especially in the fourth century,[3] it was still widely acknowledged by the end of the first century that acceptance of the true humanity of Jesus was characteristic of Christian faith (I John 4:1-3); all four canonical Gospels evidence this. On the other hand, whether Jesus was identified as a spirit or as the Spirit or as an angel or as a divinely empowered man, the range of perspectives in the churches appears to have been quite broad.

Eschatological perspectives also varied in the earliest Christian literature, but all theologies had a hope in the future blessing of God for the faith directed toward Jesus. Within great diversity, therefore, some elements of Christian faith had long standing in the Christian communities and must have played a role in the churches' decisions as to which literature was useful in their life, faith, and worship.

The "orthodox" opposition to the limited canon of Marcion or to the many collections of sacred writings of the Gnostics came from local churches, based on their understanding of Christian faith that was believed to be "normal" in the majority of the churches.[4] It is instructive that opposition to the so-called heresies of the second centuries did not come from organized Church councils, but from local church leaders.

Early creedal statements, just like all subsequent creedal formulations, were forged in particular contexts in the churches and often were formed in a controversial setting. For example, I John 4:1-3, 6, 13-16, opposed the docetic controversy of the late first century. The result was that the theology of the ancient Christian churches always developed in different directions, being heavily influenced by diverse social contexts. This, in part, is why ancient Christian theology was neither monolithic, nor was it arrived at, even when many churches agreed on its substance, at the same time in all of the churches. Amid some very basic general agreements, most everything else in the churches varied in terms of both theology and practice. At the end of the second century, while the Church was interacting with extreme diversity ("heresy") there was a growing sense of need for uniformity in the Christian community, especially in the churches of the West. This development in itself may have been subconsciously influenced by the Romans, who were already calling for uniformity in social and religious matters. The mid-third-century Roman persecutions of Christians were in large measure the result of the growing call for uniformity and the Romans' fear of nonconformity. The many moves by Constantine to involve himself in church councils were clearly to bring about harmony in the Church and not purity of Christian doctrine.[5]

Whatever his original source or motivation, the influence that Irenaeus' theology and similar theologies had on his and subsequent generations, regarding which Christian scriptures were to be recognized, was quite strong. As von Campenhausen contends, this influence spread quite rapidly, and the move toward recognizing new scriptures in this era could not be checked. Although there was broad agreement on the Gospels and Paul—even among the heretical groups—the collection of sacred Christian writings was not thereby closed. (See *Formation*, p. 210.) The result of this, as he explains, was that:

> Attempts were made to secure as comprehensive and solid a collection as possible; and in the process people from various churches naturally

liked to adopt such books as confirmed their own points of view. There was thus a danger that even recent, tendentious works would find their way into the canon, as, for example, II Peter or the Shepherd of Hermas. (*Formation*, p. 211)

With the principle of recognizing a new set of scriptures behind it, the Church then found it necessary to identify precisely what those Christian scriptures were and what they were not. Several historical factors contributed to this clarification, which we will now attempt to show.

II. The Montanists

One factor that may have functioned as a limiting force in regard to the boundaries of the Christian scriptures was the emergence of the "New Prophecy" of the Montanists from Phrygia. Around 170 C.E., a man (possibly a priest of Cybele)[6] by the name of Montanus was joined by two women, Prisca and Maximilla, in Phrygia in Asia Minor, claiming to be inspired by the Paraclete and having an announcement of the coming Parousia of the Lord. Together they made a major impact on the people of Phrygia and were received with enthusiasm by many. Their message was apocalyptic in focus, strongly advocating their interpretation of the message of the Revelation to John. They emphasized prophecy, rigid asceticism, martyrdom, and the presence and power of the Holy Spirit. Frend has pointed to the long history of prophetic movements in that region and indicates that the orthodox were not well prepared to deal with the situation.[7] Those who most vigorously opposed the Montanists in Asia Minor, the so-called *Alogi*—a term referring to those who rejected the Gospel of the Word (or John)—rejected both the fourth Gospel and the book of Revelation. The response of the rest of the greater Church at large was a rejection of the Montanist movement and a reserve toward the Gospel of John, because of its focus on the Paraclete, and a reserve toward the book of Revelation (especially in the Eastern churches in the second and third centuries) because of its apocalyptic emphasis. Raymond Collins adds that even Hebrews was called into question by the Alogi because it was linked with the Montanist crisis.[8] This was probably because of that book's view of the hopeless condition of the apostate Christian, a view that co-incided with the Montanists' harsh penitential practice.[9]

What is most surprising about the Montanists, however, is that Tertullian became their most well-known convert. Numerous suggestions have been presented to explain the reason for this, but perhaps it was because of the strong emphasis on a rigorous ascetic life-style, which enticed him. Tertullian was a disciplined man with little toleration for the more weak and undisciplined souls. He may also have been impressed with the charismatic focus of the Montanists, which was always acknowledged in the greater Church as a legitimate and authentic expression of Christian faith, but which had declined rapidly in the second-century Church.

What is more relevant here is von Campenhausen's claim that the Montanists, in their enthusiasm, generated numerous books that they claimed were divinely inspired. In response, von Campenhausen says, the greater Church felt the need to identify more precisely which literature was inspired and, therefore, authoritative in the Church. Another interesting note about the Montanists is that both men and women became prophets in their church.[10] By the year 200, they had expanded their influence to Rome and North Africa, though their influence was primarily among rural communities.[11]

A more debatable issue has to do with whether the Montanists produced any literature, a point rejected by Schneemelcher,[12] but emphasized by von Campenhausen.[13] Von Campenhausen argues that the Montanists wrote down many of their prophecies and visions in books that they claimed were inspired and that these books ("innumerable books," according to Hippolytus) were then read in their assemblies.[14] He has also observed that Tertullian strongly defended this practice.

> It is, he says, mere prejudice to heed and value only past demonstrations of power and grace. "Those people who condemn the one power of the one Holy Spirit in accordance with chronological eras should beware." *It is the recent instances to which far higher respect ought to be paid;* for they already belong to the time of the End, and are to be prized as a superabundant increase of grace, "which God, in accordance with the testimony of scripture, has destined for precisely this period of time." (Tertullian, from his "introduction" in *Passio Perpetuae* 1.1., trans. by von Campenhausen, *Formation*, p. 229)

According to von Campenhausen, the mainstream churches rejected the Montanist prophecies essentially on the grounds that their prophecies were contrary to the earlier Christian writings, now called scriptures (see *Formation*, p. 231). In a polemic against the Montanists, recorded by Eusebius, a certain Apolinarius wrote:

> For a long and protracted time, my dear Abercius Marcellus, I have been urged by you to compose a treatise against the sect of those called after Miltiades, but until now I was somewhat reluctant, not from any lack of ability to refute the lie and testify to the truth, but from timidity and scruples *lest I might see to some to be adding to the writings or injuctions of the word of the new covenant of the gospel*, to which no one who has chosen to live according to the gospel itself can add and from which he cannot take away. But when I have just come to Ancyra in Galatia and perceived that the church in that place was torn in two by this new movement [the Montanists] which is not, as they call it, prophecy but much rather, as will be shown, false prophecy, I disputed concerning these people themselves and their propositions so far as I could, with the Lord's help, for many days continuously in the church. Thus the church rejoiced and was strengthened in the truth, but our opponents were crushed for the moment and our adversaries were distressed. (*Hist. eccl.* 5.16.3-4, *LCL*, italics added)

From this and other criticisms against the Montanists, von Campenhausen maintains that the Church could no longer continue either having a roughly defined canon of scriptures or rejecting the "heretical" forgeries. Therefore, he concludes, the Montanists and their production of numerous books were the primary factors that caused the Church to define more precisely which books belonged to the NT and which did not.[15] It was at this point, von Campenhausen claims, that the last phase of the canonical process began,[16] though it will become clear that this phase was by no means complete as a result of this polemic against the Montanists. Also, if the Church at large was interested in closing the NT canon at this time, one would expect to find numerous lists of canonical literature in this period, which is precisely what is missing. As will become clearer in the following sections of this chapter, more and *later* developments in the Church were also responsible for the need to close the canon of NT literature.

III. The Gnostics

Along with the Montanists, the Gnostic Christians in the second century produced a vast amount of literature that they considered sacred. Although their roots are somewhat obscure, unlike the case with the Montanists, a significant amount of their literature has been found and is now preserved in the recently translated Coptic documents, which were discovered in Nag Hammadi, Egypt, near the upper Nile in 1945. The Nag Hammadi Library—a collection of texts now translated in entirety by a team of Coptic scholars directed by James M. Robinson (NHLE), and more recently by Bentley Layton[17]—are the best sources available on Gnostic Christianity. These Gnostic documents, which originally came from outside Egypt and were translated into Coptic, have for the first time permitted us to view Gnostic Christianity from the *gnostic* perspective. Before this discovery, all that was known about these people and their views came from their opponents—the "orthodox" Christians, especially Irenaeus, who leveled the most severe attacks against them.[18]

Generally speaking, the Gnostic Christians, like Marcion, (1) denied that the Christians' God was also the creator of the world. For them, matter was evil and was created by a Demiurge, an evil and distant emmanation from the *pleroma*, or fulness of the divine. (2) They usually rejected the OT, especially after the time of Marcion, but not always.[19] (3) They distinguished the heavenly Savior from the human Jesus of Nazareth, a view that is not unlike various positions of *docetism*, a teaching that claimed that the Christ only "seemed" human. (4) They believed that full salvation is only for the pneumatics or spiritually elite (themselves), but that a lesser degree of salvation could be obtained by those who have only faith (without gnosis). Those completely involved in the world had no hope of salvation. (5) They claimed that they had received "secret" gospels from the apostles themselves. Interestingly, the oldest gospel that purports to be of apostolic authorship—by the way, no canonical Gospel makes such a claim for itself—is the apocryphal Gospel of Thomas, a Gnostic document.[20]

The widespread esoteric writings of the Gnostics, along with their claims to secret revelations from the apostles, were rejected by

Irenaeus, who argued instead for the legitimacy of the truth of the rule of faith, which he contends was passed on in the Church by apostolic succession through the bishops. Notice, for example, his famous line of reasoning: "For if the apostles had known hidden mysteries, which they were in the habit of imparting to 'the perfect' apart and privily from the rest, they would have delivered them especially to those to whom they were also committing the leadership of the churches themselves" (adapted from *Adv. Haer.* 3.3.1, *ANF*). One can scarcely deny Irenaeus' logic here.

The presence of these Gnostic writings at the end of the second century, along with those of the Montanists, must have been a powerful incentive to the "orthodox" churches to define more precisely not only Christian proclamation, but also the boundaries or limitations of their scriptures.

IV. The Burning of Sacred Books

On February 23, 303, Diocletian, the Roman emperor, launched the last great empire-wide persecution of the Christians. The reasons for this attack are not clear, but the most notable acts of hostility against the Christians are well known. Problems of loyalty to the emperor and threats of the disintegration of the empire loomed large, especially in Britain, Persia, and North Africa. Diocletian, in an almost paranoid state of mind, significantly increased the size of the military and began large rebuilding programs, hoping to return the empire to its former years of glory. More significant for our purposes, however, were Diocletian's actions aimed at restoring the Roman virtues, whose religious roots were in earlier acts of devotion to the Roman deities. His edict (ca. 295) regarding marriages (*De nuptitis*) focuses again and again on the need to return to religious uniformity.[21]

Diocletian insisted that no blood be shed, but demanded that all Christian churches be destroyed and that the sacred scriptures of the Christians be burned. Christians in public office were removed, those in the upper classes had their privileges taken away, and Christian slaves could not be freed. Unlike the earlier Decian persecution, which required Christians to sacrifice to the emperor, the Diocletian persecution sought to destroy the organization and life of the Church by eliminating the books, buildings, and offices of the Christians. Contrary to Diocletian's original plan, however, deaths of Christians did occur in many locations where the Christians refused to turn over their scriptures. Within a short time, Christians in some locations were forced to offer sacrifices as well.[22]

One such example of the Roman authorities' attempting to destroy the Christian scriptures took place in Alexandria, Egypt, in May of 303. The following text is helpful for understanding this discussion.

> In the eighth and seventh consulships of Diocletian and Maximian, 19th May, from the records of Munatius Felix, high priest of the province for life, Mayor of the colony of Cirta, arrived at the house where the Christians used to meet. The Mayor said to Paul the bishop: "Bring out the writings of the law and anything else you have here, according to the order, so that you may obey the command."
>
> **The Bishop:** "The readers have the scriptures, but we will give what we have here."
>
> **The Mayor:** "Point out the readers or send for them."
>
> **The Bishop:** "You all know them."
>
> **The Mayor:** "We do not know them."
>
> **The Bishop:** "The municipal office knows them, that is, the clerks Edusius and Junius."
>
> **The Mayor:** "Leaving over the matter of the readers, whom the office will point out, produce what you have."
>
> Then follows an inventory of the church plate and other property, including large stores of male and female clothes and shoes, produced in the presence of the clergy, who included three priests, two deacons, and four subdeacons, all named, and a number of "diggers."
>
> **The Mayor:** "Bring out what you have."
>
> **Silvanus and Carosus** (two of the subdeacons): "We have thrown out everything that was here."
>
> **The Mayor:** "Your answer is entered on the record."
>
> After some empty cupboards have been found in the library, Silvanus then produced a silver box and a silver lamp, which he said he had found behind a barrel.
>
> **Victor** (the mayor's clerk): "You would have been a dead man if you hadn't found them."

The Mayor: "Look more carefully, in case there is anything left here."

Silvanus: "There is nothing left. We have thrown everything out."

And when the dining-room was opened, there were found there four bins and six barrels.

The Mayor: "Bring out the scripture that you have so that we can obey the orders and command of the emperors."

Catullinus (another subdeacon) produced one very large volume.

The Mayor: "Why have you given one volume only? Produce the scriptures that you have."

Marcuclius and Catullinus (two subdeacons): "We haven't any more, because we are subdeacons; the readers have the books."

The Mayor: "If you don't know where they live, tell me their names."

Marcuclius and Catullinus: "We are not traitors: here we are, order us to be killed."

The Mayor: "Put them under arrest."

They apparently weakened so far as to reveal one reader, for the Mayor now moved on to the house of Eugenius, who produced four books.

The Mayor now turned on the other two subdeacons, Silvanus and Carosus:

The Mayor: "Show me the other readers."

Silvanus and Carosus: "The bishop has already said that Edusius and Junius the clerks know them all: they will show you the way to their houses."

Edusius and Junius: "We will show them, sir."

The Mayor went on to visit the six remaining readers. Four produced their books without demur. One declared he had none, and the Mayor was content with entering his statement of the record. The last was out, but his wife produced his books; the Mayor had the house searched by the public slave to make sure that none had been overlooked. This task over, he addressed the subdeacons: "If there has been any omission, the responsibility is yours." (*Gesta apud Zenophilum* XXVI, in Stevenson, *ANE*, pp. 287-89)

Eusebius describes this persecution in significant detail, emphasizing especially the martyrs at Nicomedia (*Hist. eccl.* 8.5-6). His introduction to the Diocletian persecution specifically mentions the burning of the sacred scriptures.

> All things in truth were fulfilled in our day, when we saw with our very eyes the houses of prayer cast down to their foundations from top to bottom, and the inspired and sacred Scriptures committed to the flames in the midst of the marketplaces, and the pastors of the churches, some shamefully hiding themselves here and there, while others were ignominiously captured and made a mockery by their enemies; when also, according to another prophetic word, He poureth contempt upon princes, and causeth them to wander in the waste, where there is no way. . . .
>
> It was the nineteenth year of the reign of Diocletian, and the month Dystrus, or March, as the Romans would call it in, in which, as the festival of the Saviour's Passion was coming on, an imperial letter was everywhere promulgated, ordering the razing of the churches to the ground and the destruction by fire of the Scriptures, and proclaiming that those who held high positions would lose all civil rights, while those in households, if they persisted in their profession of Christianity, would be deprived of their liberty. Such was the first document against us. But not long afterwards we were further visited with other letters, and in them the order was given that the presidents of the churches should all, in every place, be first committed to prison, and then afterwards compelled by every kind of device to sacrifice. *(Hist. eccl.* 8.2.1, 4-5, *LCL)*

During this persecution, the Christians who gave into the persecution and handed over copies of their sacred scriptures to the Roman authorities were called the *traditores.* They were despised by the other Christians, especially by the Donatists, who were not at all forgiving of those who had betrayed their sacred scriptures. These Donatists condemned all *traditor* clergy as those who had committed a sacriligious act worthy of damnation in an everlasting fire because they sought "to destroy the testaments and divine commands of Almighty God and our Lord Jesus Christ."[23] The Christians who did not give into the persecutions and tortures and survived were called *confessors* (ὁμολογῆται). Those who suffered abuse, as well as those who died, were called *martyrs* (μάϱτυϱες). A problem emerged in the fourth-century Church on how to deal with the *traditores,* or *lapsi,* and the controversy eventually involved Constantine himself.[24]

At any rate, the matter of knowing which books could be handed over to the authorities without one's attaining the charge of being a *traditor* was evidently settled by this time in individual churches. *The handing over of scriptures to Roman authorities presupposes a knowledge on the part of the Christians at that time of what books in fact were considered scriptures,* even though *complete* agreement in all churches was not present. The act of deciding which books to hand over would have been determined certainly by the time of the Diocletian persecution, if not much sooner. This does not presuppose, however, any unified answers present in all the churches. There had been as yet no church councils dealing with the matter. Each church or region of churches had decided this question for itself. Even though wide agreement on the majority of the NT scriptures was already present, later in the fourth and fifth centuries, church councils met to deliberate the matter of which literature would serve the Church as its scriptures.

V. Constantine and the Call to Uniformity

It was noted earlier that a move toward unity and conformity in the churches was in full swing by the time of Irenaeus. Also, the move on the part of Diocletian to bring religious unity and conformity to pagan Roman worship was a characteristic trait of Roman society. In the following discussion, several examples of this same tendency toward uniformity in the reign of Constantine (306–337) will be presented. The significance of this is that during Constantine's time and thereafter many moves toward canon conformity were initiated. The clearest and most precise lists of authoritative Christian scriptures are products of this period of history.

It is indisputable that the reign of Constantine (306–337) marked the highly significant transition for the Church from the role of a community persecuted for its faith by the pagan government to a union of long duration with the state. At first, it was an especially beneficial marriage for the Church, but later this union made profound and lasting changes in the make-up and mission of the Church itself.

Constantine's "conversion" came as a result of his most famous vision (see Eusebius, *Life of Constantine*, 2:45; 3:2, 3) and led to many significant benefits for the Church. The most important of these benefits at first was, of course, the cessation of all hostilities toward the Church and the resultant freedom for Christians to worship without fear of persecution (2:14). This was accomplished especially through the Edict of Milan in 313, which gave religious freedom to all Roman subjects, not just to the Christians. The benefits for the Christians even increased later when Constantine ordered the repair of old church buildings damaged in the severe persecutions of the year 303 and following. He not only ordered the rebuilding, at Rome's expense, of those churches that were completely destroyed, but he also ordered the bestowal of extravagant gifts upon the Church (2:46; 3:1) and its leaders (3:16), including the making of extra copies of the Church's "inspired records," which had earlier been destroyed. Finally, he "took vengence" upon those who had persecuted the Christians (3:1).

These events obviously had highly significant effects on the life of the Church. Indeed, as is seen in the manner in which Eusebius describes these events, Eusebius and the Church were understandably euphoric in their reception of the new honors and blessings. They had only praise for Constantine, who is referred to by Eusebius as one "like a powerful herald of God" (2:61), "pious emperor" (2:73), "the divinely favored emperor" (3:1), and one who "thus made it his constant aim to glorify his Saviour God" (3:54).

Although Eusebius finds no fault in Constantine, the Roman emperor's "conversion" to Christianity has not been universally accepted without reservation.[25] Constantine appears to have been only fond of Christianity at first and later grew into a more complete acceptance of its teachings. He was not baptized until shortly before his death. Following his conversion, he still revered the god of his father and tended toward a *syncretistic* Christianity, in which he identified the Christian God with the sun. He made the first day of the week (the Lord's Day) a holiday and called it "the venerable day of the sun" (Sunday). Eusebius seems to have ignored many of Constantine's faults, even passing over his breaking of his pledge not to murder Licinius or his wife, Faust, and his son, Crispus.

The impact on the Church of Constantine's conversion was nonetheless a most important historical event, bringing the Church to an altogether new age. Eusebius proudly claims that with Constantine, "a new and fresh era of existence had begun to appear, and a light heretofore unknown suddenly [brought forth the Church] to the dawn from the midst of darkness on the human race" (3:1).

Constantine's involvement in the affairs of the Church was extensive. Although he was initially invited by the Christians to become involved in settling Church controversies, almost from the beginning he saw it as his duty to become involved in the decisions of the Church. This involved not only the calling (ordering?) together of the bishops and other Church leaders at various councils (3:6, 4:41-43), but also the resolving of theological disputes (for instance, the one between Alexander and Arius, 2:61), as well as disputes concerning a bishop (whether Eusebius was to go to Antioch, 3:59-61). He was even involved in settling the time for the celebration of Easter (3:6-18). He made decisions on whether and how to punish heretics (3:20, 64-65) as well as when, where, and how to build churches (3:29-43).

He not only arbitrated in such matters, but also reconvened a council when its decision went contrary to his own wishes, as in the case of the Donatist controversy in North Africa. Constantine threatened bishops under penalty of banishment if they did not obey his orders to convene at Tyre (4:41, 42), and he even sent his representative of "consular rank" (Dionysus) to ensure order at the church council as well as to remind the bishops of their duty (4:42). Finally, he ordered the same Church leaders to Jerusalem to help him celebrate the dedication of the new church building there!

It is ironic that on one occasion he even wrote that while the bishops were overseers of the internal affairs of the Church, he himself was a "bishop, ordained by God to overlook whatever is external to the church" (4:24). One is hard pressed, however, to find the "internal" issues in which he did not involve himself!

Although no one would deny the interest of Constantine in all matters related to the Church, it is clear from Eusebius that Constantine could tolerate no rivals to the rule of peace and harmony either in his empire or in the churches. Although he can in no way be considered as cruel as his predecessors toward the Church, it is still a fact that he wanted "harmony" (uniformity) at all costs. Those whose doctrines were not in keeping with the "orthodoxy" of the day were banished into exile, their writings burned, and their meeting places confiscated (3:66).

At times Constantine was gracious, generous, and even humble, but he did not easily or long tolerate differences of opinion or challenges to his authority in church matters (4:42). His understanding of "harmony" was not so much peaceful co-existence, as it was uniform thinking—that is, to bring about a consensus from the people. He, therefore, on the one hand destroyed certain temples and banned the practices of sacrificing and idol worship (2:44; 3:54-58) and on the other hand intimidated the dissident bishops into conformity to his wishes or with those of the majority of the bishops (3:13).

As with earlier emperors, Constantine seems to have viewed anything out of step as a threat to be dealt with. Several of the previous Roman rulers considered any opposition to or rejection of Roman dieties as a threat to the empire. Constantine, at times, appears only to have changed the favored religion, not the example of his predecessors. His over-riding concern does not appear to be the moral and inner transformation of the Christian faith so much as "peace at any price" in its outward social influence. Following the suppression of heresy, Eusebius with pleasure wrote: "Thus the members of the entire body became united and compacted in one harmonious whole . . . while no heretical or schismatic body anywhere continued to exist" (3:66, *NPNF*).

His example of unifying the Church under the all-powerful state, which had the right to convene councils of bishops and to discipline dissident church members, appears to have established the authoritative pattern for later popes to follow in dealing with ecclesiastical activities, heresy, and with the appointment of bishops in the Church. Constantine's title *Pontifex Maximus*, which he kept throughout his rule and perhaps influenced his decision to become actively involved in Church decisions, is not a distant example of the kind of power ultimately vested in the popes. Constantine's granting of the power of the bishop's council over decisions of local magistrates (3:20) was also followed later; it helped to politicize the clergy.

The major effects on the Church of the conversion of Constantine and the "Christianizing" of the Roman Empire not only included the cessation of the persecution of the Christians, but also guaranteed the triumph of orthodoxy (primarily Western "orthodoxy") over the whole Church. The major dissidents within the Church were all but silenced during this time. The point of this is, of course, that *the theological stance that later became identified as "orthodoxy" also became the leading position of the Church during this time.* Consequently, in terms of the subsequent identity of the Christian biblical canon, the theological views of this time, which were clearly imposed on many of the churches, also made an impact on the views about which Christian scriptures would receive priority in the churches. In this sense, Constantine's actions toward the Church surely must have had a significant effect on the formation of the Christian biblical canon.

The role of Constantine in the closing of the Christian biblical canon is not inconsiderable when one considers that he also asked Eusebius to supervise the production of fifty copies of the scriptures (presumably both OT and NT) for use in the new capital city of Constantinople. If the matter of which books belonged in the Christian Bible was not finalized before then, as one can surmise from Eusebius' comments in *Ecclesiastical History* (3.25.1-7) that the issue was not settled for the Church earlier, then it probably was at least for him by the time he finalized the fifty copies of the Christian scriptures. In Eusebius' words, the production of these copies of sacred scriptures went as follows.

> Ever careful for the welfare of the churches of God, the emperor addressed me personally in a letter on the means of providing copies of the inspired oracles, and also on the subject of the most holy feast of Easter. For I had myself dedicated to him an exposition of the mystical import of that feast; and the manner of which he honored me with a reply may be understood by anyone who reads the following letter. (Chapter 34)

> "VICTOR CONSTANTINUS, MAXIMUS AUGUSTUS, to Eusebius:
> "It is indeed an arduous task, and beyond the power of language itself, worthily to treat of the mysteries of Christ, and to explain in a fitting manner the controversy respecting the feast of Easter, its origin

as well as its precious and toilsome accomplishment. For it is not within the power even of those who are able to apprehend them, adequately to describe the things of God. I am, notwithstanding, filled with admiration of your learning and zeal, and have not only myself read your work with pleasure, but have given directions, according to your own desire, that it be communicated to many sincere followers of our holy religion. Seeing, then, with what pleasure we receive favors of this kind from your sagacity, be pleased to gladden us more frequently with those compositions, to the practice of which, indeed, you confess yourself to have been trained from an early period, so that I am urging a willing man, as they say, in exhorting you to your customary pursuits. And certainly the high and confident judgment we entertain is a proof that the person who has translated your writings into the Latin tongue is in no respect incompetent to the task, impossible though it be that such version should fully equal the excellence of the works themselves. God preserve you, beloved brother." Such was his letter on this subject: and that which related to the providing of copies of the Scriptures for reading in the churches was to the following purport. (Chapter 35)

"VICTOR CONSTANTINUS, MAXIMUS AUGUSTUS, to Eusebius:

"It happens, through the favoring providence of God our Saviour, that great numbers have united themselves to the most holy church in the city which is called by my name. It seems, therefore, highly requisite, since that city is rapidly advancing in prosperity in all other respects, that the number of churches should also be increased. Do you, therefore, receive with all readiness my determination on this behalf. I *have thought it expedient to instruct your Prudence to order fifty copies of the sacred Scriptures,* the provision and use of which you know to be most needful for the instruction of the Church, to be written on prepared parchment in a legible manner, and in a convenient, portable form, by professional transcribers thoroughly practiced in their art. The catholicus of the diocese has also received instructions by letter from our Clemency to be careful to furnish all things necessary for the preparation of such copies; and it will be for you to take special care that they be completed with as little delay as possible. You have authority also, in virtue of this letter, to use two of the public carriages for their conveyance, by which arrangement the copies when fairly written will most easily be forwarded for my personal inspection; and one of the deacons of your church may be en-

trusted with this service, who, on his arrival here, shall experience
my liberality. God preserve you, beloved brother!" (Chapter 36)

Such were the emperor's commands, which were followed by the
immediate execution of the work itself, which we sent him in magnif-
icent and elaborately bound volumes of a threefold and fourfold
form. This fact is attested by another letter, which the emperor wrote
in acknowledgement, in which, having heard that the city Constan-
tia in our country, the inhabitants of which had been more than commonly devoted to superstition, had been impelled by a sense of
religion to abandon their past idolatry, he testified his joy, and approval of their conduct. (Chapter 37) (Eusebius, *The Life of Constantine*, Book 3, *NPNF*, italics added)

By the time of Constantine's request (ca. 334–336, perhaps), one
can presume there was a fairly well-defined collection of both OT
and NT scriptures, even though several books of the NT as well as
some books that did not make it into the NT canon continued to be
debated in later councils of the Church.

VI. Summary

A brief summary of the developments of the Christian canon up
to this point is in order for the sake of clarity before advancing the
discussion. (1) The primary authority of the earliest Christian community was Jesus himself. Not only was the early Church's faith
related to his death and resurrection, but it was also focused on the
sayings of Jesus. These sayings were at first and for some time later
passed on in oral form in the Church, but many of them were also
written down quite early and circulated among the Christians, even
though the books in which they were found (the Gospels) were not
yet viewed as scripture. The scripture of the first century Christians
was the OT, which was not yet well defined by either the Christians
or the Jews. (2) In the second century, along with the OT and the
Church's oral tradition, the Christian writings, especially the Gospels, began to be referred to with greater frequency in the life of the
Church. At first the words of Jesus, when written down, functioned
as scripture. The collection of Pauline letters was also revered in the
Church by many Christians (not all), and they were used in admo-
nitions to Christians (I Clem. 47). The many allusions to the Pauline

literature in the Apostolic Fathers at least shows deep respect for Paul and a willingness to hear his advice. By the end of the first century C.E., collections of Paul's writings probably circulated freely among many churches along with one or more of the canonical Gospels. (3) Marcion, whose primary concern was to eliminate all Jewish influences from the Christian message, including the OT itself, created a limited collection of what he probably considered to be sacred Christian scriptures.[26] (4) Justin (ca. 160) defended the OT as *Christian* scripture and also indicated that the Church regularly used the Gospels ("memoirs of the apostles") in its worship alongside (or on occasion possibly instead of) the OT scriptures. (5) With Irenaeus came the first clear designation of Christian writings as scripture and also of a "New Testament" collection of scriptures separate from the OT scriptures. Irenaeus had a closed gospel canon, but he was not precise on the boundaries of the rest of the Christian scriptures; so far as can be determined from his writings, apart from the four canonical Gospels he did not clarify what was NT scripture and what it was not. (6) The emergence of fringe, or "heretical," groups such as the Montanists and the Gnostic Christians must surely have forced the Church to come to grips with its authoritative literature, though as yet there was no Christian concensus on exactly what was and was not considered to be scripture. The major sections of what was later called the NT literature, however, were generally (though not completely) acknowledged at the end of the second century as scripture. (7) Diocletian's edict forcing the Christians to hand over their sacred scriptures for burning must also have been a significant factor in causing many churches to come to grips with the question of which books among those they possessed were in fact sacred. Many Christians were willing to hand over nonscriptural writings in an attempt to satisfy the authorities, but this act, of course, presumes a knowledge of what was and was not scripture. (8) Constantine himself may have played a decisive role in the churches' agreement on the broad outlines of the canon by his many actions promoting unity and uniformity in the Church. A study of his life shows that unity and peace were more important to him than what he called the "trifling" matter of the person of Christ. In his letter to Alexander, the bishop of Alexandria, and to Arius the Presbyter, he states clearly his purpose for writing.

VICTOR CONSTANTINUS, MAXIMUS AUGUSTUS, to Alexander and Arius.

"I call that God to witness, as well I may, who is the helper of my endeavors, and the Preserver of all men, that I had a twofold reason for undertaking that duty which I have now performed. (Chapter 64)

"My design then was, first, to bring the diverse judgements formed by all nations respecting the Deity to a condition, as it were, of settled uniformity; and, secondly to restore to health the system of the world, then suffering under the malignant power of a grievous distemper. Keeping these objects in view, I sought to accomplish the one by the secret eye though, while the other I tried to rectify by the power of military authority. For I was aware, that if I should succeed in establishing, according to my hopes, a common harmony of sentiment among all the servants of God, the general course of affairs would also experience a change correspondent to the pious desires of them all. (Chapter 65) (Eusebius, *The Life of Constantine*, Book II, *NPNF*)

But going on to the christological issue, which was dividing the Church, he states unambiguously:

And yet, having made a careful inquiry into the origin and foundation of these differences, I *find the cause to be of a truly insignificant character*, and quite unworthy of such fierce contention. Feeling myself, therefore, compelled to address you in this letter, and to appeal at the same time to your unanimity and sagacity, I call on Divine Providence to assist me in the task, while I interrupt your dissension in the character of a minister of peace, and with reason: for if I might expect, with the help of a higher Power, to be able without difficulty, by a judicious appeal to the pious feelings of those who heard me, to recall them to a better spirit, even though the occasion of the disagreement were a greater one, how can I refrain from promising myself a far easier and more speedy adjustment of this difference, *when the cause which hinders general harmony of sentiment is intrinsically trifling and of little moment?* (Eusebius, *The Life of Constantine*, chapter 68, *NPNF*, italics added)

One is led to believe that peace and harmony were Constantine's major doctrines. The doctrines he favored were held by the majority of the churches, and he expected all others to conform to them. His call for the production of fifty copies of the Christian scriptures shows that at least Eusebius, the one charged with the duty, was aware of or soon became aware of the parameters of this collection of scriptures. This is not to say that all Christians agreed on what books belonged in the cannon of Christian scriptures. As the next chapter will show, voices expressing differences of opinion on what is sacred scripture in the Church have never been completely silenced, in spite of the decisions of Church councils.

S I X

ANCIENT COLLECTIONS OF CHRISTIAN SCRIPTURES

Many scholars have discussed the various collections of ancient Christian scriptures that date for the most part sometime after the first half of the fourth century.[1] *Some* of these "lists" of sacred writings are in fact no more than a collection of allusions, citations, or quotations from the NT and other ancient literature used by the Church Fathers. They are not necessarily closed canons. Some scholars have collected and tabulated these references, concluding that they constitute some kind of canon, but such collections say no more than that the theology of the early Church Fathers was informed by those earlier Christian writings that make up our present biblical canon. The references for the most part do not in themselves prove that the literature was necessarily considered to be scripture or that the collection of such references from an author's extant writings constitutes his "canon" of NT scriptures. This inference is perhaps the biggest weakness of Alexander Souter's otherwise very helpful work on the canon; the same could be said of Kummel[2] to a lesser degree and also of William R. Farmer.[3] Although the study of such references can be extremely valuable, especially as one examines the context in which each of these allusions or citations is found,[4] a common error in the study of the biblical canon is viewing all these references as citations of "scripture." For this reason, it is altogether important to add a few cautionary comments at the beginning of this section before looking at the so-called "lists."[5]

First, the presence of citations or references to the NT literature in the writings of the Church Fathers in themselves do not necessarily prove that the documents referred to were viewed as sacred scripture.[6] Second, the absence of a particular Christian document from the writings of one of the Church Fathers does not necessarily mean that he was either unaware of it or that he did not believe it was scripture. Often the writings we do possess from antiquity were produced in response to a problem in the Church, and the writer would seldom have the occasion in such *ad hoc* writings to cite all of the works he considered to be inspired scriptures. Third, the writings of one Church Father in one area are not necessarily representative of all Christians in that area or even less in other areas. Finally, only a small portion of the total number of ancient written documents is known today. Many were destroyed by the enemies of the Church, and some were destroyed by Christians themselves in "heresy hunts." Some of these writings were simply lost (a part of Paul's Corinthian correspondence) and still others were at some point no longer deemed relevant to the local church and were either discarded or stored in an as yet undiscovered location. The possibility still exits that discoveries such as those at Qumran and Nag Hammadi will reveal documents that give us even greater insight into the perplexing questions about the Christian canon. With these cautionary notes, let us proceed.

Although no part of the NT was consciously written as a part of an already existing collection of documents, these writings did begin to appear together in the second century. It is not unreasonable to think that such a collection of Paul's epistles was grouped together and circulated in many churches by the end of the first century,[7] and at least three of the Gospels were grouped together by Justin (ca. 160) and all four by Irenaeus (ca. 170–180). R. M. Grant believes that the first collection of Christian scriptures arose in Alexandria, Egypt, in the early second century and possibly even earlier. He contends that Basilides, who wrote during the reign of Hadrian (ca. 117–138), made explicit what other Christians already believed in that region—namely, that the writings of Paul and the Gospels (Matt., Luke, John) were considered to be scriptures on a par with the OT.[8] He further believes that NT writings were first called scriptures there and even suggests that the author of II Peter (see II Pet. 3:15) may have come from Alexandria.[9] Whatever the case, Grant depends heavily on Hippolytus, who wrote against Basilides in his *Refutations of All Heresies* (ca. 220–230), a source that not all scholars consider reliable. No precise collection of NT writings is attributed to him by Hippolytus, and certainly no closed canon. The earliest possibility that we have from the second century for a limited collection of scriptures is Marcion; this survey of collections will, therefore, begin with him.

What becomes obvious in all such listings or collections of NT documents from the time of Marcion and later is the absence of any early—or present—agreement on what such a grouping means and whether these collections should be considered sacred scriptures. We can find no agreement on this matter in the ancient churches. As will be argued later, only at the end of the fourth century was a general consensus reached on most of the twenty-seven books that make up our present NT, but, as we will see, unanimity did not prevail even then. Kurt Aland has correctly observed that it took centuries longer for a consensus on our present twenty-seven books to be reached.[10] The following "lists" are intended to give the reader an indication of the variety of views in the ancient churches on what literature informed the theologies of the earliest Christian communities and what was considered authoritative in those communities for "faith and practice." Although not all of the writings in these lists were specifically called "scripture," for the most part they seem to function in that way in the churches. These lists indicate to some extent that there was broad acceptance in the early churches in regard to the majority of the books that now constitute our present NT canon.[11]

I. Marcion (ca. 140–155, d.ca. 160)

The first documented "closed" collection of Christian scriptures was set forth by Marcion around the mid-second century. Since we have no Marcionite sources or documents, we depend completely on his critics, especially Irenaeus and Tertullian, for information. Fortunately, their reports are extensive and generally considered reliable.

Marcion, for reasons discussed earlier, rejected the whole of the OT and accepted only an edited form of the Gospel of Luke and ten of Paul's epistles. Marcion's canon did not include the Pastoral epistles, and it is not likely that he knew of them. Helmut Koester suggests that they may have been written after the time of Marcion and in response to him (see I Tim. 6:20).[12] He notes that they are found in p^{46}, the oldest extant manuscript of the Pauline epistles, which dates ca. 200.[13] Tertullian argued, however, that Marcion rejected the Pastoral letters, indicating that he was aware of them. Commenting on Marcion's acceptance of Philemon and his rejection of the Pastorals, Tertullian writes:

> I wonder, however, when he received . . . this letter which was written but to one man, that he rejected the two epistles to Timothy and the one to Titus, which all treat of ecclesiastical discipline. His aim, was, I suppose to carry out his interpolating process even to the number of (St. Paul's) epistles. *(Adv. Marc. 5.21, ANF)*

II. Valentinus (ca. 135–160)

It is possible that some awareness of a collection of writings was known earlier than the time of Marcion, who lived in Rome ca. 135–160. Tertullian states that Valentinus, in contrast to Marcion, used all the scriptures and perverted them, while Marcion excised with the knife what he did not like.[14] The text reads as follows.

> One man perverts the Scriptures with his hand, another their meaning by his exposition. For although Valentinus seems to use *the entire volume*, he has none the less laid violent hands on the truth only with a more cunning mind and skill than Marcion. Marcion expressly and openly used the knife, not the pen, since he made such an excision of the Scriptures as suited his own subject-matter. Valentinus, however, abstained from such excision, because he did not invent Scriptures to square with his own subject-matter, but adapted his matter to the Scriptures; and yet he took away more, and added more, by removing the proper meaning of every particular word, and adding fantastic arrangements of things which have no real existence. *(Praescript. 38.4 ff., ANF, italics added)*

The words *entire volume* (Latin, *integro instrumento*) appear to be a reference to a collection of scriptures, probably NT writings but possibly a reference to OT scriptures. The context favors the reference to NT writings, since Tertullian asks both Marcion and Valentinus what right they have to use that scripture received from the apostles[15], which, of course, could not refer to the OT writings. Tertullian evidently believed that Valentinus, unlike Marcion, used a collection of NT writings similar to his own. Bruce M. Metzger has pointed out that the recent discovery of *Evangelium Veritatis* ("The Gospel of Truth"), believed by some scholars to have been written by Valentinus, shows acquaintance with the four Gospels, several of Paul's Epistles, Hebrews, and Revelation.[16] If an early dating of this work is preferred, this is the earliest such collection we possess that has a decidedly Western orientation. The book of Revelation, for example, is a part of that collection; however, it is possible that Tertullian's judgment of Marcion and Valentinus was in part based on a general awareness of the status or understanding of the NT scriptures from his own time (ca. 200 C.E.) and not from theirs when the status of both the NT writings and those writings that did not eventually become canonical literature were vaguer and still in a state of flux.

III. Irenaeus (ca. 130–200)

Irenaeus did not make a "list" of authoritative Christian writings as such but referred frequently to many NT passages for support of his positions. This practice was not presented as something new, but was for him a reflection of a long-standing tradition in the Church.[17] As was shown earlier, Irenaeus considered the NT literature as scripture on a par with the OT, even though he did not clearly define the parameters of the NT scriptures.[18] If references or citations are any indication of what Irenaeus considered authoritative, then apparently he did not consider Hebrews equal in authority to the other NT writings, but rather appears to have acknowledged the authority of the Shepherd of Hermas. Also, there is no mention of James, Jude, or II Peter. The scriptures, for Irenaeus, were evidently made up of the still fluid collection of the OT writings and at least the four Gospels. In an overly optimistic statement about the interpretation of scripture, he states, *"the entire Scriptures, the prophets and the Gospels,* can be clearly, unambiguously understood by all" (*Adv. Haer.* 2.27.2, *ANF,* italics added). Later, however, he seems to reverse himself regarding the clarity of the scriptural writings by saying that if we fail to understand some parts of these scriptures we should leave these matters with God since the Scriptures "are indeed perfect since they were spoken by the Word of God and His Spirit" (2.28.2, *ANF*).

In regard to the books cited by Irenaeus, it should be recalled that the failure to mention an ancient source does not necessarily mean that such a source was either unknown or not viewed as authoritative by him. The *ad hoc* nature of Irenaeus' writings must have had a considerable effect on which literature he cited to support his positions. Nonetheless, contrary to the arguments of William Farmer and others, apart from the four-Gospel canon, we are unable to find in Irenaeus a canon of NT scriptures. So far as his surviving writings are concerned, we are unable to find a list or collection of inspired documents similar to our present NT writings. Irenaeus does recognize the "Apostles" as a distinct collection from the Gospel writers, but there are no clear statements on what writings make up the "Apostles" (see *Adv. Haer.* 1.3.6). Apart from Irenaeus' closed Gospel canon, nothing in his writings suggests how he might have carried out this "canonizing" procedure on the rest of the NT literature. Since he often cited literature that was not later canonized by the Church—Hermas, I Clem., it is not easy to discover what would have made up his collection of sacred scriptures.

IV. Tertullian (ca. 160–225)

A well-educated native of Carthage, in Africa, and often called the "Father of Latin Theology" in the Church, Tertullian, like Irenaeus, acknowledged all four canonical Gospels, but added that they were written by the apostles or those whose masters were apostles. He writes: "Of the apostles, therefore, John and Matthew first *instill* faith into us; whilst of apostolic men, Luke and Mark *renew* it afterwards. These all start with the same principles of faith" (Tertullian, *Adv. Marc.* 4.2.2, *ANF,* italics added). Both here and elsewhere he seems to have relegated Luke and Mark to lower than Matthew and John, and he does not fail to criticize Marcion for selecting Luke as his Gospel instead of an "apostolic" gospel.

> Now, of the authors whom we possess, Marcion seems to have singled out Luke for his mutilating process. Luke, however, was not an apostle, but only an apostolic man; *not a master, but a disciple, and so inferior to a master*—at least as far subsequent to him as the apostle whom he followed . . . was subsequent to the others. (*Adv. Marc.* 4.2.5., *ANF*, italics added)

For Tertullian, apostolicity was the chief criterion for recognizing the authority of the Gospels. This same apostolic authority, which was passed on by them through the succession of bishops, guaranteed the truthfulness of the Gospel. The apostolic writings formed for him the *Novum Testamentum*.

> If I fail in resolving this article (of our faith) by passages which may admit of dispute out of the Old Testament, I will take out of the New Testament a confirmation of our view, that you may not straightway attribute to the Father every possible (relation and condition) which I ascribe to the Son. Behold, then, I find both in the Gospels and in the (writings of the) apostles a visible and an invisible God (revealed to us), under a manifest and personal distinction in the condition of both. *(Adv. Prax. 15, ANF)*

For him, the NT apparently consisted of the four Gospels, thirteen epistles of Paul, Acts, Revelation, I John, I Peter, and Jude; however, he did not produce a list of these works, even though he cited them frequently in an authoritative manner. Beare has noted that before Tertullian became a Montanist he also included in his canon the Shepherd of Hermas, but later dismissed it with scorn, and he surprisingly treated Hebrews as marginal.[19] Beare, like other scholars, seems to overstate the case when he claims that Tertullian had a closed canon of NT scriptures, and he does not support this claim with any clear references.[20] None of the books Tertullian appears to have accepted as authoritative was later rejected, except, of course, the Montanist prophecies.

V. Clement of Alexandria (ca. 150–215)

Probably born in Athens, Clement came to study under Pantaenus (ca. 190), the director of the Catechetical School in Alexandria, and he succeeded Pantaenus as director of the school. Like others before him, Clement referred to or cited as scripture many of the writings of the NT—the four canonical Gospels, Acts, fourteen epistles of Paul (Heb. was attributed to Paul), I and II John, I Peter, Jude, and Revelation. He made no mention, however, of James, II Peter, or III John. What is more interesting is that he also quoted variously to support his ideas from The Epistle of Barnabas, I Clement, the Shepherd of Hermas, the Preaching of Peter, the Sibylline Writings and the Didache. Eusebius' description of the writings that informed Clement's theology is interesting.

> Now in the *Stromateis* [Clement] has composed a patchwork, not only of the divine Scripture, but of the writings of the Greeks as well, if he thought that they also had said anything useful, and he mentions opinions from many sources, explaining Greek and barbarian alike, and moreover sifts the false opinions of the heresiarchs; and unfolding much history he gives us a work of great erudition. With all these he mingles also the opinions of philosophers, and so he has suitably made the title of the *Stromateis* to correspond to the work itself. And in them he has also made use of testimonies from the disputed writings, the book known as the Wisdom of Solomon, the Wisdom of Jesus the Son of Sirach, and the Epistle to the Hebrews, and those of Barbabas, and Clement, and Jude; and he mentions Tatian's book *Against the Greeks*, and Cassian, since he also had composed a chronography, and moreover Philo and Aristobulus and Josephus and Demetrius and Eupolemus, Jewish writers, in that they would show, all of them, in writing, that Moses and the Jewish race went back further in their origins than the Greeks. And the books of Clement, of which we are speaking, are full of much other useful learning. In the first of these he shows with reference to himself that he came very near to the successors of the Apostles; and he promises in them also to write a commentary on Genesis. (*Hist. eccl.* 6.13.4-8, *LCL*)

And in the *Hypotyposeis*, to speak briefly, he has given concise explanations of all the Canonical [ἐνδιαϑήκου, literally, "testamented"] Scriptures, not passing over even the disputed writings, I mean the Epistle of Jude and the remaining Catholic Epistles, and the Epistle of Barnabas, and the Apocalypse known as Peter's. And as for the Epistle to the Hebrews, he says indeed that it is Paul's, but that it was written for Hebrews in the Hebrew tongue, and that Luke, having carefully translated it, published it for the Greeks; hence, as a result of this translation, the same complexion of style is found in this Epistle and in the Acts: but that the [words] "Paul the apostle" were naturally not prefixed. For, says he, "in writing to Hebrews who had conceived a prejudice against him and were suspicious of him, he very wisely did not repel them at the beginning by putting his name." *(Hist. eccl.* 6.14.1-3, *LCL)*

And again in the same books Clement has inserted a tradition of the primitive elders with regard to the order of the Gospels, as follows. He said that those Gospels were first written that include the genealogies, but that the Gospel according to Mark came into being in this manner: When Peter had publicly preached the word at Rome, and by the Spirit had proclaimed the Gospel, those present, who were many, exhorted Mark to make a record of what was said as one who had followed him for a long time and remembered what had been spoken. He did this and distributed the Gospel among those who had asked him. And when the matter came to Peter's knowledge, he neither strongly forbade it nor urged it forward. But John, last of all, who was conscious that the outward facts had been set forth in the Gospels, was urged on by his disciples and divinely moved by the Spirit to compose a spiritual Gospel. This is Clement's account. (adapted from *Hist. eccl.* 6.14.5-7, *LCL)*

Metzger has appropriately observed that Clement "delighted to welcome truth in unexpected places!"[21] Even though Clement apparently did not acknowledge them as scripture (that is, normative), he certainly knew of the *Gospel of the Hebrews, The Gospel of the Egyptians,* and *The Tradition of Matthias* and did not condemn them as heretical documents.[22]

What is most surprising about Clement is his high regard for Greek philosophy as a means of preparing one to receive the Christian message.

Even if Greek philosophy does not comprehend the truth in its entirety and, in addition, lacks the strength to fulfill the Lord's command, yet at least it prepares the way for the teaching which is royal in the highest sense of the word, by making a man self-controlled, by moulding his character, and by making him ready to receive the truth. *(Strom. 7.20, ANF).*[23]

If Clement of Alexandria had a closed canon of Christian scripture, it is nowhere apparent. In his pursuit of the knowledge of God, he was prepared to be informed from a broad selection of literature.

VI. Origen (ca. 184–235)

Sundberg claims that the transition from the authority of *oral* tradition to the authority of *written* traditions, which began with Irenaeus, was completed with Origen.[24] Like Clement of Alexandria, Origen drew from the four canonical Gospels, fourteen epistles of Paul (he appears to have included Hebrews, even though he did not believe Paul wrote it), I Peter, I John, and Revelation. Again, Eusebius is our primary[25] witness to what Origen considered to be scriptural.

In the first of his *Commentaries on the Gospel according to Matthew,* defending the canon of the Church, he gives his testimony that he knows only four Gospels, writing somewhat as follows "As having learned by tradition concerning the four Gospels, which alone are unquestionable in the Church of God under heaven. The first was written by *Matthew,* who was once a tax-collector but afterwards became an apostle of Jesus Christ, and he published it for those who came from Judaism to believe in Christ. Matthew's Gospel was composed in the Hebrew language. Second, *Mark,* who wrote his Gospel in accordance with Peter's instructions, whom also Peter acknowledged as his son in the catholic epistle [I Peter 5:13], spoke in these terms: 'She that is in Babylon, elect together with you, saluteth you; and so doth Mark my son.' And third, *Luke,* who wrote his Gospel for those who came to believe from among the Gentiles, which was the Gospel that was praised by Paul. After them all came the Gospel according to *John.*"

And in the fifth of his *expositions on the Gospel according to John* the same person says this with reference to *the epistles of the apostles:* "But he who was made sufficient to become a minister of the new covenant, not of the letter but of the spirit, even Paul, who fully preached the Gospel from Jerusalem and round about even unto Illyricum, did not so much as write to all the churches that he taught; and even to those to whom he wrote he sent but a few lines (ὀλίγους στίχους). And Peter, on whom the Church of Christ is built, against which the gates of Hades shall not prevail, has left *one* acknowledged epistle (μίαν ἐπιστολὴν ὁμολογουμένην) and, *it may be* (ἔστω δὲ), a second also; for it is doubted. Why need I speak of him who leaned back on Jesus' breast, John, who has left behind one Gospel, confessing that he could write so many that even the world itself could not contain them; and he wrote also the Apocalypse, being ordered to keep silence and not to write the voices of seven thunders? He has left also *an epistle* of a very few lines, and *it may be, a second and a third;* for not all say that these are genuine. Only, the two of them together are not a hundred lines long."

Furthermore, he thus discusses the Epistle to the Hebrews, in his Homilies upon it: "That the character of the diction of the epistle entitled 'To the Hebrews' has not the apostle's rudeness in speech, who confessed himself rude in speech, that is, in style, but that the epistle is better Greek in the framing of its diction, will be admitted by everyone who is able to discern differences of style. But again, on the other hand, that the thoughts of the epistle are admirable and not inferior to the acknowledged writings (ὁμολογουμένων γραμμάτων) of the apostle, to this also everyone will consent as true who has given attention to reading the apostle."

Further on, he adds the following remarks: "But as for myself, if I were to state my own opinion, I should say that the thoughts are the apostle's, but that the style and composition belong to one who called to mind the apostle's teachings and, as it were, made short notes of what his master said. If any church, therefore, holds this epistle as Paul's, let it be commended for this also. For not without reason have the men of old time handed it down as Paul's. But who wrote the epistle, in truth God knows. Yet the account that has reached us is twofold, some saying that Clement, who was bishop of the Romans, wrote the epistle, others that it was Luke, he who wrote the Gospel and the *Acts*." (adapted from *Hist. eccl.* 6.25.3-14 *LCL*)

A. C. Sundberg[26] and Everett Kalin[27] have argued that Origen's "canonical list" is a creation of Eusebius in the fourth century, seventy-five years after the death of Origen. They contend that Eusebius' source may well have been his own collection of Origen's references or citations to the NT literature in Origen's writings. Kalin maintains that all such canonical lists were produced in the fourth century and later. He further stresses that the second-century heresies in the Church were not fought with a canon of scripture, but with the canon of faith.[28]

According to Eusebius, Origen accepted the four canonical Gospels and an unspecified number of Paul's epistles as well as I John, Revelation, Hebrews with some doubt, and evidently with some question II Peter and II and III John.[29] Further, he made use of James and Jude with some hesitation due to their lack of general recognition,[30] but does not clearly refer to them as scripture (or "Recognized" ὁμολογούμενα). He also refers to Barnabas, Shepherd of Hermas, and the Didache, but again, it is not clear that he acknowledged them as scripture. However, if one is prone to claim that Origen acknowledged James and Jude because he made use of them, then the same conclusion should also be made for Barnabas, Shepherd of Hermas, and the Didache.

Metzger, evidently seeking to support Origen's acceptance of the NT literature, has noted that Origen never wrote a commentary on a book *not* found in the later NT.[31] It should be added, however, that so far as our information goes, neither did Origen write a commentary on every book of the NT.

Before leaving Origen, Rufinus' (ca. 400 C.E.) well known translation of the Homily on Joshua ought to be noted for the sake of completeness, though as noted above, there is not much confidence today in the accuracy of his translation.

Jericho was destroyed by the trumpets of the priests. . . . When our Lord Jesus Christ came, whose coming that former son of Nun represented, he sent as his priests his apostles, carrying the "finely hammered trumpets" of the proclamation of the sublime and heavenly teaching. Matthew sounded the first priestly trumpet in his gospel; Mark also, and Luke and John individually played their priestly trumpets; Peter, moreover, makes the two trumpets of his epistles resound; James also and Jude. And no less does John add to this by playing a trumpet through his epistles [and Apocalypse] and Luke in describing the Acts of the apostles. Last of all comes he who said, "I think God displays us apostles last of all," and thundering on the 14 trumpets of his epistles he tore right down to the foundations the walls of Jericho. (Origen, *Homily 7 on Joshua*, translated by Rufinus in Kahlin, "Re-examining")

Everett Kahlin has shown by comparison with Eusebius that Rufinus' translation is unreliable. His arguments include: (1) in his introduction to the passage, Eusebius states that Origen was upholding the "ecclesiastical canon" of the Church—its statement of faith—but Rufinus states that Origen is setting forth his "NT canon"; (2) while Origen does not number Paul's epistles, Rufinus states clearly that Paul had fourteen "trumpets"; (3) while Origen, according to Eusebius, acknowledged only one epistle for Peter and had some doubts about a second, Rufinus clearly claims that Peter wrote two, even though some doubt it; and (4) while Origen, according to Eusebius, claims that John wrote one acknowledged epistle and perhaps a second and third, Rufinus again claims that John wrote three epistles, though some have doubts about two of them.[32]

The main problem with a supposed canon of Origen is that we have no solid evidence from him as to what that canon might be. Kahlin is probably right when he concludes about Rufinus and Eusebius that he does not believe that Homily 7 on Joshua presents us with Origen's NT canon any more than does Eusebius' *Hist. eccl.* 6.25. He is convinced that Origen never had a closed canon of NT scriptures.

VII. Eusebius (ca. 325–330 for his *Ecclesiastical History*)

It was Eusebius, bishop of Caesarea, who set forth the first 'clearly identifiable list, or canon, of NT scriptures. His canon was not, however, as clear as many subsequent theologians would have hoped. His list of recognized (ὁμολογουμένα) NT scriptures emerges in the midst of uncertainty, some of the books that are found in his list are undisputed, while others are disputed, and still others are listed as spurious. The books he listed as having wide acceptance and as "recognized" or "admitted"[33] as authoritative NT scripture ("canonical" or "testamented," Greek ἐνδιάθηκον) without qualification ("undisputed" ἀναμφιλέκτῳ 3.3.1, 5) are the four Gospels, Acts, *fourteen* epistles of Paul,[34] I Peter, I John, and possibly Revelation. Second, he listed some disputed (ἀντιλεγομένα) books that were known to most churches (*Hist. eccl.* 3.25.3). Those disputed books included James, Jude, II Peter,[35] II John, and III John. He also classified as "spurious" ("among those [books] reckoned not genuine"—ἐν τοῖς νόθοις—see 3.25.4) the Acts of Paul, the Shepherd (of Hermas), the Apocalypse of Peter, the Didache, and possibly Revelation (3.25.4). The text in which most of this information is found is highly significant and merits close attention.

At this point it seems reasonable to summarize the writings of the New Testament which have been quoted. In the first place should be put the holy tetrad of the Gospels. To them follows the writing of the Acts of the Apostles. After this should be reckoned the Epistles of Paul. Following them the Epistle of John called the first, and in the same way should be recognized the Epistle of Peter. In addition to these should be put, if it seem desirable, the Revelation of John, the arguments concerning which we will expound at the proper time. These belong to the Recognized [ὁμολογουμένοις] Books. Of the Disputed [τῶν δ' ἀντιλε-γομένων] Books which are nevertheless known to most are the Epistle called of James, that of Jude, the second Epistle of Peter, and the so-called second and third Epistles of John which may be the work of the evangelist or of some other with the same name. *Among the books which are not genuine* [ἐν τοῖς νόθοις] must be reckoned the Acts of Paul, the work entitled the Shepherd, the Apocalypse of Peter, and in addition to them the letter called of Barnabas and the so-called Teachings of the Apostles. And in addition, as I said, the Revelation of John, if this view prevail. For, as I said, some reject it, but others count it among the *Recognized Books*. Some have also counted the Gospel according to the Hebrews in which those of the Hebrews who have accepted Christ take a special pleasure. These would all belong to the *disputed books*, but we have nevertheless been obliged to make a list of them, distinguishing between those writings which, according to the tradition of the Church, are true, genuine, and recognized, and those which differ from them in that they are *not canonical* [οὐκ ἐνδιαθήκ-ους] but disputed, yet nevertheless are known to most of the writers of the Church, in order that we might know them and the writings which are put forward by heretics under the name of the apostles containing gospels such as those of Peter, and Thomas, and Matthias, and some others besides, or Acts such as those of Andrew and John and the other apostles. To none of these has any who belonged to the succession of the orthodox ever thought it right to refer in his writings. Moreover, the type of phraseology differs from apostolic style, and the opinion and tendency of their contents is widely dissonant from true orthodoxy and clearly shows that they are the forgeries of heretics. They ought, therefore, to be reckoned not even *among spurious* [ἐν νόθοις] books but shunned as altogether wicked and impious. (*Hist. eccl.* 3.25.1-7, LCL, italics added; see also 3.3.1-2, 6.)

What apparently comes out of Eusebius' threefold classification of Christian writings, which is also similar to the classification attributed to Origen, is that there was still no unanimity in the greater Church of Eusebius' time about which writings were authoritative NT scripture. Twenty of the NT books appear to have been widely recognized, but Hebrews, James, II Peter, II and III John, Jude, and Revelation were still questioned by many. Indeed, it is difficult to establish from Eusebius that he accepted as canonical any more NT writings than the first twenty books, which he himself listed as authoritative scripture. He had doubts about some of the others and had especially strong negative feelings about the final category. Eusebius saw, as Metzger has pointed out, that "it is not always possible to give a definite affirmative or negative answer to the question whether a book should be in the Canon ("Canon," p. 125). His observation that some books could be held in question, however, did not prevail in the churches after Eusebius. As time went on, the churches preferred certainty over acceptable ambiguity, even though historically it was never able to agree unanimously on precisely which books should receive the normative status of scripture.

Up to this point, there appears to have been wide agreement in the greater Church on most of our NT writings, and this without any council decisions by gathered leaders in the Church. It might be said that this collection of twenty NT writings was widely recognized from the "grass roots" of the Church, but later the remaining seven were determined more by the hierarchy of the Church through council decisions. Up to and including the generation of Eusebius, however, no hierarchical council had been involved in any decision regarding the status of Christian writings, and very few lists of NT scriptures were produced. From the time of Eusebius, numerous lists of authoritative NT writings began circulating in the Church, and it is highly probable that Eusebius was the leader of a move toward the stabilization of the canon in the Eastern churches. This may have come as a result of his being asked by Constantine to produce the fifty copies of the Church's scriptures, but that is not certain. Later, Jerome became the primary leader in the West in helping the Church determine which writings were authoritative scriptures.

VIII. The Muratorian Fragment (ca. 350)

In 1740 Lodovico Antonio Muratori discovered in the Ambrosian Library of Milan what many canonical scholars believe is one of the most important documents for establishing a late second-century date for the formation of a NT canon. The document he found is a seventh- or eighth-century fragment of a larger document, translated into Latin from the Greek and commonly called the "Muratorian Canon" or Muratorian Fragment" (MF). It is usually dated ca. 180-200. Recently it has been hailed as "the oldest extant list of sacred books of the New Testament."[36] Because of the significant amount of scholarly attention the MF has received, it may justifiably be called either the "final proof" or the "Achilles heel" of canonical research for evidence of a late second-century NT canon. The full text of the MF is as follows.

[1] At which, however, he was present and so he has set it down. The third Gospel book [is] that according to Luke. This physician Luke after Christ's ascension (resurrection?), since Paul had taken him with him as an expert in the way (of the teaching), composed it in his own name according to (his) thinking. Yet neither did he himself see the Lord in the flesh; and therefore, as he was able to ascertain it, so he begins to tell the story from the birth of John.

[2] The fourth of the Gospels [was written by] John [who was one] of the disciples. When his fellow-disciples and bishops urged him, he said: Fast with me from today for three days, and what will be revealed to each one let us relate to one another. In the same night it was revealed to Andrew, one of the apostles, that, whilst all [of them] were to go over (it), John in his own name should write everything down. And therefore, though various [elements] (or tendencies?) are taught in the several Gospel books, [nevertheless] that matters nothing for the faith of believers, since by the one and [sovereign] Spirit everything is declared in all [of the Gospels]: concerning the birth, concerning the passion, concerning the resurrection, concerning the [life] with his disciples and concerning his two comings, the first [time he came he was] despised in lowliness, which has come to pass [but] the second [time he will come] glorious[ly] in kingly power, which is yet to come. What wonder [is it] then if John, being thus always true to himself, adduces particular points in his epistles also,

where he says of himself: What we have seen with our eyes and have heard with our ears and our hands have handled, that have we written to you. For so he confesses (himself) not merely [to be] an eye and ear witness, but also a writer of all the marvels of the Lord in [their] order.

[3] But the acts of all the apostles are written in one book. For the "most excellent Theophilus" Luke summarizes the several things that in his own presence have come to pass, as also by the omission of the passion [death] of Peter he makes quite clear, and equally by (the omission) of the journey of Paul, who from the city (of Rome) proceeded to Spain. The epistles, however, of Paul themselves make clear to those who wish to know it which there are (i.e. from Paul), from what place and for what [purpose] they were written. First of all to the Corinthians (to whom) he forbids the heresy of schism, then to the Galatians (to whom he forbids) circumcision, and then to the Romans, (to whom) he explains that Christ is the rule of the Scriptures and moreover their principle, he has written at considerable length.

[4] We must deal with these [individually], since the blessed apostle Paul himself, following the rule of his predecessor John, writes by name only to seven churches in the following order: to the Corinthians the first (epistle), to the Ephesians the second, to the Philippians the third, to the Colossians the fourth, to the Galatians the fifth, to the Thessalonians the sixth, to the Romans the seventh. Although he wrote to the Corinthians and to the Thessalonians once more for their reproof, it is yet clearly recognizable that over the whole earth one church is spread. For John also in the Revelation writes indeed to seven churches, yet speaks to all. But to Philemon [Paul wrote] one [letter], and to Titus one, and to Timothy two, (written) out of goodwill and love, are yet held sacred to the glory of the catholic Church for the ordering of ecclesiastical discipline.

[5] There is current also (an epistle) to the Laodiceans, another to the Alexandrians, forged in Paul's name for the sect of Marcion, and several others, which cannot be received in the catholic Church; for it will not do to mix gall with honey. Further an epistle of Jude and two with the title . . . John are accepted in the catholic Church, and the *Wisdom written by friends of Solomon* in his honour. Also of the revelations we accept only those of John and *Peter*, which (latter) some of our people do not want to have read in the Church.

[6] *But Hermas wrote the Shepherd quite* [recently] *in our time* in the city of Rome, when on the throne of the church of the city of Rome the bishop Pius, his brother, was seated. And therefore it ought

indeed to be read, but it cannot be read publicly in the Church to the people either among the prophets, whose number is settled, or among the apostles to the end of time.

[7] But we accept nothing whatever from Arsinous or Valentinus and Miltiades(?), who have also composed a new psalm book for Marcion, together with Basilides of Asia Minor, the founder of the Cataphrygians.[37]

The primary reason many scholars date the original text of the Latin fragment at or before the end of the second century is mainly because of the passage in the fragment that reads, "But Hermas wrote the Shepherd quite lately [or recently] in our time" *(vero nuperrime temporibus nostris)*.[38] Hermas lived roughly ca. 100–145 and, therefore, was not of the apostolic era. The author of the fragment evidently separated the apostolic times from all other times. Further, one of the reasons this document is called an early Western text by von Campenhausen is that the fragment lists the apocalypses of both John and Peter as acceptable books. The Eastern churches in the second and third centuries, he claims, routinely rejected these apocalypses. Another argument usually put forward to support a Western origin of the fragment is the absence of any mention of Hebrews in the list.[39] Von Campenhausen argues that this fragment could not have been written later than the end of the second century because:

> At a later period it is hardly conceivable that the Catholic Epistles would be limited to three or four, with no mention of those attributed to Peter, or, on the other hand, that the Apocalypse of Peter and the Wisdom of Solomon would have been acknowledged as part of the New Testament Canon. Furthermore, the heretics and heresies named by the Muratorianum [the MF] all still belong to the second century. (*Formation*, p. 244.)

On the other hand, A. C. Sundberg,[40] in a major study of the fragment, has argued against the traditional conclusions about the dating and understanding of this document.[41] He concludes that the fragment was written ca. 350–400 in the East and not in the West. His main arguments are (1) that permission was granted to read the Shepherd of Hermas even though it was considered outside of the canon. In the time of Irenaeus and Tertullian (see above) Hermas was considered authoritative and not an outside book. Only later in the West was Hermas excluded. (2) The Apocalypses of John and Peter are in equivocal positions[42] that Sundberg claims are more characteristic of the Eastern than of the Western churches in the third and fourth centuries. (3) The closest parallel to this list is that of Eusebius (ca. 325) in the East and (4) there are no similar lists in the second century anywhere.[43] (5) The argument that Hermas was written "quite recently in our time" should be understood in terms of how the ancient churches distinguished the apostolic times from their own; "our times" is a reference to a *post-apostolic* era as opposed to the times of the apostles. Sundberg gives several examples of this practice, including one from Irenaeus, who uses "our times" *(temporibus nostris)* of an event one hundred years before his time![44]

Admittedly, Sundberg's last point is probably the weakest in his line of reasoning, but whichever view one takes in regard to these words, they are still problematic since no one today seriously dates Hermas as late as 180–200 (the most commonly appealed to date for the MF). Along that same line, Pius, the brother of Hermas, is several successions of bishops before the bishop of Rome in the last two decades of the second century or even in the time of Irenaeus.[45] If the manuscript must be dated in the second century, why not stress the most logical time of ca. 140–150, which would place the MF in the time of Hermas? This date would be more in keeping with the words "quite recently in our time" than a late second century dating of the manuscript suggests. The most likely reason that no one wants to date the MF as early as the time of Hermas is probably because no scholar can find a biblical canon this complete that early in the second century. However, since no one suggests such an early dating (140–50), two other conclusions are possible. First, it is possible that the original form of the fragment has been tampered with in its translation from the Greek text to the Latin. If this is so, even the so-called technical term for the city of Rome *(urbs Romana)*, which Metzger claims is evidence for a Roman origin of the fragment, could have originated in the translation. But second, and much more likely, the MF most probably originated in the fourth century, since all of the closest parallels to it date after the mid-fourth century C.E.

On the whole, I believe that Sundberg's arguments are considerable. Since there are no parallels to the fragment until after the time of Eusebius, the document should probably be dated sometime after Eusebius (sometime after the mid-fourth century) and located in the East. Metzger, following the very significant critique of Sundberg by Everett Ferguson,[46] has good arguments against this fragment's coming from the East, but they appear to be based on the terminology used of Rome in the fragment, which may in fact have been more widespread than he allows.[47] This is, of course mere speculation, but the problems of dating the MF in the late second century appear to be more speculative.

Although Ferguson's and von Campenhausen's arguments for a later second century date of the fragment are considerable, it is not as clear as von Campenhausen claims that all of the catholic epistles were accepted by the majority of churches in the late second century. Further, after the fourth century, acceptance of the Revelation of John in the Eastern churches appears to have been more widespread than earlier, possibly owing to the decline of the Montanists by that time. It should be added that not all of the leaders of the Eastern churches of the fourth century rejected Revelation. (Eusebius does not reject it outright, but Athanasius and Dionysius clearly accepted it as a part of their canons.)

Again, the main problem with accepting a second century date for the Muratorian fragment is that it is simply too far advanced for that period, and its only close parallels all come from the fourth century.[48] If the MF could be established as a late second-century document, then it should also be recognized that we cannot find where it influenced any other writer for at least a hundred years!

IX. Athanasius of Alexandria

The ambiguity of Eusebius' list of NT canonical literature in general continued *in practice* after him, even though with some modifications. The most famous of the lists of NT canonical scriptures which eventually carried the day is found in Athanasius' *Festal Letter* from Alexandria which corresponds to the twenty-seven books of the NT which are acknowledged in the Church today. The *Letter* in part reads:

(1.) Since, however, I have spoken of the heretics as dead but of ourselves as possessors of the divine writings unto salvation, I am actually afraid lest in any way, as Paul said in writing to the Corinthians, a few of the undefiled may be led astray from their simplicity and purity by the craftiness of certain men and thereafter begin to pay attention to other books, the so-called sacred books. Therefore, because of this fear of your being deceived by these books possessing the same names as the genuine books and because of the present stress of the Church, I exhort you to bear with me for your own benefit as I actually make mention of these heretical writings, which you already know about.

(2.) As I am about to mention such matters, I will back up my venturesomeness by following the example of the evangelist Luke. And I will also say that since certain men have attempted to arrange for themselves the so-called secret writings and mingle them with the God-inspired Scripture, concerning which we have been fully informed even as they were handed down to our fathers by those who were eye-witnesses and servants of the word from the beginning, having been encouraged by true brethren and learning all from the beginning, I also resolved to set forth in order the writings that are in the list and handed down and believed to be divine. I have done this so that each person, if he has been deceived, may condemn those who led him astray, and that he who has remained stainless may rejoice, being again reminded of the truth.

(3.) There are then of the Old Testament books . . . [omitted here].

(7.) Those of the New Testament I must not shrink from mentioning in their turn. They are these: four Gospels, according to Matthew, according to Mark, according to Luke, and according to John.

(8.) Then after these are the Acts of the Apostles and the seven letters of the apostles, called the "Catholic" letters, which are as follows: one from James, two from Peter, three from John, and after these one from Jude.

(9.) In addition, there are fourteen letters of Paul the apostle, written in the following order: the first to the Romans, then two to the Corinthians, and thereafter one to the Galatians, one to the Ephesians, one to the Philippians, one to the Colossians, two to the Thessalonians, one to the Hebrews, and, without a break, two letters to Timothy, one to Titus, and one written to Philemon. Last, from John again comes the Revelation.

(10.) These are springs of salvation, so that he who is thirsty may be filled with the divine responses in them; in these alone is the good news of the teaching of true religion proclaimed; *let no one add to them or take anything away from them*. It was in regard to these that the Lord was ashamed of the Sadducees, saying: "You are being led astray, since you do know not the scripture," and he exhorted the Jews, saying, "Search the scriptures, for they are the very writings that witness concerning me."

(11.) But for the sake of being more exact in detail, I also add this admonition, writing out of necessity, that there are also other books apart from these that are not indeed in the above list, but were produced by our ancestors to be read by those who are just coming forward to receive oral instruction in the word of true religion. These include: the Wisdom of Solomon, the Wisdom of Sirach, Esther, Judith, Tobias, the so-called Teaching of the Apostles, and the Shepherd.

(12.) And nevertheless, beloved, though the former writings *be in the list* [or "are listed," κανονιζομένον] and the latter are read, nowhere is there any mention of the secret writings (the apocrypha). They are, rather, a device of heretics, who write them when they will furnishing them with dates and adding them, in order that by bringing them forth as ancient books they may thus have an excuse for deceiving the undefiled.[49]

Athanasius was probably the first to use the term *canon* (κανών) in reference to a body of sacred literature, and also appears to be the first to list the twenty-seven books of our current NT canon.[50] The verb form κανονιζομένον ("canonized" or "listed") in verse 12 of Athanasius' letter is also used here. One should not conclude by this, however, that all subsequent Church leaders agreed with Athanasius' NT canon, as the examples from the following sections will show. (Compare also his OT canon with the other OT lists in *Appendix B*.)

X. Cyril of Jerusalem (ca. 360–386)

Cyril gave a list of "Divine Scriptures" similar to that of Athanasius, only he excluded Revelation. His NT collection is described in the following manner.

But the four Gospels alone belong to the New Testament; the rest happens to be pseudepigrapha and harmful. The Manicheans also wrote [The] Gospel according to Thomas, which indeed, having been camouflaged by the sweetness of its title derived from an evangelist, corrupts the souls of the simpler ones. But accept also the Acts of the twelve Apostles. In addition to these [accept] the seven Catholic Epistles: [the one] of James and [the two] of Peter and [the three] of John and [the one] of Jude; and accept lastly as the seal of all, even of the disciples, the fourteen Epistles of Paul. Let all the rest, however, be placed in secondary [rank]. *And those which are not read in the Church, do not even read them privately as you have heard,* "So much" then about these. (*Cyrillus Catecheses* 4.36, italics added, trans. in Theron, *Evidence*, p. 117)

XI. Other Related Lists

Amphilochius, Bishop of Iconium (after 394 C.E.), appears to have accepted all of the books in Athanasius' canon except Revelation (which he called spurious), though he also raised doubt about Hebrews and the catholic epistles, questioning whether there should be seven epistles or three (see Theron, *Evidence*, p. 117). He appears to be the second person to use *canon* (*κανών*) in reference to a list of Christian scriptures.[51] Further examples of differences of opinion about what in fact comprised the NT canon include, as Metzger has observed, that Chrysostom (407 C.E.) never alluded to Revelation or the last four catholic epistles and also that the *Apostolic Constitutions* (no earlier than the fourth century) adds to Athanasius' list I and II Clement and the eight books of the *Constitutions* themselves, but omits Revelation.[52] Some Eastern churches rejected Revelation, even though they appear to have been in substantial agreement regarding most of the other Christian literature in Athanasius' canon. It is interesting that Dionysius of Alexandria (ca. 230) accepted Revelation as authoritative scripture, but did not believe that the apostle John had written it. He made one of the earliest critical assessments of the text, noting that the vocabulary and style of Revelation were not John's. Dionysius' evaluation of the text of Revelation is preserved in Eusebius and is instructive, though not necessarily typical, of the critical skills of that day. He writes:

In a word, it is obvious that those who observe their character throughout will see at a glance that the Gospel [John] and Epistle

[I John] have one and the same complexion. But the Apocalypse is utterly different from, and foreign to, these writings; it has no connexion, no affinity, in any way with them; it scarcely, so to speak, has even a syllable in common with them. Nay more, neither does the Epistle (not to speak of the Gospel) contain any mention or thought of the Apocalypse, nor the Apocalypse of the Epistle, whereas Paul in his epistles gave us a little light also on his revelations, which he did not record separately.

And further, by means of the style one can estimate the difference between the Gospel and Epistle and the Apocalypse. For the former are not only written in faultless Greek, but also show the greatest literary skill in their diction, their reasonings, and the constructions in which they are expressed. There is a complete absence of any barbarous word, or solecism, or any vulgarism whatever. For their author had, as it seems, both kinds of word, by the free gift of the Lord, the word of knowledge and the word of speech. But I will not deny that the other writer had seen revelations and received knowledge and prophecy; nevertheless I observe his style and that his use of the Greek language is not accurate, but that he employs barbarous idioms, in some places committing downright solecisms. These there is no necessity to single out now. For I have not said these things in mockery (let no one think it), but merely to establish the dissimilarity of these writings." *(Hist. eccl.* 7.25.22-27, *LCL)*

Koester has noted that Revelation is absent from many of the Greek manuscripts of the NT literature.[53] This may well have had as much to do with the uncertainty over who wrote the book, as Dionysius shows, as it did with the contents of the book.

Still further, several ancient manuscripts containing Christian literature—*Codex Claramontanus* (D) (ca. fifth to sixth century), also include some noncanonical early Christian writings;[54] *Codex Alexandrinus* (A) (fifth century) contains both I and II Clement; *Codex Constantinopolitanus* (C), dating from the eleventh century, includes I and II Clement, Barnabas, the Didache, and an interpolated text of the Epistles of Ignatius; the Epistle of Barnabas is also included as one of the books of the NT in the fourth century *Codex Sinaiticus* (‎ℵ). Kirsopp Lake has observed that Barnabas, along with I Clement and Hermas, became canonical literature in some circles, was quoted by Clement of Alexandria as scripture, and was even called a "catholic epistle" by Origen.[55]

XII. Summary

Enough has been shown in the above collections to argue reasonably that the notion of a closed NT canon was not a second-century development in the Church and that there were still considerable differences of opinion about what should comprise that canon even in the fourth and fifth centuries. We have argued that the NT collection of Christian scriptures was developed into a closed collection of scriptures for the first time in the fourth and fifth centuries. But even then, there was never a time in the fourth or fifth centuries when the *whole* Church adopted as scripture all of the twenty-seven books of the NT and those books alone. The four Gospels, for example, were set aside in the Syrian churches in favor of Tatian's *Diatessaron* until after ca. 400. Many Christians continued to reject in practice parts of the greater Church's canon long after there was a general recognition of it.[56]

Only in the time of the Reformation did Roman Catholics achieve "total unity" on the NT canon by the decree of the Council of Trent, but by that time Luther had already denied full canonical status to James, Hebrews, Jude, and Revelation—not to mention the deutero-canonical books (the Apocrypha)! The Protestants have affirmed, with Luther, the shorter OT canon, while the Eastern Orthodox have had a longer one than the Roman Catholics. Quite apart from these traditional church communions, the Ethiopian church, which can claim the tradition of the fourth century Church, continues to maintain a biblical canon of some eighty-one books.[57] At no time in history has the whole Church agreed completely on what should make up its canon of scriptures. There has been a general agreement in the early churches from the third century regarding the authoritative, or scriptural, status of the four Gospels, Acts, Paul's epistles, I Peter, and I John. However, there has been no unanimity. The rest of the NT canon appears to have been decided in councils based perhaps on wide church use, but within individual churches, reservations have continued to linger about the "doubted" books in the NT canon.

The results of our examination of the above lists and their many variations must be to raise the question of whether the Church was correct in perceiving the need of a closed canon since historically it did not agree, indeed it has never completely agreed, on what must go into that canon of scriptures. As will be shown in the next chapter, even the criteria the Church used to define its scripture and canon are somewhat vague and imprecise. If the earliest Christians ever intended for the Church that followed them to have a closed canon of scriptures, either OT or NT, there is no clear tradition from them to make that clear.

The historical context of the fourth and fifth centuries may be the major key to our understanding of why the Church began to try to close its canon of scriptures. The theological controversies (Marcionism, Gnosticism, Montanism) of the second and third centuries no doubt gave the initial impetus to the Church to define more precisely what was believed to be Christian and what was not. However, the era of conformity that characterized the reign of Constantine and the Roman world probably gave the Church its major push toward the conformity and unity it desired. The development of a closed biblical canon of authoritative scriptures and the exclusion (and in some cases, destruction) of all other Christian writings must surely have helped much to secure the unity the Church desired.

CHAPTER SEVEN

THE CRITERIA FOR A NEW TESTAMENT CANON:

Another Look

Thus far we have presented some of the processes by which the early Church came to recognize and employ certain of its literature as sacred scripture, and we have shown that there were many ambiguities as well as disagreements over such matters in the ancient Church. We now turn our focus to the inevitable questions related to the criteria the ancient Church used either consciously or unconsciously to distinguish its sacred literature from all other ancient Christian literature. In the case of Marcion, as was shown above, the answer is obvious; he sought to recognize only the literature that he thought would show the separation of Christianity from Judaism. But what was it that separated the NT literature from all other ancient Christian literature? The traditional "criteria" of apostolicy, orthodoxy, antiquity, inspiration, and Church use will be examined in the following discussion. Following this, we will raise several important questions that this investigation poses for the modern study of the Christian canon.

I. Apostolicity

In a carefully written essay on the matter, G. W. H. Lampe shows that the Church's most readily available weapon against the Gnostic Christians and other "heretics" was its apostolicity, which was guaranteed by historical succession and preserved in its oral and written traditions.[1] This "apostolic deposit," he claims, became the core of the authoritative NT literature and determined the formation of the canon of those writings.[2] He maintains that this was true even though the early Church "did not possess the critical or historical equipment to define the canon quickly, uniformly or exactly; but it gradually succeeded in isolating such works . . . as it believed to embody the general doctrinal tradition of the apostles."[3] Oscar Cullmann, going one major step further than Lampe, asserts that the "intrinsic apostolic authority" of the books that later became those that made up the Church's canon "forced themselves upon the church" because Christ speaks through them.[4] Cullmann is not clear, however, on how one can determine with precision the "intrinsic apostolic authority" in an ancient work.

Robert Funk also recognizes the importance for the early Church of the apostolic witness to the traditions they followed. He rightly concludes that it is not too much to say that "the church sought to ground its tradition in the apostles and Jesus."[5] It was an insistence upon grounding its faith in Jesus, represented by the apostles' teaching, that has historically led the Church to contend for the apostolic authorship of a given NT writing. This has been done to ensure the reliability of those documents and to maintain that the Church's tradition was not severed from its historical roots.[6]

The problem the application of the criterion of apostolicity presents for canonical studies is most pronounced in an age in which historical-critical methods of assessment enable the scholar to question whether *most* of the literature of the NT was written by any of the apostles. It can be argued fairly convincingly that John the apostle was not the author of all the literature that traditionally bears his name.[7] Although a case could possibly be made for the apostolic authorship of I Peter, I John, and possibly Jude (*if* he was the brother of Jesus and James), the arguments even then are not conclusive, and there is no consensus among scholars on the matter. No one seriously believes today—as was widely suspected quite early in the history of the Church—that Paul (or any apostle) wrote Hebrews. Again, there are strong questions about Paul's authorship of Ephesians, Colossians, and especially the Pastoral epistles, even though some authentic Pauline traditions may be carried on in them; how Paul died may be accurately portrayed in II Timothy 4:6-17. James, even if he were the brother of Jesus and wrote the epistle that bears his name, was still not an apostle. It is impossible for anyone today to argue credibly that the apostle Peter wrote II Peter. Further, the Gospels of Mark and Luke have no claim to apostolicity, even though they *may* have been written shortly after the apostolic period (ca. 30–65) of the Church. Ernest Best rightly concludes that a contemporary examination of what comprises apostolic documents is considerably different today from the conclusions promoted by the early Church on the matter.[8]

If apostolicity was the ancient criterion that determined the recognition of the authority of a work, as it most assuredly was for most churches,[9] then it must be admitted that this criterion was not carefully and consistently applied, however well intentioned the Church might have been. In the case of Hebrews, the attributing of it to Paul may have been more political than well intentioned in order to help the book gain acceptance among the churches, since many in the ancient Church rejected Pauline authorship of it. The above mentioned testimony of Origen (chapter 6, sect. VI) on this matter illustrates many of the doubts about Hebrews, at least in the Eastern Churches.

Finally, Koester has made the observation that the "apostolic" criterion itself is useless "when Christian movements that were later condemned as heretical can claim genuine apostolic origin."[10] The Gnostic Christians of the second century and the Donatists of the fourth century also claimed to have apostolic support for their teachings.[11] The Gnostic Gospel of Thomas, interestingly, is the first gospel that specifically claims apostolic authorship. Indeed, some of the sayings of Jesus in it are acknowledged today by some scholars to be as early as some of the sayings in the canonical Gospels and may also contain some authentic sayings of Jesus.[12]

II. "Orthodoxy"

It has frequently been argued that one of the unifying and distinguishing factors in the NT literature is the *truth*, or canon of faith, it presents.[13] However, as one examines the NT literature carefully, it becomes quite clear that there was no unified view of "orthodoxy" in the early apostolic Church. For example, can the eschatology of the Synoptic evangelists be harmonized with that of the fourth evangelist? Does Paul's view of the death of Christ "for our sins" square with Luke's lack of interest in that matter?[14] In another instance, compare Paul's argument in Romans 13:1-3, that we ought to be subject to the governing authorities (which are appointed by God) and that those who resist such authorities resist God with Peter's and John's attitude in Acts 4 and 5, which rejects the authority of governing officials in favor of obedience to God. Apart from relativizing the message of Paul to a specific context, how can these texts be harmonized?[15] Compare also the baptismal formulas in the book of Acts (2:38; 10:48; 19:5) with that in Matthew 28:19. Again, can the organizational structure of the early Church in Acts, Paul, John, the Pastorals and Matthew 16:18-19 be easily harmonized? Many other examples could be listed here to show that there is a fair amount of diversity in the NT literature. Kelsey concludes that the scriptures of the Church are "a 'whole' of irreducibly different parts"[16] and calls into question an almost universal assumption, characteristic of the time following Irenaeus, that is still present with us in more conservative churches—namely, that the faith of the early apostolic Church was "unified and pure" and that the Church was united in a "normative orthodoxy" from which it subsequently fell in the postapostolic age.[17] He properly dismisses this assumption primarily because there are no first-century witnesses who give that picture. Ernst Käsemann boldly asserts that "this variability [in early Christianity] is already so wide even in the New Testament that we are compelled to admit the existence not merely of significant tensions, but, not infrequently, of irreconcilable theological contradictions."[18] Krister Stendahl, in the same unambiguous manner, asserts that the many variations and differences in the NT are real and that "they cannot be overcome by harmonization. Or we could even say: When they are overcome by harmonization, the very points intended by the writers are dulled and distorted."[19]

If the NT has a theological core that is everywhere acknowledged or reasonably assumed, it is that "Jesus-the-man-now-exalted"[20] is worthy of faithful obedience and that the promise of the blessing of God awaits all who follow him. Even this confession, however, is not confined to the NT literature alone, but is affirmed in numerous non-canonical Christian writings.[21] The NT writings nonetheless were unquestionably *believed* by the Church to have conveyed reliably the message of and about Christ. Apostolicity witnessed to this, but apostolicity could not take priority over what was testified to.[22]

The very presence of creedal formulations in the Church following the formation of a biblical canon within the Christian communities has manifestly demonstrated that "orthodoxy" itself was based on a "canon within the canon."[23] In other words, if the NT literature alone was considered sufficient for faith, many of the subsequent creedal formulations hammered out in lengthy debates and often under great stress would probably not have been deemed necessary.

What Rolf Knierim says of the OT literature at this point applies also to the NT. In a thoughtful essay, Knierim contends that the primary problem in studying the OT is that it "contains a plurality of theologies."[24] One of the problems in the study of the OT, he goes on to say, is the assumption of most OT theologians that it must be understood as a whole. He shows that this approach is indefensible and that the theologian who deals with the plurality of those theologies cannot regard them all as equal even though they all belong to the OT canon.[25] He also stresses that the theologies of the OT are neither the same nor are they equal, and they must be prioritized. What is it that unites the OT canon and shows correspondence or relationships among the theologies? Knierim says it is not the traditionally emphasized notions, such as monotheism,[26] the kerygma (or Word of God), liberation theology, salvation history, or even the covenant motif. Rather, the ultimate concern in the OT theologies is for the *"universal dominion of Yahweh in justice and righteousness."*[27] Citing Hebrews 1:1, which tells of God's having spoken "in many and various ways" in the past, Knierim stresses that this does not mean that all such ways are equal or should have the same place and function for the theologian and preacher. Instead, he proposes that the minister not pick and choose at will what to emphasize, but rather he or she should choose in terms of "the true biblical priorities." For Knierim, the task of the biblical theologian is to establish those priorities. The same can be said about the NT theologies, even though the differences there are not nearly so great as in the OT. The task of the interpreter of the NT should, therefore, be to find the "true biblical priorities" in that literature and allow the literature to take priority in the Church's witness.

Koester has shown convincingly that there were other voices (trajectories) in early Christianity, which, though having lost the battle with later standards of "orthodoxy," may not have been so heretical by early Church standards.[28] Walter Bauer even claimed that in the postapostolic age the so-called "orthodox" Christians, who were in fact Christians of a "Roman" church distinction, were actually fewer in number than the so-called "heretics," later so designated.[29] It should be noted, however, that two scholars have recently disputed this last claim by Bauer, the most recent of whom argues that Bauer did not carefully interpret Celsus, one of his major sources for his views on the numerical superiority of the so-called "heretics."[30]

Frederik Wisse, in a helpful advance of the discussion of heresy in the early Church, agrees with Bauer that heresy was prior to orthodoxy, but he does so for different reasons. He contends that more diverse groups were present in the early Church than simply the "orthodox" and the Gnostic Christians, whose views fell out of vogue with the Christians at Rome. He notes that most of the literature Eusebius cites is only vaguely appealed to and that most of it was lost because orthodoxy of the fourth century rejected what was polemical and/or not uniform; in the fourth century, uniformity and not diversity, was in vogue. Wisse asks why most of the Gnostic literature is not polemical, like much of the "orthodox" literature that survived the second century, and concludes that it was because Gnostic Christianity was in the majority position during that time and did not need to respond in kind.[31] As to why most of the accepted literature of the first through the third centuries disappeared by the fifth century, Wisse argues that orthodoxy that gained preeminence in the fourth century viewed it in a heresiological manner and consequently as a threat. He also answers the question of why most of the early Christian polemics were *ad hominem*, or directed against persons, rather than *ad doctrinam*, or directed against established doctrines. Wisse's response is that at the time the polemics were going on there were no accepted *ad doctrinam* standards by which to judge.[32] That is probably an overstatement, but Wisse's point about theological diversity in the early Church is important.

All of this is not to say, however, as some theologians are prone to conclude, that all theologies of the Bible and outside of the Bible equally represent the proclamation of the earliest Christian community. David Kelsey appears unwilling to venture among the plurality of theologies in the Bible to prioritize them in order to search for the distinguishing marks that identify authentic Christianity.[33] However, Knierim's comments about the task of OT theologians are again equally true for NT theologians.[34] There were justifiable reasons *historically* and *exegetically* for the ancient Church to reject the Gnostic esoteric and ahistorical interpretation of Christian faith.[35] The NT scholar must also sift carefully through the literature of the NT and other ancient documents in order to prioritize those elements that are essential to Christian faith and those that are not. Many theologians today are far too anxious to omit this admittedly complex inquiry and conclude in some vague way that all ancient theologies are essentially equal. Although the Christian proclamation of the first century is much broader than the late second-century orthodoxy in Rome, we do contend that all ancient theologies are *not* equally representative of the faith of the earliest Christian communities.

III. Antiquity

Oscar Cullmann has argued that only the tradition that comes from the "period of incarnation" can claim acceptance as authoritative for the Church.[36] The author of the Muratorian Fragment opposed the acceptance of Hermas as an authoritative document for the Church, specifically because it was not written in the apostolic age but more recently, in his own age—that is, any time after the apostolic age. Therefore, antiquity, perhaps linked with apostolicity and a "rule of faith," appears to have been an important criterion for canonicity for some of the churches.

However, once again the more developed critical tools of investigation today have enabled the biblical scholars to show fairly convincingly that some literature of the NT—especially II Peter, probably the Pastorals, and possibly other literature as well—was written later than other noncanonical Christian books—later than the Didache, I Clement, the Epistles of Ignatius, Polycarp, Barnabas, Hermas, and possibly even II Clement. A strong argument can be made at least for the earlier dating of this literature than some of the canonical literature, which is enough to show that the criterion of antiquity was not as carefully applied in the patristic Church as is possible today.

Helmut Koester maintains that if "antiquity" be used as a criterion for acceptance by the Church, then we should give special consideration to the study of some of the apocryphal gospels, which he argues are representative of the earliest strands of Christianity. He maintains that some of these writings have a rightful claim to as early a date of composition as some of the canonical Gospels and possibly even earlier. He notes that the evidence for an early dating of about a dozen noncanonical gospels—before the end of the first century C.E.—compares quite well with the evidence for the canonical Gospels.[37] He suggests that the Gospel of Thomas should be dated sometime around the end of the first century and that it contains some very early sayings of Jesus. Koester especially makes his case in regard to the Egerton Papyrus, (also called the Unknown Gospel), which, he contends, may have been used by John to compose his more elaborate discourses. He also makes a similar claim of antiquity for the Dialogue of the Savior, the Apocryphon of John, and the Gospel of Peter.[38] He states unequivocally that these five sources are as old and as valuable as the canonical sources for knowledge of the earliest development of the traditions about Jesus. Further, he adds that they are significant witnesses for the development of the NT Gospel literature in its formative stages.[39]

In another study, Koester has shown the relevance of the study of Gnostic apocryphal gospels by using them to identify traditional sayings of Jesus found in John but not in the Synoptic Gospels. He maintains that further comparisons of John (other than just the one in John 8:12-59) to the apocryphal sayings will demonstrate that there was an even broader "sayings" tradition than is found in the Synoptic tradition. Such a comparison, he adds, will give clues for understanding the often elusive process of the composition of the Johannine discourses as well as aid in the identification of the traditional sayings of Jesus used in them.[40] Although there may be some "gall mixed with honey" in the Gnostic gospels, there is little doubt that a serious study of them will produce important results for our study of early Christianity, and especially the sayings of Jesus.[41]

If Koester is correct in his assessment of the five sources mentioned above, we need to raise again the significance of antiquity. If the goal of the canonizing process is in part to reach back through the literature of the NT era to the earliest sayings and deeds of Jesus that were held to be authoritative for the Church, then those five sources ought to be given a fair hearing, and we should allow for the possibility that they may contain legitimate elements of the earliest traditions of Jesus should be considered.[42]

In most discussions of canonicity, an implied value is put on antiquity. The older the document, the more reliable it is presumed to be. Ernest Best questions this assumption, contending that an earlier interpretation of the facts of Christianity is not necessarily more reliable than later understandings. He suggests the opposite when, by way of analogy, he declares that "the understanding of life which we find in Shakespeare is almost always more profound than that in the chronicles which he used as sources for many of his plots."[43] If antiquity alone were the chief criterion for canonicity, a great deal of rethinking would need to be done regarding the present biblical canon; however, it would be unwise to build a canon of scriptures on such an everchanging and imprecise criterion, which the best of scholars cannot agree on. The earlier writings cannot by that fact alone be considered more reliable or, indeed, more "inspired." Given that word of caution, the aim of recovering the earliest and most reliable tradition about Jesus has always been one of the goals of the Christian Church, and especially of its teachers. Regardless of recent attempts of Brevard Childs to focus attention on the final form of a given biblical text as *the* canonical and, therefore, authoritative text for the Church, the aim at recovering the earliest traditions of the Christian community cannot be an ill-informed quest.[44] This does not necessarily mean that the Christian biblical canon ought to be either broadened or even paired down based on the criterion of antiquity. Metzger appears to be apprehensive about mixing the gall of Gnosticism with the honey of the authentic traditions of Jesus, urging on us that the criteria of apostolicity and orthodoxy should be followed more closely, disallowing traditions that are too far away from the traditional pictures of Jesus in the canonical Gospels. For example, he rejects the acceptance of the Gospel of Thomas into the biblical canon because in it "the voice of the Good Shepherd is heard only in a muffled way."[45] Many contemporary scholars are also confident that "the voice of the Good Shepherd" is somewhat muffled in the canonical Gospels. The same methods employed in our study of the canonical Gospels to determine the authentic sayings of Jesus can also be applied to the noncanonical Christian literature with significant value in our overall understanding of the origins of the Christian faith. I believe that the antiquity of these Christian documents is sufficient reason to examine them carefully to determine whether they may help in our quest to understand better the one who gave rise to the Christian faith. If in that examination it is determined with some sense of confidence that an authentic saying of Jesus is couched in one of the Gnostic texts, then would it not be prudent on the part of the Church to listen to that voice?

IV. Inspiration

Each of the ancient Church Fathers believed that his canon of scriptures was inspired. Certainly no ancient voices denied the inspiration of those scriptures, but to what extent did an awareness of the inspiration of the NT literature play a part in the canonizing process? Origen is quite explicit that the scriptures were written by inspiration of God (or inspired by the Holy Spirit). Note, for example, his emphasis that "the Scriptures were written by the Spirit of God, and have a meaning, not such only as is apparent at first sight, but also another which escapes the notice of most."[46] Again, while seeking to discredit the authenticity of the treatise the Doctrine of Peter, he writes in the same text, "We can show that it was not composed by Peter or by any other person inspired by the Spirit of God." Later in his discussion of the Holy Spirit, in which he presented his best evidence for a Son belonging to God, he wrote:

> We, however, in conformity with our belief in the doctrine, which we assuredly hold to be divinely inspired, believe that it is possible in no other way to explain and bring within the reach of human knowl-

edge this higher and diviner reason as Son of God, than by means of those Scriptures alone which were inspired by the Holy Spirit, i.e., the Gospels and Epistles, and the Law and the Prophets, according to the declaration of Christ himself. *(De Prin.,* Preface 8, ANF)[47]

Theophilus of Antioch (ca. 180), also believed that the scriptures had their origins in God and expressed the relationship between scriptures ("holy writings") and inspiration. "And hence the holy writings teach us, and all the spirit bearing [inspired] men . . . showing that at first God was alone, and the Word in Him" *(Ad Autolycum* 2:22, ANF).

There is no question that the early Church believed its scriptures were inspired by God, but the biggest problem with using inspiration as a criterion for canonicity is that *the canonical scriptures were not the only ancient literature believed to be inspired by God.* Hermas, for example, who uses none of the traditional scripture formulae when referring to any OT or NT literature, does in fact employ a scriptural formula when he quotes the noncanonical apocalypse of Eldad and Modat (now lost). He writes, "The Lord is near those that turn to him, as it is written (ὡς γέγραπται) in the Book of Eldad and Modat, who prophesied to the people in the wilderness" *(Shepherd, Vis.,* 2.3.4, LCL).[48] The author of II Clement quotes I Clement 23:3, 4 with the introductory words, "For the *prophetic word also says*" (λέγει γὰρ καὶ ὁ προφητικὸς λόγος) (11:2), which are the usual words to designate works deemed inspired and authoritative. Again, the author of the Epistle of Barnabas in 16:5 introduces a passage from II Enoch 89:56, 66, 67 with the words, "For the scripture says" (λέγει γὰρ ἡ γραφή)[49] Theophilus apparently also included Sibyl as an inspired document along with the prophets of God (2:9).[50]

In a somewhat different light, Clement of Rome (ca. 95) recommended the teaching of the apostle Paul in I Corinthians, which he claimed Paul wrote "with true inspiration" (ἐπ᾽ ἀληθείας πνευματικῶς) *(I Clem.* 47:3, LCL). Yet, on the other hand, he also said that his own epistle was "written by us through the Holy Spirit" (ὑφ᾽ ἡμῶν γεγραμμένοις διὰ τοῦ ἁγίου πνεύματος) (63:2, LCL). Similarly, Ignatius expressed his own awareness of his speaking by the power of the Holy Spirit when he commented:

I spoke with a great voice, —*with God's own voice.* . . . But some
suspected me of saying this because I had previous knowledge of the
division of some persons: but he in whom I am bound is my witness
that I had no knowledge of this from any human being, *but the Spirit
was preaching and saying this* (τὸ δὲ πνεῦμα ἐκήρυσσεν λέγον τάδε).
(*Ign. Phld.*, 7:1b-2, *LCL*, italics added)

There are, in fact, numerous other examples in the postapostolic
and early patristic communities, in which various authors either
claimed or were acknowledged by others to have been inspired by
the Spirit to talk or to write.[51]

It has often been argued, however, that the NT word for inspiration (θεόπνευστος, II Tim. 3:16) was used only in reference to the
biblical scriptures. Even though that is normally the case, the term
is also used of individuals, and not just those who did not write
scripture. Kalin, for example, shows that Gregory of Nyssa (ca.
330–395), when commenting on Basil's commentary on the creation
story, claimed that Basil (ca. 330–379) was inspired and that his
words even surpassed those of Moses in terms of beauty, complexity
and form.[52] Kalin also notes that the famous epitaph of Abercius
from ca. the fourth century was called an "inspired inscription"
(θεόπνευστον ἐπίγραμμα),[53] as well as a synodical epistle of the
council of Ephesus (ca. 433), which described the council's condem-
nation of Nestorious (d. ca. 451) as "their inspired judgment" (or
"decision") (τῆς αὐτῶν θεοπνεύστου κρίσεως).[54]

The conclusion one is led to from even such a limited gathering of
examples is that inspiration as such was not believed to have been
limited to the OT or NT literature alone. It also cannot be claimed
that inspiration was limited to literature alone. Justin Martyr, for
example, who is certainly in harmony with the literature of the NT,
believed that inspiration and the Holy Spirit's power were the pos-
sessions of the whole Church. He writes: "For the prophetical gifts
remain with us even to the present time. And hence you ought to
understand that [the gifts] formerly among your nation [the Jewish
nation] have been transferred to us" (*Trypho* 82, *ANF*).[55]

Kalin notes that even in the ancient fragments that dealt with the
Montanist controversy[56] he could find no evidence from the early
Church that inspiration was confined to the apostolic age, which

was already past, or even to a collection of sacred writings.[57] Hence
the traditional belief that *only* the canonical writings were deemed
inspired by the early Christians must surely be called into question.
The ancient Jewish belief that limited inspiration to the OT scriptures, claiming that "When the last prophets, Haggai, Zechariah
and Malachi, died, the holy Spirit ceased out of Israel" (*Tosefta
Sotah* 13:2),[58] was not carried over into the postapostolic Church.
Kalin, following a study by Krister Stendahl,[59] further notes that the
distinction between "inspired" writings and "non-inspired" writings was that the latter lay outside the whole life of the Christian
community; such writings were heretical.[60] He continued to state
that his own investigation of the Church Fathers up to 400 C.E.
failed to turn up one example that an orthodox writing outside of
the NT was ever called uninspired. That designation was only for
heretical authors. He concludes, "If the Scriptures were the *only*
writings the Fathers considered inspired, one would expect them to
say so, at least once in a while."[61] Kahlin adds that in the early
Church inspiration was applied not only to all scripture, but also to
the Christian community as it bore "living witness of Jesus Christ."
Only heresy was considered to be noninspired because it was contrary to this "living witness of Jesus Christ."[62]

The views of LaSor, Hubbard, and Bush in regard to inspiration
and canonicity apparently do not take the above examples into consideration, since they conclude: "Canonicity and inspiration cannot
be separated. The ultimate basis for canonicity is simply this: if the
writing is inspired (God-breathed) it is canonical. If it is not inspired it is not canonical."[63] Similarly, this traditional view is also
found in the earlier official Roman Catholic statement of Vatican I,
which stated in part that the books of scripture "are held to be sacred and canonical . . . because they were written under the inspiration of the Holy Spirit."[64]

James Barr has correctly expressed the basic thrust of the traditional view of inspiration and the canon of scriptures as follows: "If
we take a really strict old-fashioned view of inspiration, all books
within the canon are fully inspired by the Holy Spirit, and no books
outside it, however good in other respects, are inspired."[65] As he
later stressed, one of the difficulties in the whole idea of the canon in
the early Church was the difficulty the Church had of distinguish-

ing inspired and noninspired writings.[66] The problem the early Church had in deciding what literature was or was not inspired, which demonstrates a lack of agreement on the meaning of inspiration,[67] is illustrated by the differences in ancient "lists" of authoritative books.[68]

Von Campenhausen, observing that "inspiration" was originally attached to prophetic utterance in the OT (II Tim. 3:16) and subsequently also in the NT, adds that it was with Origen that a transition took place in which all scriptures of both testaments were acknowledged as inspired. This unhistorical application of inspiration to all of the Bible, he says, was modified somewhat in time, but was never overcome in the Church. (See *Formation*, p. 332.)

Throughout history, the Church has never had a coherent definition of inspiration, nor has it been able to articulate clearly the distinction between the inspiration of a biblical writing and the inspiration resident in the ongoing life of the Church and in the act of preaching. The continuing prophetic ministry of the Spirit of the first century, which called individuals through the proclamation of the Good News to faith in Christ, was clearly believed by the Church of the second and following centuries to be resident in *their* community of faith and in *their* ministry as well. The Christian community believed that God continued to inspire individuals in their proclamation *just as God did* the writers of the NT literature. *The Spirit was believed by the early Church to be the gift of God to the whole Church and not simply the possession of its writers of sacred literature.* Does this conclusion then pose an affront to the uniqueness, inspiration, and authority of the biblical literature? Kalin says that would be true if the only unique factor of that literature were its inspiration.[69] Inspiration was not the distinguishing factor that separated either the apostles from subsequent Christians or the Christian scriptures from all other Christian literature. Krister Stendahl is right when he concludes:

> Inspiration, to be sure, is the divine presupposition for the New Testament, but the twenty-seven books were never chosen because they, and only they, were recognized as inspired. Strange as it may sound, inspiration was not enough. Other standards had to be applied. ("Apocalypse of John," p. 245)

Enough evidence has been presented here to make it possible to argue that inspiration was not in itself the criterion by which a book of the NT was given the status of scripture and later placed into the canon. What was true or not true concerning the message of and about Jesus—the canon of faith—appears more to have been a determining factor of what was authoritative in the life of the early Church than a notion of what was and was not inspired. However, as was shown in the preceding section, even (orthodoxy) was not the only factor leading to the recognition of a writing as scripture and its subsequent canonization.

V. Use

The question of whether a book should be regarded as scripture and placed within a canon seems to have been determined ultimately by early Church use. If use refers to the widespread recognition of a document in the ancient Church, then, of course, one of the earliest testimonies for this criterion is Eusebius. Notice, for example, how he shows an acceptance of I John and a reluctance to accept II and III John and Revelation because, along with the Gospel of John, I John

> has been *accepted without controversy by ancients and moderns alike but the other two are disputed,* and as to the Revelation there have been many advocates of either opinion up to the present. This, too, shall be similarly illustrated by *quotations from the ancients* at the proper time. (*Hist. eccl.,* 3.24.18, *LCL,* italics added)

Further, Eusebius separated (rejected?) the "disputed" books (James, Jude, II Pe., II and III John, and possibly Rev. as well as the Acts of Paul, Herm., Apoc. Pet., Barn., and Did.) from those that were recognized based on the tradition of recognition in the Church. Notice why he says that he separates them.

> But we have nevertheless been obliged to make a list of them, distinguishing between those writings which, *according to the tradition of the Church,* are true, genuine, and recognized, and those which differ from them in that they are not canonical but disputed, yet nevertheless are known to most of the writers of the Church. (*Hist. eccl.* 3.25.6, *LCL,* italics added)

Wide use in the churches appears to be the best explanation of why some writings were recognized and preserved as authoritative in some churches but not in others; some writings met the worship and instructional needs of churches, but others did not. The writings that did not survive in the Church did not meet the needs of the greater Church. Koester, though acknowledging a modified form of apostolicity—that is, authorship by the apostles or their disciples—claims that the final criterion for accepting or rejecting a book as part of the Church's canon was "the teachings of the churches in the earliest period, meaning whichever of these writings had actually remained in use since that time."[70]

Although church use was probably one of the controlling factors in determining canonicity, this alone does not answer all of the questions concerning the selection process.[71] It is not at all clear that some writings of the NT—Philemon, II Peter, Jude, II and III John, and possibly others—were cited, referred to, or even used as frequently in the life of the churches as were several extra-biblical sources—I Clement, the Shepherd of Hermas, the Didache, and possibly also Barnabas, Ignatius and Polycarp. Raymond Collins, arguing that the historic "canon of truth" about Christ that was passed on in the early churches, concludes that not all of the teachings of the current NT canon are of equal value for Christian faith and ministry, nor are they necessarily more important or closer to that canon of truth than are several other nonbiblical Christian writings. While still acknowledging the strong influence of the present twenty-seven-book NT canon on Christian thought, Collins is surely on target when he goes on to say that

> a concern for the truth of history calls for the admission that some
> books within the canon have had a more influential function in shap-
> ing the expression of the Church's faith than have others within the
> canon, and that some books outside of the canon have had a more
> striking impact on the formulation of the Church's faith than have
> some individual books among the canonical twenty-seven. In effect,
> the canon of the New Testament must be considered with the utmost
> seriousness, yet it can be no more simply equated with the canon of
> truth in our day than it was at the time of Irenaeus. (*Introduction*,
> p. 39)

Another side of the criterion of use is what F. F. Bruce calls the criterion of "catholicity."[72] By it he means the unwillingness of a church to be out of step with other churches in regard to which documents were recognized as authoritative. Although this concern probably had a considerable influence on many of the churches from time to time, especially the influence of the larger churches on the smaller ones, still the variety in canonical lists of the fourth century shows that this criterion of catholicity was far from absolute.[73]

Not only use, but also other historical circumstances helped determine which books were included in the Church's authoritative list. After the reaction to Montanism, prophetic literature was much more suspect and tended to be neglected, especially in the East. The Apocalypse of Peter was not looked on as authoritatively after the Montanist controversies, as before, and even the book of Revelation had a stormy reception, especially through the fourth century. Although the criteria the Church used to establish its canon of sacred scriptures are still somewhat imprecise, probably all of the above criteria played a role to some extent in various churches' decisions about the canon, with the exception of the criterion of inspiration. This is true regardless of how consistently the churches carried out the use of those criteria.

Ultimately, it appears that the writings that were believed to have best conveyed the earliest Christian proclamation and that also best met the needs of the local churches in the third and fourth centuries were the writings they selected for their sacred scriptures. Conversely, it appears that the literature that was no longer deemed relevant to the Church's needs, even though it may have been considered such at an earlier time, was simply eliminated from consideration. If that conclusion is true, this would not be the first time the Church focused on literature that was most relevant to its own historical situation. Why else do "canons within the canon" arise? NT scholars have long recognized that the *Sitz im Leben* of the early Church (the social circumstances of the life of the Church) played a significant role in the selection, organization, and editing of the materials that form the NT Gospels. The relevance of those Gospels and other literature to the life of the emerging churches in subsequent generations no doubt also played a major role in their preservation as well as in their sometimes forced[74] and/or gradual disappearance because they ceased being relevant and useful to the Church. This explanation seems to answer best the question regarding the differing lists of both OT and NT authoritative books in the ancient Church. Although the leaders of the Church in the fourth century and later pushed for a unity in the recognition of which books were inspired, authoritative, and canonical, such unanimity could hardly have been achieved due to the variation in the churches' historical circumstances. Use in this sense, as well as in the sense of wide use in the larger churches of the third through the fifth centuries, is probably the primary key to understanding the preservation and canonization of these books by the Church.

CHAPTER
E I G H T

FINAL REFLECTIONS

It has been argued in the discussion up to this point that the earliest Christians recognized above all others the authority of Jesus in the living witness of the apostolic community.[1] From the beginning they also appear to have accepted the predictive witness of the partially opened OT collection of scriptures to the Christ event as an apologetic for Christian preaching. There was little occasion in the first century C.E. when the followers of Jesus saw the need for anything more than that. While the memory of the apostolic witness was still fresh, there was little need to give attention to written records. Also, to the degree that the early Church believed it could find adequate witness to Jesus the Christ and the kerygma about him in the OT scriptures, there was no need to focus on the priority of "apostolic" documents.[2] Quite early, however, the ancient Church circulated and often referred to such documents, and/or the oral tradition behind them, as a resource for Christian identity and guidance in the ongoing life of their churches, even though this literature was not yet put on a par with the OT scriptures.

In the middle to late second century, however, and largely as a result of the challenges to what was believed at that time to be the norm for Christian faith and practice, many of the leaders of the

Church began to defend the legitimacy and truthfulness of their message by appealing to the succession of the apostolic preaching—the "apostolic deposit"—which was believed to have eyewitness authority.[3] The Church believed also that this "deposit" was conveyed faithfully in succeeding generations through the bishops. It was affirmed not only that the bishops carefully handed on this canon of faith in the churches, but also that some early Christian literature was believed to have faithfully conveyed that same apostolic message. Throughout the last half of the second century, no closed "orthodox" canon of authoritative Christian writings was universally so acknowledged,[4] but the literature that was believed to have faithfully transmitted the message of Christ began to be widely recognized and played a useful role in the life and worship of the Church.

As was shown earlier, some of that literature was acknowledged early on as scripture—possibly in the early decades of the second century, though that would have been an exception rather than the rule at that time. In the last quarter of the second century, some "core" documents (mainly the four Gospels and Paul) emerged as authoritative scriptures in the life and worship of the Church on a par with the OT. These writings were not, however, a closed biblical canon at that stage; closed canons began to emerge in the fourth and fifth centuries. The practice of drawing up closed lists of authoritative NT scriptures appears to have started with Eusebius, and within a short time such lists began to appear everywhere in both the East and the West. With the possible exceptions of Melito and Origen, the Christian OT canons also began to appear in the fourth century.[5] These two exceptions are only found in Eusebius' *Ecclesiastical History*, a fourth-century document. Prior to this time, one searches in vain for such canonical lists of sacred scriptures. At first, these lists were products of individuals and subsequently (especially in the fifth century) began to grow out of council decisions.

To what extent were these developments a result of the Church's response to heresy or to a proliferation of "inspired" writings thrust upon the Christian community by Gnostic and Charismatic communities or to the conscious decisions at grass roots levels regarding which books could be handed over to be burned? To what extent were these natural developments in view of the Roman influence, which called for conformity and consensus? In what way was the biblical canon affected by contemporary and parallel notions of "canon" in the ancient world? Why did a need for such a precisely defined collection of sacred scriptures arise in the churches? What are the roots of the notion of a canon of scripture? Why does such an idea come forth (first of all in Judaism) only after Alexander the Great and during a time when other canons were widely used in the Hellenistic world?[6] To what extent was the biblical canon strongly influenced by the idea of a perfect guide in the Hellenistic world, or of peace and harmony in the Roman world? Was that a legitimate influence on the Church, which has always claimed to have been made free in Christ and alive in the power of the Spirit? In other words, are fixed scriptural canons Christian?[7]

Whatever our response to these and other related questions, a careful survey of the literature that makes up the present Christian canon of both OT and NT scriptures shows clearly that the Church was not of one mind in the matter of which writings should be accepted as sacred scripture. As our historical survey has shown, final agreement on the scope of the biblical canon was not reached through a general recognition or consensus in the churches. Rather, attempts were made to arrive at a consensus by council decisions of the Church hierarachy, whose decisions were not always followed by the churches themselves. Also, the precise boundaries of the Christian faith, or beliefs that defined the nature of Christianity, were never fully agreed upon either, even though there was finally some agreement by the "orthodox" churches (those of a "Roman bent") that the Church was not broad enough to allow for the presence of Docetics, Gnostics, Marcionites, Ebionites, and, to some extent, even the Montanists.

The primary criterion by which the ancient Church established its canon of authoritative scriptures was clearly a modified form of apostolicity, but the task of determining what was "apostolic" was not easy since even the "heretical" Christians claimed to have an apostolic heritage. Eventually the view that carried the day was that the "apostolic deposit," or genuine witness to and from Christ (the Church's true canon), was transmitted faithfully from the apostles to the Church through its succession of bishops. What does not appear to have been given serious consideration in the late second-century Church is that the earliest apostolic community may not have been so monolithic in its passing on of a single "orthodox" tradition as the later Church apparently supposed.[8] It is quite clear that what the Church eventually did recognize as "apostolic" was in no way monolithic or uniform throughout the churches in Irenaeus' day. That lack of theological and historical agreement, however, may not have been a fault if one sees from the literature of the NT itself that the Church thereby "canonized" breadth and diversity.[9]

Nevertheless, did the Church need a fixed catalogue of scriptures for its continuing existence in order to function as well as to deal with the various "heresies" in the community of faith? There can be no doubt about the advantages of possessing an early written reflection of the Christ event, which called the Church into existence. What else could have reminded the Church of its true identity when the oral tradition of and about Jesus began to fade in the Church's memory by the middle to late second century? Since Christianity is a historical religion—its faith is directed toward one who is believed to have lived, died, and rose again in Palestine ca. 30 C.E.—how could it fail to have an interest in documents close to those events, purporting not only to report those events, but also to express their significance? Possibly the reason why a fixed collection of Christian writings, like the one put forth by Irenaeus, was not as important to the Church in earlier times—before Marcion—[10] may have been because the continuing circulation of oral tradition was still fresh in the early second century and was deemed sufficient for the Church's needs. It is perhaps also likely that the heretical threats to the Church by the Judaizers and the Docetics were such that they could be identified and dealt with easier by the oral tradition of the Church than at a later time, when the Church faced both Marcionite and Gnostic heresies as well as the rapidly increasing amount of Christian literature produced by the Montanists (which they also believed was "inspired").[11]

The obvious difficulty the Church had in defining the precise limits of its canon, as well as the problem of the lateness in time when a closed canon began to emerge in the Church, not to mention the problem which that canon had in defining the nature of Christian faith adequately,[12] raises several important questions.

First of all, and most important of course, is whether the Church was right in perceiving the need for a closed canon of scriptures. If the term *Christian* is to be best defined by the examples and beliefs passed on by the earliest followers of Jesus, then we must at least ponder the question of whether the notion of a biblical canon is necessarily "Christian." From our best available information about the earliest followers of Jesus, we see that they did not have such canons as the Church presently possesses today, nor did they indicate that their successors should draw them up. Even in regard to the OT canon, it has been shown that their collection of OT scriptures (there were no NT scriptures then) were considerably broader than those presently found in either the Catholic or Protestant canons and with much more flexibility than our present collections allow. To the extent that this is true, one is forced to ask again the question of whether biblical canons are in fact "Christian"?

Second, one must ask today whether in fact the present biblical canon has not legitimized for all time the practice of slavery[13] and proclaimed the inferiority and subjugation of half of the human race, which has an equal claim to having been created in the image of God.[14] In other words, does the biblical canon as the Word of God ever become a "letter of the Law," thereby missing the true Gospel, which is liberating? Stendahl, observing how the Bible has been used throughout the history of the Church to justify the unjustifiable, claims that "there never has been an evil cause in the world that has not become more evil if it has been possible to argue it on biblical grounds."[15] More specifically, Stendahl argues that slavery in the Western world would have vanished quicker were it not that slavery is neither condemned nor discouraged in the Bible.[16]

Third, does such a move toward a closed canon of scriptures ultimately (and unconsciously) limit the presence and power of the Holy Spirit in the Church? More precisely, does the recognition of the absoluteness of the biblical canon minimize the presence and activity of God in the Church today? Does God act in the Church today by the same Spirit? On what biblical or historical basis has inspiration been limited to the written documents the Church now calls its Bible?

Fourth, in regard to the OT, should the Church be limited to an

OT canon to which Jesus and his first disciples were clearly not limited? We have shown that writings from a much broader perspective informed the theology and practice of the early Christian community. Also, we have shown at least the possibility that the final limits of the OT canon used by the Protestants may in part have been defined by Judaism in a polemic against the Church. What obligations does the Church have to limit itself today to a canon of scriptures that was not the canon of the earliest Christians?

Fifth, if apostolicity is still a legitimate criterion for canonicity of the NT literature as it was for the churches that first began to draw up biblical canons, should the Church today continue to recognize the authority of II Peter, the Pastorals, and other nonapostolic literature of the NT? If the Spirit was not limited to apostolic documents alone, as we have shown in the previous chapter, can we make other arguments for the inclusion of other literature in the biblical canon?

Sixth, one must surely ask about the appropriateness of tying the Church of the twentieth century to a canon that emerged out of the historical circumstances in the second to fifth centuries C.E. Are we necessarily supposed to make absolute the experience of that Church for all time, even though its historical context is not the same of either the earliest Christian community or that of the present Church? Those who would argue for the infallibility or the inerrancy of scripture logically should also claim the same infallibility for the churches in the fourth and fifth centuries, whose decisions and historical circumstances have left us with our present Bible. This is apparently what would be required if we were to acknowledge only the twenty-seven NT books that were set forth by the Church in that context. Did the Church in the Nicene and post-Nicene eras make an infallible decision or not?[17]

Finally, if the Spirit only inspired the written documents of the first century, does that mean that the same Spirit does not speak today in the Church about matters that are of *more* significant concern now than then—the use of contraceptives, abortion, liberation, ecological responsibility, equal rights, euthanasia, nuclear proliferation, global genocide, and so on?

In an age when the tools of biblical scholarship have advanced our understanding of the historical context of the early Church and the background and interpretation of its biblical literature beyond the critical skills of the ancient Church that first dealt with the notion of a canon of Christian scriptures, it may be that the time has come for the Church to examine anew the above series of questions related to its canon of scriptures. To do so, of course, would be to open up "Pandora's box," and it is doubtful whether we could ever hope to arrive at a consensus in the Church on precisely what books should make up any new canon. It might be that as a result of this inquiry the Church could feel freer to allow other ancient (or modern) voices to inform its understanding of God today, even though I for one am not in favor of rejecting the present biblical canon in order to create a new closed canon of scriptures. The Church could trade in its present Bible for another only at the Church's own peril. The documents we possess sufficiently inform the Church of the core of the gospel—the good news of God in Christ. More important, they inform us that *Jesus Christ alone is the true and final canon* for the child of God (Matt. 28:18). There should be no fear, however, of allowing other ancient literature to inform our faith, since, as was argued earlier, some of that extra-biblical literature (the Apocrypha and Pseudepigrapha as well as other early Christian literature) informed the faith of the earliest Christians and even later ones. In the case of gospel literature, some of the noncanonical gospels may indeed contain authentic strands of the teaching of Jesus and even possibly some earlier strands of the same traditional sayings of Jesus. If so, why should Christians avoid listening to them, at least in a careful and critical manner? In spite of a reasonable and important call to listen to other ancient voices, it must be stressed in closing that there are no other ancient documents that are on the whole more reliable in informing the Church's faith than our present biblical canon. Nevertheless, it must be stressed that the final authority of the Church is not the Bible, but the Lord.[18]

My aim in this study has not been to destroy the Church's Bible, as if that could ever be done, but to bring some light to the often dimly lit corridors that led to the formation of our Bible and, in that process, to remind the reader of the true canon of faith for the Church: our Lord Jesus Christ. The Bible is still the Church's book without which the Christian faith would only be a blur. I believe that a careful study of the biblical message in its historical environment and in the community of faith in which it was first acknowledged as scripture and canon will prove invaluable to the Church. Lessons learned from this approach will not only free the Church from inappropriate loyalties, but also will help the Church to focus more clearly on the true object and final authority of its faith.

APPENDIX
A

New Testament Citations and Allusions to Apocryphal and Pseudepigraphal Writings*

Matt.	4:4	Wisd. of Sol.	16:26
	4:15	1 Macc.	5:15
	5:2ss	Sirach	25:7-12
	5:4		48:23
	5:5	1 En.	5:7
	5:11	3 Esd.	7:14
	5:15	Baruch	4:1
	5:28	Sirach	9:8
	6:7		7:14
	6:9		23:1, 4
	6:10	1 Macc.	3:60
	6:12	Sirach	28:2
	6:13		33:1
	6:20	3 Esd.	7:77;
		Sirach	29:10s
	6:23		14:10
	6:26	Psa. Sol.	5:9ss
	6:29	3 Esd.	1:4
	6:33	Wisd. of Sol.	7:11
	7:12	Tobit	4:15;
		Sirach	31:15
	7:13	3 Esd.	7:6-14
	7:16	Sirach	27:6
	8:11	4 Macc.	13:17;
		Baruch	4:37
	8:21	Tobit	4:3
	9:38	1 Macc.	12:17
	10:16	Sirach	13:17
	10:22	3 Esd.	6:25
	10:28	4 Macc.	13:14
	11:14	Sirach	48:10
	11:22	Judith	16:17
	11:23	Psa. Sol.	1:5
	11:25	Tobit	7:17;
		Sirach	51:1
	11:28		24:19;
			51:23

Matt.	11:29		6:24s;
			6:28s;
			51:26s
	12:4	2 Macc.	10:3
	13:3	4 Esd.	8:41;
			9:31ss
	13:5	Sirach	40:15
	13:6	Psa. Sol.	18:6s
	13:39	4 Esd.	7:113;
		1 En.	16:1
	13:44	Sirach	20:30s
	16:18	Wisd. of Sol.	7:11
	16:22	1 Macc.	2:21
	16:27	Sirach	35:22
	17:11		48:10
	18:10	Tobit	12:15
	19:28	Psa. Sol.	26:29
	20:2	Tobit	5:15
	21:12	Psa. Sol.	17:30
	22:13	Wisd. of Sol.	17:2
	22:14	4 Esd.	8:3;
			8:41
	22:32	4 Macc.	7:19;
			16:25
	23:38	Tobit	14:4
	24:15	1 Macc.	1:54;
		2 Macc.	8:17
	24:16	1 Macc.	2:28
	25:31	1 En.	61:8;
			62:2s;
			69:27
	25:35	Tobit	4:17
	25:36	Sirach	7:32-35
	26:13	1 En.	103:4
	26:24		38:2
	26:38	Sirach	37:2
	26:64	1 En.	69:27

*Adapted from Kurt Aland and Barbara Aland, eds., *The Text of the New Testament* (Grand Rapids: Wm. B. Eerdmans, 1979), pp. 769-75. Used by permission of the publisher.

Book	Verse	Source	Ref
Matt.	27:24	Susanna	46
	27:43	Wisd. of Sol.	2:13, 18-20
Mark	1:15	Tobit	14:5
	3:27	Ps. Sol.	5:3
	4:5	Sirach	40:15
	4:11	Wisd. of Sol.	2:22
	5:34	Judith	8:35
	6:49	Wisd. of Sol.	17:15
	8:29	1 En.	46:10
	8:37	Sirach	26:14
	9:31	Ep. of Jer.	2:18
	9:48	Judith	16:17
	12:25	1 En.	15:6s; 51:4
	13:8	4 Esd.	13:30-32
	13:13		6:25
	14:14		8:41; 9:31ss
	14:34	Sirach	37:2
	15:29	Wisd. of Sol.	2:17s
Luke	1:17	Sirach	48:10
	1:19	Tobit	12:15
	1:42	Judith	13:18;
		Apoc. Bar.	54:10
	1:52	Sirach	10:14
	2:11	Ps. Sol.	17:32
	2:14		18:10
	2:29	Tobit	11:9
	2:37	Judith	8:6
	6:12	4 Macc.	3:13-19
	6:24	1 En.	94:8
	6:35	Wisd. of Sol.	15:1
	7:22	Sirach	48:5
	9:8		48:10
	10:17	Tobit	7:17
	10:19	Sirach	11:19
	10:21		51:51
	12:19	Tobit	7:10;
		1 En.	97:8-10
	12:20	Wisd. of Sol.	15:8
	13:27	1 Macc.	3:6
	13:29	Baruch	4:37
	13:35	Tobit	14:4
	15:12		3:17;
		1 Macc.	10:29 [30]
	16:9	1 En.	39:4; 63:10
Luke	16:23	4 Macc.	13:15
	16:26	4 Esd.	7:36;
		1 En.	22:9ss
	18:7	Sirach	35:22
	19:44	Wisd. of Sol.	3:7
	20:37	4 Macc.	7:19; 16:25
	21:24	Ps. Sol.	17:25;
		Tobit	14:5;
		Sirach	28:18
	21:25	Wisd. of Sol.	5:22
	21:28	1 En.	51:2
	22:37	Ps. Sol.	16:5
	24:4	2 Macc.	3:26
	24:31	2 Macc.	3:34
	24:50	Sirach	50:20s
	24:53		50:22
John	1:3	Wisd. of Sol.	9:1
	1:14	Jub.	7:6
	3:8	Sirach	16:21
	3:12	Wisd. of Sol.	9:16; 18:15s
	3:13	Baruch	3:29;
		4 Esd.	4:8
	3:21	Tobit	4:6
	3:27	Jub.	5:3s
	3:29	1 Macc.	9:39
	4:9	Sirach	50:25
	4:48	Wisd. of Sol.	8:8
	5:18		2:16
	5:22	Jub.	69:27
	6:35	Sirach	24:21s
	7:38		24:40, 43 [30s]
	7:42	Jub.	17:21
	8:44	Wisd. of Sol.	2:24
	8:53	Sirach	44:19
	10:20	Wisd. of So.	5:4
	10:22	1 Macc.	4:59
	12:26	4 Macc.	17:20
	14:15	Wisd. of Sol.	6:18
	15:9s		3:9
	15:25	Jub.	7:1
	17:3	Wisd. of Sol.	15:3
	20:22		15:11
Acts	1:8	Ps. Sol.	8:15
	1:10	2 Macc.	3:26
	1:18	Wisd. of Sol.	3:17
	2:4	Sirach	48:12

Acts	2:11		36:7
	2:39		24:32
	4:24	Judith	9:12
	5:2	2 Macc.	4:32
	5:7	3 Macc.	4:17
	5:21	1 Macc.	12:6;
		2 Macc.	1:10
	5:39		7:19
	7:36	As. Mos.	3:11
	9:1-29	2 Macc.	3:24-40;
		4 Macc.	4:1-14
	9:2	1 Macc.	15:21
	9:7	Wisd. of Sol.	18:1
	10:2	Tobit	12:8
	10:22	1 Macc.	10:25;
			11:30,
			33, *etc.*
	10:26	Wisd. of Sol.	7:1
	10:30	2 Macc.	11:8
	10:34	Sirach	35:12s
	10:36	Wisd. of Sol.	8:3 *etc.*
	10:63		6:7
	11:18		12:19
	12:5	Judith	4:9
	12:10	Sirach	19:26
	12:23	1 Macc.	7:41;
		2 Macc.	9:9;
		Judith	16:17;
		Sirach	28:7
	13:10		1:30
	13:17	Wisd. of Sol.	19:10
	14:14	Judith	14:16s
	14:15	4 Macc.	12:13;
		Wisd. of Sol.	3:17
	15:4	Judith	8:26
	15:29	4 Macc.	5:2
	16:14	2 Macc.	1:4
	16:23, 25	T. Jos.	8:5
	17:23	Wisd. of Sol.	14:20;
			15:17
	17:24		9:9;
		Tobit	7:17
	17:24, 25	Wisd. of Sol.	9:1
	17:26		7:18
	17:27		13:6
	17:29		13:10
	17:30	Sirach	28:7

Acts	19:27	Wisd. of Sol.	3:17
	19:28	Bel and Dragon	18:41
	20:26	Susanna	46
	20:32	Wisd. of Sol.	5:5
	20:35	Sirach	4:31
	21:26	1 Macc.	3:49
	22:9	Wisd. of Sol.	18:1
	24:2	2 Macc.	4:6
	24:14	4 Macc.	12:17
	26:18	Wisd. of Sol.	5:5
	26:25	Judith	10:13
Romans	1:4	T. Levi	18:7
	1:18	1 En.	91:7
	1:19-32	Wisd. of Sol.	13-15
	1:19	Apoc. Bar	54:17s
	1:21	4 Esd.	8:60;
		Wisd. of Sol.	13:1;
		1 En.	99:8
	1:23	Wisd. of Sol.	11:15;
			12:12
	1:25	As. Mos.	5:4
	1:26	T. Jos.	7:8
	1:28	2 Macc.	6:4;
		3 Macc.	4:16
	1:29-31	4 Macc.	1:26;
			2:15
	2:3	Jub.	15:8
	2:4	Wisd. of Sol.	11:23
	2:5	Jub.	9:5;
		T. Levi	3:2
	2:11	Sirach	35:12s
	2:15	T. Reu.	4:3;
		Wisd. of Sol.	17:11;
		Apoc. Bar.	57:2
	2:17	Jub.	17:1;
		Apoc. Bar.	48:22
	2:22	T. Levi	14:4
	2:29	Jub.	1:23
	3:3		8:28
	4:13	Sirach	44:21;
		Jub.	19:21
			etc.;
		Apoc. Bar.	14:13;
			51:3
	4:17		48:8
	5:3	T. Jos.	10:1
	5:5	Sirach	18:11
	5:12	4 Esd.	3:21s, 26;

Book	Verse	Source	Reference
Romans		Wisd. of Sol.	2:24;
		Apoc. Bar.	23:4; 54:15
	5:16	4 Esd.	7:118s
	7:7	4 Macc.	2:5s
	7:10	Jub.	14:1
	7:12	4 Esd.	9:37
	7:23		7:72
	8:18	Apoc. Bar.	15:8; 32:6
	8:19	4 Esd.	7:11; 7:75
	8:22		10:9
	8:28	Psa. Sol.	4:25, etc.
	9:4	Sirach	44:12; 44:18, etc.;
		2 Macc.	6:23
	9:16	As. Mos.	12:7
	9:19	Wisd. of Sol.	12:12
	9:21		15:7
	9:22	Apoc. Bar.	59:6
	9:24	Jub.	2:19
	9:31	Wisd. of Sol.	2:11;
		Sirach	27:8
	10:6	4 Esd.	4:8;
		Baruch	3:29
	10:7	Wisd. of Sol.	16:13
	11:4	2 Macc.	2:4
	11:15	Sirach	10:20s
	11:25	4 Esd.	4:35s:
		T. Zeb.	c.9 *fin*
	11:33	Wisd. of Sol.	17:1;
		Apoc. Bar.	14:8ss
	12:1	T. Levi	3:6
	12:15	Sirach	7:34
	12:21	T. Ben.	4:3s
	13:1		4:27;
		Wisd. of Sol.	6:3s
	13:9	4 Macc.	2:6
	13:10	Wisd. of Sol.	6:18
	15:4	1 Macc.	12:9
	15:8	Sirach	36:20
	15:33	T. Dan.	5:2
	16:27	4 Macc.	18:24
Gal.	1:5		18:24
	2:6	Sirach	35:13
	4:4	Tobit	14:5

Book	Verse	Source	Reference
Gal.	4:10	1 En.	72–82
	6:1	Wisd. of Sol.	17:17
	6:17	3 Macc.	2:29
Eph.	1:6	Sirach	45:1; 46:13
	1:17	Wisd. of Sol.	7:7
	3:9	3 Macc.	2:3
	4:14	Sirach	5:9
	4:24	Wisd. of Sol.	9:3
	6:13		5:17
	6:14		5:18
	6:16		5:19, 21
Phil.	4:5		2:19
	4:13		7:23
	4:18	Sirach	35:6
Col.	1:22	1 En.	102:5
	2:3	Sirach	1:24s;
		1 En.	46:3
	5:8	Wisd. of Sol.	5:18
1 Thess.	1:3	4 Macc.	17:4
	1:8		16:12
	3:11	Judith	12:8
	4:6	Sirach	5:3
	4:13	Wisd. of Sol.	3:18
	5:1		8:8
	5:2		18:14s
	5:3	1 En.	62:4;
		Wisd. of Sol.	17:14
2 Thess.	2:1	2 Macc.	2:7
1 Tim.	1:17	Tobit	13:7, 11
	2:2	2 Macc.	3:11;
		Baruch	1:11s
	3:16	4 Macc.	6:31; 7:16; 16:1
	6:15	2 Macc.	12:15; 13:4;
		3 Macc.	5:35
		Sirach	46:5
2 Tim.	2:19	Sirach	23:10 *vl;* 35:3
	3:11	Ps. Sol.	4:23
	4:8	Wisd. of Sol.	5:16
	4:17	1 Macc.	2:60
Titus	2:11	2 Macc.	3:30;
		3 Macc.	6:9
	3:4	Wisd. of Sol.	1:6
Heb.	1:3	Wisd. of Sol.	7:25s
	2:5	Sirach	17:17

Book	Ref	Source	Citation
Heb.	4:12	Wisd. of Sol.	7:22-30; 18:15s
	4:13	1 En.	9:5
	4:15	Ps. Sol.	17:36
	5:6	1 Macc.	14:41
	6:12	Ps. Sol.	12:6
	7:22	Sirach	29:14ss
	9:26	T. Levi	18:9
	11:5	Sirach	44:16;
		Wisd. of Sol.	4:10
	11:6		10:17
	11:10	2 Macc.	4:1;
		Wisd. of Sol.	13:1
	11:17	1 Macc.	2:52; 44:20
	11:25	4 Macc.	15:2; 15:8
	11:27	Sirach	2:2
	11:28	Wisd. of Sol.	18:25
	11:35	2 Macc.	6:18–7:42
	11:37	Mar. Isa.	5:11-14
	12:1	4 Macc.	16:16; 17:10-15
	12:4	2 Macc.	13:14
	12:7	Ps. Sol.	10:2; 14:1
	12:9	2 Macc.	3:24
	12:12	Sirach	25:23
	12:17	Wisd. of Sol.	12:10
	12:21	1 Macc.	13:2
	13:7	Sirach	33:19;
		Wisd. of Sol.	2:17
	13:15	Ps. Sol.	15:2, 3
James	1:1	2 Macc.	1:27
	1:2	Sirach	2:1;
		Wisd. of Sol.	3:4s
	1:3	4 Macc.	1:11
	1:4		15:7
	1:13	Sirach	16:12
	1:14	1 En.	98:4
	1:19	Sirach	5:11
	1:21		3:17
	2:13	Tobit	4:10
	2:23	Wisd. of Sol.	7:27
	3:2	Sirach	14:1
	3:6, 10		5:13
	3:6	1 En.	48:7
	3:9	Sirach	23:1, 4
James	3:10		28:12
	3:13		3:17
	4:2	1 Macc.	8:16
	4:7	T. Naph.	8:4
	4:8	T. Dan.	4:8
	4:11	Wisd. of Sol.	1:11
	4:13	1 En.	97:8-10
	5:1		94:8
	5:3	Judith	16:17;
		Sirach	29:10
	5:4	Tobit	4:14
	5:6	Wisd. of Sol.	2:10; 2:12; 2:19
	5:10	4 Macc.	9:8
1 Pet.	1:3	Sirach	16:12
	1:7		2:5
	1:12	1 En.	1:2; 16:3
	2:25	Wisd. of Sol	1:6
	3:19	1 En.	9:10; 10:11-15
	4:19	2 Macc.	1:27
	5:7	Wisd. of Sol.	12:13
2 Pet.	1:19	4 Esd.	12:42
2 Pet.	2:2	Wisd. of Sol.	5:6
	2:4	1. En.	10:4s; 11-14; 91:15
	2:7	Wisd. of Sol.	10:6
		3 Macc.	2:13
	3:6	1 En.	83:3-5
	3:9	Sirach	35:19
	3:18		18:10
1 John	4:6	Jub.	8:14
	5:21	Ep. of Jer.	72
Jude	4	1 En.	48:10
	6		10:6; 12:4; 22:11
	13	Wisd. of Sol.	14:1;
		1 En.	18:15s; 21:5s
	14		1:9; 60:8; 93:3
	16		5:4
Rev.	1:18	Sirach	18:1
	2:10	2 Macc.	13:14

Rev.	2:12	Wisd. of Sol.	18:16 [15]	Rev.	13:14	1 En.	54:6
	2:17	2 Macc.	2:4-8		15:3		9:4
	2:27	Ps. Sol.	17:23s		16:5		66:2
	3:18		17:43		17:9		21:3
	4:11	3 Macc.	2:3;		17:14	2 Macc.	13:4;
		Wisd. of Sol.	1:14;			3 Macc.	5:35;
		Sirach	18:1			1 En.	9:4
	5:7		1:8		18:2	Baruch	4:35
	5:11	1 En.	14:22;		19:1	Tobit	13:18;
			40:1			Ps. Sol.	8:2
	7:9	2 Macc.	10:7		19:11	2 Macc.	3:25;
	8:1	Wisd. of Sol.	18:14				11:8
	8:2	Tobit	12:15		19:16		13:4
	8:3		12:12		19:20	1 En.	10:6
	8:7	Sirach	39:29		20:3		18:16;
		Wisd. of Sol.	16:22				21:6
	8:8	1 En.	18:13;		20:12s	Sirach	16:12
			21:3		20:13	1 En.	51:1;
	8:10		86:1				61:5
	9:3	Wisd. of Sol.	1:14		21:19s	Tobit	13:17
	11:19	2 Macc.	2:4-8		22:1	1 En.	14:19
					22:2	Ps. Sol.	14:3

B*

Lists of Old Testament Books in the Eastern Churches

Melito of Sardis (died ca. 190)	Origen (ca. 185–254)	Athanasius (ca. 367)	Cyril of Jerusalem (ca. 315–86)	Epiphanius (ca. 315–403)
Gen.	Gen.	Gen.	Gen.	Gen.
Ex.	Ex.	Ex.	Ex.	Ex.
Num.	Lev.	Lev.	Lev.	Lev.
Lev.	Num.	Num.	Num.	Num.
Deut.	Deut.	Deut.	Deut.	Deut.
Josh.	Josh.	Josh.	Josh.	Josh.
Judg.	Judg.	Judg.	Judg.	Judg.
Ruth	Ruth	Ruth	Ruth	Ruth
**I–IV Ki.	I–II Ki.	I–II Ki.	I–II Ki.	Job
I–II Chr.	III–IV Ki.	III–IV Ki.	III–IV Ki.	Ps.
Ps.	I–II Chr.	I–II Chr.	I–II Esd.	Prov.
Prov.	I–II Esd.	I–II Esd.	Esther	Eccles.
Eccles.	Ps.	Ps.	Job	Song
**Song	Prov.	Prov.	Ps.	I Ki.
Job	Eccles.	Eccles.	Prov.	II Ki.
Isa.	Song	Song	Eccles.	III Ki.
Jer.	Isa.	Job	Song	IV Ki.
**Twelve	Jer.	Twelve	Twelve	I Chr.
Dan.	Lam.	Isa.	Isa.	Isa.
Ezek.	Ep. of Jer.	Jer.	Jer.	Twelve
Esd.	Dan.	Baruch	Baruch	Isa.
	Ezek.	Lam.	Lam.	Jer.
	Job	Ep. of Jer.	Ep. of Jer.	Lam.
	Esther	Ezek.	Ezek.	Ep. of Jer.
		Dan.	Dan.	Baruch
				Ezek.
				Dan.
				I Esd.
				II Esd.
				Esther

---

*These lists are taken selectively from a much larger collection found in Albert C. Sundberg, Jr., *The Old Testament of the Early Church* (Cambridge: Harvard University Press, 1964), pp. 58-9, who footnotes the ancient sources for each. Special note should also be given to the *order* in which the books appear in the collections. Used by permission of the publisher.

**I and II Ki. (Kings) = I and II Samuel
   Song = Song of Solomon

III and IV Ki. = I and II Kings
Twelve = the 12 Minor Prophets

Lists of Old Testament Books in the Western Churches

Hilary of Poitiers (ca. 315–67)	Jerome (ca. 342–400)	Augustine (ca. 350–430)	Codex Vaticanus (B, ca. 350)	Codex Sinaiticus (ℵ, ca. 350)	Codex Alexandrinus (A, ca. 400–50)
5 books of Moses	Gen.	Gen.	Gen.	Gen.	Gen.
Josh.	Ex.	Ex.	Ex.	Num.	Ex.
Judg.	Lev.	Lev.	Lev.	I–II Chr.	Lev.
Ruth	Num.	Num.	Num.	I–II Esd.	Num.
I–II Ki.	Deut.	Deut.	Deut.	Esther	Deut.
III–IV Ki.	Job	Josh.	Josh.	Tobit	Josh.
I–II Chr.	Josh.	Judg.	Judg.	Judith	Judg.
I–II Esd.	Judg.	Ruth	Ruth	I–II Macc.	Ruth
Ps.	Ruth	I–IV Ki.	I–IV Ki.	Isa.	I–IV Ki.
Prov.	Sam.	I–II Chr.	I–II Chr.	Jer.	Twelve
Eccles.	III–IV Ki.	Job	I–II Esd.	Lam.	Isa.
Song	Twelve	Tobit	Ps.	Twelve (incomplete)	Jer.
Twelve	Isa.	Esther	Prov.	Ps.	Baruch
Isa.	Jer.	Judith	Eccles.	Prov.	Lam.
Jer.	Ezek.	I–II Macc.	Song	Eccles.	Ep.
Lam.	Dan.	I–II Esd.	Job	Song	Ezek.
Ep. of Jer.	Ps.	Ps.	Wisd.	Wisd.	Dan.
Dan.	David	Prov.	Sirach	Sirach	Esther
Ezek.	Solomon	Song	Esther	Job	Tobit
Job	Esther	Eccles.	Judith		Judith
Esther	I–II Chr.	Wisd.	Tobit		I–II Esd.
(some add Tobit, Judith)	Ezra–Neh.	Sirach	Twelve		I–IV Macc.
		Twelve	Isa.		Ps.
		Isa.	Jer.		Job
		Jer.	Baruch		Prov.
		Dan.	Lam.		Eccles.
		Ezek.	Ep. of Jer.		Song
			Ezek.		Wisd.
			Dan.		Sirach
					Ps. Sol.

Chapter 1: The Bible as Canon

1. The terms *Old Testament* and *New Testament* were not used regularly for the Hebrew scriptures and the early Christian scriptures until the middle of the fourth century, when, for instance, in canon 59 of the Synod of Laodicea (ca. 360) we read, "[It is decreed] that private psalms should not be read in the church, *neither uncanonized books, but only the canonical* [books] *of the New and Old Testament* (οὐδὲ ἀκανόνιστα βιβλία, ἀλλὰ μόνα τὰ κανονικὰ τῆς καινῆς καὶ παλαῖς διαθήκης)", see Theron, *Evidence*, p. 125. However, the terms first appear in the writings of Irenaeus (ca. 180): "Inasmuch, then, as in both Testaments there is the same righteousness of God (displayed) when God takes vengeance, in the one case indeed typically, temporarily, and more moderately; but in the other, really, enduringly, and more rigidly. . . . 2. For as, in the New Testament, that faith of men [to be placed] in God has been increased, receiving in addition [to what was already revealed] the Son of God, that man too might be a partaker of God" *(Adv. Haer.* 4:28.1-2, ANF). See also Tertullian (ca. 200), "If I fail in resolving this article [of our faith] by passages which may admit of dispute out of the Old Testament, I will take out of the New Testament a confirmation of our view, that you may not straightway attribute to the Father every possible (relation and condition) which I ascribe to the Son" *(Adv. Prax.* 15, ANF). At about 220 in Alexandria, Origen commented, "It appears to me, therefore, to be necessary that one who is able to represent in a genuine manner the doctrine of the Church, and to refute those dealers [the gnostics] in knowledge, falsely so-called, should take his stand against historical fictions, and oppose to them the true and lofty evangelical message in which the agreement of the doctrines, found both in the so-called Old Testament and in the so-called New, appears so plainly and fully" *(Commentary on John 5.4, ANF).* Eusebius (ca. 325 C.E.), describing Josephus' canon of scripture, writes, "In the first of these he gives the number of the canonical scriptures of the so-called Old Testament, and showed as follows which are undisputed among the Hebrews as belonging to ancient tradition" *(Hist. eccl.* 3.9.5, LCL). Later, while speaking of the NT, he says, "At this point it

---

*For full bibliographical information of some cited works, see the list of abbreviations, beginning on page 21.

seems reasonable to summarize the writings of the New Testament which have been quoted" *(Hist. eccl.* 3.25.1, *LCL).* Both Edgar Hennecke *(NT Apo,* 1:24) and Grant *(Formation,* 161) appear to have missed the references to a "New Testament" in Irenaeus and Tertullian.

2. The most disappointing aspect of William T. Farmer and Denis M. Farkasfalvy's recent, and otherwise excellent, work on the canon, *The Formation of the New Testament Canon* (New York: Paulist Press, 1983), is that both scholars appear to employ the "old assumptions of canonical research, *viz.* (1) if an ancient author cited a NT writing, he must have considered it as scripture; (2) if one author called a text "scripture," then everyone in his general era and location did the same; and (3) the compilation of all of the citations, quotations, or allusions to biblical literature by an ancient author constitute his canon of scriptures. Since the publication of von Campenhausen's formidable work on the canon, we should have laid to rest these assumptions.

3. James A. Sanders, *Canon,* p. xvii. See also his *Torah and Canon* (Philadelphia: Fortress Press, 1972) and more recently *Sacred Story,* especially pp. 155-72, where he contrasts his own view of the canonical text, which the church receives, with the view of Brevard Childs. Also important in that section is his emphasis on the value of history and historical criticism, which Childs tends to deemphasize in his work.

4. See Brevard Childs' two most important volumes on this topic, *OT as Canon* and *NT as Canon.* See also his *OT Theology.*

5. Childs, *NT as Canon,* pp. 41 and 48, and more recently, *OT Theology,* pp. 11-12.

6. Ibid. It is at this point that Metzger, *Canon* 268-69, is most critical of Childs for not clarifying what that "best text" or "received text" is.

7. Ibid., 51.

8. See the discussion of Tertullian in chapter 6, sec. IV.

9. See *Adv. Haer.* 3.3.3. cited in chap. 4, sect. V of this book.

10. See the full text of the fragment in chapter 6, sec. VIII, but notice especially lines 70-80.

11. Metzger, *Canon,* pp. 268-670, chides Childs for not being more clear on which text is *the* canonical and "received text" that the Church is to adopt.

12. See Ernest Best, "Scripture, Tradition, and the Canon of the New Testament." 61 (1979):259.

13. Childs, *OT as Scripture,* pp. 311-38.

14. Stephen Fowler's criticism of Childs at this point (in "The Canonical Approach of Brevard Childs." *ET* 96 [1985]:173-75) is significant. He shares a concern with James Sanders for Childs' seeming lack of concern for the original historical context of a writing or an event in favor of the final *interpretation* of the writing or event. James Sanders also criticizes Childs' apparent lack of appreciation for the historical development of a given biblical text (that is, ignoring a *diachronic* approach) in favor of the leveling of that tradition by seeing it as a whole without any development (a *synchronic* approach). See Sanders, *From Sacred Story to Sacred Text,* pp. 165-70, in which he notes his frustration with Childs' acceptance of the biblical text at a single "frozen point."

15. Peter Ackroyd, "Original Text and Canonical Text." *USQR* 32, nos. 3-4 (1977):166-73.

16. Ibid, p. 172.

17. These two distinctions are from James Smart, *The Strange Silence of the Bible in the Church* (Philadelphia: Westminster Press, 1970), p. 25.

18. See Childs, *NT as Canon,* p. 38.

19. Metzger, *Canon,* p. 1.

Chapter 2: Scripture and Canon

1. Gottlob Schrenk, "γραφή, κτλ." *TDNT,* vol. 1, pp. 744-56. The secondary text of John 7:53–8:11, even if genuine, would hardly qualify as a written document.

2. Barr, *Scripture,* p. 5.

3. Many of the Psalms, especially 19 and 119, which focus on meditation on the word,

law, precepts, statues, and so on, of God, are almost certainly pre-exilic in origin, but most of these probably do not date before the time of Josiah's finding of the book of the Law (probably Deuteronomy) ca. 622–621 B.C.E. (compare II Kings 18:20a with 22:3-13).

4. Barr, *Scripture*, p. 5.

5. See chapter 6, which lists and compares several important ancient collections of NT books.

6. Krister Stendahl, "The Apocalypse of John and the Epistle of Paul in the Muratorian Fragment." In *Current Issues in New Testament Interpretation: Essays in Honor of Otto A. Piper*, eds. W. Klassen and G. T. Snyder (New York: Harper, 1962), p. 240.

7. See, for example, how both Matthew and Luke drop the first part of Mark's quotation, which was erroneously attributed to Isaiah but which originated with Malachi 3:1. Compare Mark 1:2 with Matthew 3:3 and with Luke 3:4.

8. Q is an abbreviation of the German word *Quelle*, meaning "source." This is a convenient way to designate a source containing sayings of Jesus that are common to both Matthew and Luke, but not found in Mark, that may have been partially oral in form.

9. L. G. Patterson, "Irenaeus and the Valentinians: The Emergence of a Christian Scripture" (unpublished article obtained from the author). Irenaeus does, of course, refer to "both of the covenants" in which the righteousness of God is displayed. See *Adv. Haer.* 4.28.1-2, cited in chapter 1, note 1.

10. For example, Q; see also Luke 1:1-4.

11. Hans von Campenhausen, *Formation*, pp. 62-63. The same could be argued for the ancient Jewish community of faith, as has been done by Barr in *Scripture*, pp. 2-7.

12. Because the notion of the term *Old Testament* is not found in the Christian community until the end of the second century C.E. in the writings of Irenaeus and Tertullian, it is perhaps premature to speak thusly of the Jewish scriptures, which only later received that designation in the Church. As will be stated more clearly later, even the precise limits of the later designated "Old Testament" scriptures were not clear for a considerable time after the "apostolic" era. However, because of the clumsiness of finding any precise designation for these scriptures (even "Hebrews scriptures" is not precise), "Old Testament" will be used throughout this study with the understanding that it will often be used as a term projected back on the Jewish scriptures.

13. Leaney has rightly observed that the early Christians were concerned with finding a scripture "to fit a fact, and were far from inventing a fact to fit the Scripture." See A. R. C. Leaney, "Theophany, Resurrection, and History." In *Studia Evangelica*, vol. 5, ed. F. L. Cross (Berlin: Akademie Verlag, 1968), p. 112.

14. Edward Farley, *Ecclesial Reflection* (Philadelphia: Fortress Press, 1982), p. 58. See also David H. Kelsey, *Uses*, pp. 89-94.

15. *Gnostic Scriptures*, p. 18.

16. Ibid, pp. xix-xxi.

17. Schrenk, "γραφή." In *TDNT*, vol. 1, pp. 759-61. See also Barr, *Scripture*, pp. 14-5, and Kümmel, *Introduction*, p. 335.

18. See the helpful descriptions of the use of the term by Hermann Wolfgang Beyer, "κανών." In *TDNT*, vol. 3, pp. 596-602 and Robert W. Funk, *Parables and Presence* (Philadelphia: Fortress Press, 1982), pp. 151-53. A brief, but careful, theological and historical description of the use of the term in the church is found in Paul J. Achtemeier, *The Inspiration of Scripture* (Philadelphia: Westminster Press, 1980), pp. 118-23. See also Metzger, *Canon*, pp. 289-93, for a helpful discussion of the use of the term in the early Church and in the Church fathers.

19. Clifford H. Moore, trans., "Introduction." In *Tacitus II, The Histories*, LCL, (Cambridge, Mass.: Harvard University Press, 1930), p. xiii.

20. It is disappointing that almost every significant investigation of the Christian canon today omits any serious discussion of the Greco-Roman historical and sociological influences on the notion of canon in the ancient Christian community. The recent English translation of Dieter Georgi's study of II Corinthians (*The Opponents of Paul in Second*

Corinthians [Philadelphia: Fortress Press, 1986]), includes a most welcome epilogue on the subject of "canon consciousness" in the Greco-Roman world. See especially the questions he raises and his observations (on pp. 427-34) and also his excellent bibliography and footnotes (on pp. 435-45). A doctoral seminar, which Georgi directed at the Harvard Divinity School in the fall of 1979, produced a number of important, but as yet unpublished, papers on the topic. Unfortunately, the papers are still on the closed shelves of the Andover Library!

21. The precise meaning of this phrase is difficult to determine. It could refer to the Christian message and its implications, which had been passed on in the Church, or to a common code of church ethics or to a reference to the Christian use of the OT scriptures. The context suggests that the first of these options was intended.

22. See Clement of Alexandria, *Stromata*, 6.15.125, in which *canon* ($\kappa\alpha\nu\dot{\omega}\nu$) is the harmony between the Law and the Prophets on the one side and the covenant instituted by the incarnation of the Lord on the other.

23. Herman Wolfgang Beyer, "$\kappa\alpha\nu\dot{\omega}\nu$." In *TDNT*, pp. 600-601. See also Edgar Hennecke, *NT Apo.*, pp. 22-24, and G. W. H. Lampe, "The Early Church." In *Scripture and Tradition*, ed. F. W. Dillistone (London: Lutterworth Press, 1955), pp. 244 ff.

24. See the complete text of this letter in chapter 6, sect. IX.

25. A. C. Sundberg, "The Making of the New Testament Canon." In *The Interpreter's One Volume Commentary of the Bible*, ed. Charles M. Laymon (Nashville: Abingdon Press, 1971), p. 1216. This will be discussed in chapter 3.

26. This matter will be discussed in more detail in chapter 7.

27. Sundberg, "The Making of the New Testament Canon," p. 1217. A careful description of the canonical process is found in James A. Sanders, *Canon*, pp. 21-45. Sanders' most recent work, *Sacred Story* (pp. 127-47 and 175-90, has an excellent discussion of the process of recognition of the authority and the stabilization of the OT biblical text. He makes points that are applicable to both OT and NT canonical inquiry. See also his "Text and Canon: Old Testament and New." In *Mélanges Dominique Barthelemy: Etudes bibliques*, eds. Pierre Casetti, Othmar Keel, and Adrian Scheuber (Friebourg: Editions Universitaires; Göttingen: Vandenhoeck & Ruprecht, 1981), pp. 373-94.

28. See Hennecke's discussion in *NT Apo*, 1:39-42. R. P. C. Hanson, in his *Origen's Doctrine of Tradition* (London: S.P.C.K., 1954), pp. 133-45, has argued convincingly that Origen's classification system was probably an invention of Eusebius. He claims that Origen had neither a NT list of books nor any notion of a NT canon.

29. Both Origen's and Eusebius' lists are included in chapter 6.

30. Sanders, *Sacred Story*, pp. 18-19.

31. This is not uncharacteristic midrashic exegesis. Notice the example of the changing of the text from *receiving* gifts to *giving* gifts in Ephesians 4:8 (compare Ps. 68:18) and observe how the author of Hebrews changes the focus of Psalm 8:4-6 in 2:6-8. He makes a temporal interpretation of the *LXX* words $\beta\varrho\alpha\chi\dot{\upsilon}$ $\tau\iota$, which is clearly not in the context of the Psalm so he might have a predictive witness from the Psalm to Jesus.

32. Although many of the variants in the NT manuscripts can be explained away as simple scribal mistakes or glosses (Rom. 5:1 and the evidence for either $\ddot{\varepsilon}\chi o\mu\varepsilon\nu$ or $\ddot{\varepsilon}\chi\omega\mu\varepsilon\nu$, but also 8:1, 4, and so on), clearly many changes or additions in the texts were not accidental, but were in fact deliberate (John 3:13; Acts 8:37; I John 5:7).

33. Observe, for example, the changes of Mark 4:10-12, which were added to the original parable of Jesus. Quite possibly the interpretation in 4:13-20 was also added later by the Church.

Chapter 3: The Christian Old Testament

1. LaSor et al., *OT Survey*, p. 17. See also F. F. Bruce, *The Books and the Parchments* (Old Tappan, N.J.: Revell, 1963) p. 127, for a similar view.

2. Ibid., p. 21. See also R. K. Harrison, *Introduction to the Old Testament* (Grand Rapids: Wm. B. Eerdman's, 1969), p. 286, which claims that the OT canon in all of its

essentials was complete by 300 B.C.E.! David Ewert, *From Ancient Tablets to Modern Translations* (Grand Rapids: Zondervan, 1983), p. 71, also agrees with this conclusion.

3. Roger Beckwith, *OT Canon*, p. 406. See also his "Canon of the Old Testament," in *The Illustrated Bible Dictionary*, eds. J. D. Douglas and Norman Hillyer (Wheaton, Ill.: Tyndale House, 1986), vol. 1, pp. 235-39. Both works essentially set forth a traditionally conservative approach to the OT canon, maintaining that it was closed well before the time of Jesus. Beckwith also assumes that the Jews had the "right" canon, but that the Christians later misunderstood what the canon of the OT was, and they mistakenly added to it. The Christian errors, according to Beckwith, were evidently corrected during the Protestant Reformation, when a return to the Jewish canon was recovered.

4. Ibid. See his reasoning on pp. 339-408. One of Beckwith's major weaknesses is his failure to show convincingly his belief that the Hebrew canon was closed well before the time of Jesus. He tries to show that Judaism distinguished between the OT canonical books and the Apocryphal and Pseudepigraphical literature from the first century B.C.E. to the second century C.E., contending that the canonical documents were believed by Judaism of that day, as well as by early Christianity, to be inspired, but that the latter documents were not. He does not, however, establish any clear separation in the use of these documents. When the latter is used and appealed to authoritatively in the developing Christian communities, Beckwith's explanations are at their weakest. When, for example, the author of Jude 14 makes use of I Enoch 1:9 in support of an argument, Beckwith contends that Jude was simply using that text as "edifying" literature but not necessarily as historical literature! (See p. 403.) Later in the same chapter, he suggests that Jude viewed the Pseudepigraphical literature as "edifying" but did not confer authority upon it. It is here that his argument is at its weakest, since it is especially in the appeal to and use of such literature that one can see that the earliest Christian community recognized Pseudepigraphical literature as authoritative and, therefore, scriptural. It is precisely in Jude's recognition of that literature's "edifying" qualities that one must conclude that for him, at least, the book was considered inspired and, therefore, truthful and historical! (See the section on the criterion of inspiration in chapter 7, sect. IV. Dieter Georgi is more on target when he contends that if such a widely accepted closed canon of scriptures did exist, as Beckwith argues, then one would hardly expect such a multifarious range of diversity about the matter and especially the wide ranging styles of interpretation that are found in Jewish literature from 300 B.C.E. to 100 C.E. See Georgi, *Opponents*, p. 361. See also p. 382, nn 30, 32.

5. Beckwith, *OT Canon*, p. 405.

6. Barr, *Scripture*, pp. 6-7.

7. David Noel Freedman, "Canon of the OT." In *IDBSup*, pp. 132-34.

8. R. H. Pfeiffer, "Canon of the OT." In *IDB*, vol. 1, p. 507.

9. There were at least three related men by that name. However, it is likely that Artaxerxes I, who authorized Ezra's mission of Jerusalem in 458 B.C.E. (Ezra 7:8-26), was - intended.

10. Other ancient references to this, which date after 70 C.E., are noted by Sundberg, *OT Early Ch*, pp. 113-19; however, David Aune, *Prophecy in Early Christianity* (Grand Rapids: William B. Eerdmans, 1983), pp. 103 ff., has challenged the notion of a widespread belief that prophecy in Israel had ceased in Judaism during the fifth century B.C.E. He shows evidence from the *Tosefta Sotah* (ca. 300 C.E.) that the Jews were informed during that period by oracles *(bat qol)*. Aune contends that only the sages of Israel made the claim that prophecy had ceased in Israel since they did not consider themselves inspired but only the interpreters of the Mosaic Law and the successors of the prophets. He shows numerous examples within Judaism of the first century B.C.E. and C.E. to underscore the possibility that there was a strong belief during that time that prophecy and the presence of the Spirit had not ceased in Israel. *Ibid.* (See pp. 104-52.)

11. Perhaps it should be stressed that when members of any religious movement believe that the authentic voice of divine authority—the voice of the prophet—is no longer present,

the writings produced in that community's past, when such religious authority was believed to be present, are then set aside by that community as its sacred literature. This could well be the reason why a closed collection of scriptures emerges quite late in Israel's history when a belief developed among some of the Jews that prophecy had ceased in Israel (I Macc. 4:46; 14:41). This could also be one reason for the development of the notion of a Christian scripture in the second century C.E. In that period, the diminishing role of the NT prophet in the Church was felt—the rise of Montanism seems to suggest that this was the case—and the recognized need for an authoritative voice of the past in the Church may have led to the recognition of some of its literature as scripture. See Arthur Jeffery, "The Canon of the Old Testament." In *IB*, vol. 1, p. 33.

12. The Hebrew word *Ketubhim* means "things written down." The Greek equivalent is *Hagiographa*, meaning "sacred writings" or "holy writings."

13. Barr, *Scripture*, pp. 56-57, does not believe that an actual council was empowered at Jamnia to determine which books would be included in the third part of the Jewish canon of scriptures. See also Jack P. Lewis, "What Do We Mean by Jabneh?" *JBR* 32 (1964):125-32. In a more recent article, Jack N. Lightstone, "The Formation of the Biblical Canon in Judaism of Late Antiquity: Prolegomenon to a General Reassessment." *SR* 8, no. 2 (1978):135-42, argues similarly and calls into question whether much of anything was really settled at Jamnia regarding the Jewish canon.

14. It is not likely that this reference to the Psalms in Luke can be taken to include *all* of the Writings so designated later as the third part of the Jewish canon. Kümmel, *Introduction*, p. 335, also argues this point. This passage is a further argument that the third part of the Jewish canon had not yet been clearly delineated in the time of Jesus or later when Luke was writing his Gospel.

15. Barr, *Scripture*, pp. 55-56.

16. Ibid.

17. Observe, for example, in the book of I Macc. the Jewish resistance to these changes.

18. The authenticity of this account has been unanimously rejected by scholars for more than 400 years. No one today seriously believes that it is an eyewitness account or that many of its features are anything more than fictitious stories intended to argue for the inspired status of the Greek OT. It has been dated as early as 200 B.C.E. by a few scholars, but the majority place it somewhere between 130-70 B.C.E., with a few scholars suggesting that it was not written until ca. 30–35 C.E., the *terminus ad quem* since it is referred to by Philo. See the discussion of this in Herbert Andrews, "The Letter of Aristeas"; Charles, *Apoc./Pseud.*, vol. 2, pp. 83 ff.; and Gunther Zuntz, "Aristeas." *IDB*, vol. 1, pp. 219-21.

19. That is, before 200-198 B.C.E., when the rule over Palestine shifted to the Selucid dynasty in Syria.

20. The Greek translation of the Law was undoubtedly an Alexandrian project, but the writer of the Letter of Aristeas may be correct in suggesting that some help for the project came from Palestine.

21. See *Ep. Arist.* 50 in R. H. Charles' translation in *Apoc./Pseud.*, vol. 2, p. 100.

22. Ibid, vol. 2, no. 307, p. 121.

23. Eduard Lohse, *The New Testament Environment* (Nashville: Abingdon Press, 1974), p. 129 and Helmut Koester, *Introduction to the NT*, vol. 1, p. 252.

24. So argue J. W. Wevers, "Septuagint," *IDB*, vol. 4, p. 273, and A. R. C. Leaney, *Jewish and Chr World*, p. 153.

25. The basis for this conclusion is found in the *Prologue of Ecclesiasticus*. See chap. 3, sect. I.

26. Some Greek fragments of the Hebrew scriptures were discovered at Qumran, and they may be sections of the *LXX*. They are, however, quite small, and it is difficult to speak here with certainty.

27. Henry M. Shires, *Finding*, p. 82.

28. Ibid. He lists several other examples of the NT's preference for the *LXX* on pp. 82-84.

29. Christians may have been the ones who tampered with these texts, since Christians had

taken on the responsibility of preserving and copying the *LXX* as well as using it in their worship and instruction.

30. Wevers, "Septuagint," p. 275.
31. *Appendix B* contains a helpful listing of these ancient OT scriptures.
32. R. H. Pfeiffer, "Canon," p. 510.
33. Ibid. His case for the Alexandrian canon is on pp. 510-14.
34. The best refutation of Pfeiffer's position is still A. C. Sundberg's significant *OT Early Ch*, especially pp. 51-79.
35. George W. Anderson, "Canonical and Non-Canonical." In *CHB*, p. 159.
36. Sanders, *Canon*, p. 9, agrees that this was one of surviving Judaism's most important issues during the time following the destruction of Jerusalem in 69–70 C.E.
37. Sid Z. Leiman, "Inspiration and Canonicity: Reflections on the Formation of the Biblical Canon." In Sanders, *Self Definition*, p. 61. Leiman contends that no *new* book was considered after ca. 150 B.C.E., even though the canonicity of some widely known books—Ecclesiastes, Song of Songs—was debated at a later time.
38. Ibid.
39. George F. Moore, "The Definition of the Jewish Canon and the Repudiation of Christian Scripture." In *The Canon and Masorah of the New Hebrew Bible*, ed. Sid Z. Leiman (New York: KATV Publishing House, Inc., 1974), 101 ff. See also J. Bloch, "Outside Books," in the same book, pp. 202-23.
40. Moore, "Definition," pp. 122-23.
41. A. C. Sundberg, "The 'Old Testament': A Christian Canon," *CBQ* 30 (1968):154.
42. See R. M. Grant, "The New Testament Canon." In *CHB*, vol. 1, p. 300. Grant believes that this development probably led the "orthodox" Church to evaluate the NT literature as well.
43. It is also interesting that Athanasius' *Festal Letter* (367 C.E.), which lists for the first time the twenty-seven books of our New Testament, also gives us a larger OT canon than the Protestants accept; he adds Baruch and the Epistle of Jeremiah. If Athanasius' NT canon should have such a large influence in the history of the canon, one wonders why Protestants ignore his OT canon but continue to value his NT canon!
44. Sundberg, *OT Early Ch*, pp. 54-55. See *Appendix A* for an updated and larger list.
45. Shires, *Finding*, p. 21.
46. Lasor et al., *OT Survey*, p. 23.
47. I and II Clement, The Letters of Ignatius, Polycarp, the Didache, Shepherd of Hermas, Epistle of Barnabas.
48. This observation is from Arthur Jeffrey, "Canon of OT," p. 40.
49. David Dungan also raises this question in his article "The New Testament Canon in Recent Study." *Int* 29, no. 4 (Oct. 1975):340-42.
50. Avery Dulles, "The Authority of Scripture: A Catholic Perspective," *Scripture in the Jewish and Christian Traditions* (Nashville: Abingdon Press, 1982), p. 35.
51. Von Campenhausen, *Formation*, pp. 244 ff. and especially pp. 82-102.
52. R. R. Williams, *Authority in the Apostolic Age* (London: SCM Press, Ltd., 1950), pp. 32 ff.
53. James L. Kugel and Rowan A. Greer, *Early Biblical Interpretation* (Philadelphia: Westminster Press, 1986), p. 114. Greer claims that on the whole, the Hebrew scriptures played less of a role in the early Christian community than has previously been supposed. Also relevant are his examples of this in the writings of the early Church Fathers (pp. 126-54). Greer, pp. 113-16, has a helpful discussion of the Church's attempts to maintain both continuity and discontinuity with its Jewish heritage.
54. Ibid, p. 202.
55. Shires, *Finding*, pp. 31 ff.
56. Numerous examples of this are listed in Shires, *Finding*, pp. 183-84. His work on this topic is still one of the best.
57. Ibid., pp. 38-39. See also Shires' discussion of the OT predictions of Christ on pp. 43-

51, in which he observes that Christians made the OT "their own special possession whose meaning relates directly to their situation" (p. 51).

Chapter 4: The Recognition of Christian Writings as Scripture

1. Although any critical interpretation of the book of Acts is plagued because of numerous historical and theological difficulties in the book, I believe that the depiction of the faith and life of the early church in Acts is a fair representation of the actual state of affairs. The presence of charismatic preachers, called prophets, in the early Church (I Cor. 12:28; Eph. 2:20; 4:11, and so) is further evidence of the widespread belief that the presence of the Spirit and the arrival of the age of fulfillment had begun in the event of Jesus.

2. See, for example, I Corinthians 7:10, 17; 9:14; and 11:23, but also John 2:22, 6:63; 12:48-50, and the much later text II Peter 3:2. Notice that the role of the Paraclete in John 14:26 is to bring to mind what Jesus *said*. In Revelation 3:8ff., Jesus praised the Christians in Philadelphia because they "have kept my word and not denied my name." Other examples are in sect. II below.

3. For example, *Q*, Luke 1:1-4, the earliest form of Mark 16:9-20, some of the sayings from *Gos. Thom.*, and probably an earlier form of Mark.

4. Von Campenhausen believes that it may be possible to date Papias as early as the end of the first century, but more likely in the second or third decade of the second century. He also believes that it is unlikely that Papias knew of more Gospels than Matthew and Mark. See von Campenhausen, *Formation*, pp. 129-30, 133.

5. Eusebius, *Hist. eccl.* 3.29.4, *LCL*. Papias' statement is evidence not only of the growing use and significance of the Gospels (at least Matthew and Mark) in the Church, but also of their not yet equal status with the OT scriptures. There is at this time (ca. 140) no reliable witness that the Gospels were read liturgically in the Church.

6. F. C. Baur, cited by von Campenhausen in *Formation*, p. 135. It is also quite likely that the author of the *Did.* used Matthew or a tradition shared with Matthew as well as oral traditions circulating at the end of the first century. See Grant, "The New Testament Canon," *CHB*, vol. 1, p. 290.

7. See Barr, *Scripture*, p. 12. Barr suggests that this perspective may also be behind the Pauline text in II Corinthians 3:6.

8. Robert M. Grant, "NT Canon," pp. 299-300.

9. Pheme Perkins, *The Gnostic Dialogue* (New York: Paulist Press, 1980), pp. 196-201.

10. Von Campenhausen, *Formation*, pp. 103-21.

11. Perkins, *Dialogue*, p. 197.

12. Ibid.

13. It is interesting to note in passing that even though the primary focus of the NT Gospels is on the words and deeds of Jesus, in the Apostolic Fathers, the OT texts are referred to more frequently than the words of Jesus. Ignatius of Antioch is, of course, a major exception to this, and Clement of Rome is the example *par excellence*. See Kurt Aland, *Canon*, p. 3.

14. Robert M. Grant, "From Tradition to Scripture and Back." In *Scripture and Tradition*, ed. Joseph F. Kelley (Notre Dame: Fides Publishers, 1976), pp. 14-15.

15. C. E. B. Cranfield, "The Gospel of Mark." *IDB*, vol. 3, p. 271.

16. The teaching that the resurrection was already past, that it was a spiritual event (II Tim. 2:18), that persons should abstain from marriage (I Tim. 2:15; 4:3; 5:14) as well as from certain foods (I Tim. 4:3; 5:23; Titus 1:15), and the references to the myths and genealogies (I Tim. 1:4; Titus 3:9) all suggest some form of gnosticizing tendencies in the Church, but because of the focus on the Law, there was perhaps also some form of a Jewish flavored heresy in the community addressed in the letter (I Tim. 1:7-11). It should also be noted that the need to clarify the function of various offices

and ministries in the Church (I Tim. 3–5) probably suggests a more developed Christian community, which was most likely post-apostolic.

17. For example, *Q*, Paul's epistles, the four canonical Gospels.
18. Romans 1:9-15; 15:24; II Corinthians 1:13-16; Colossians 4:15-16; I Thessalonians 3:5, *passim*. Paul's frequent desire to see his converts was often hindered by other pressing concerns, so he sent messengers with letters to the churches to inform them of his wishes for them. See also II John 12 and III John 13. Similarly, Raymond E. Brown, "Canonicity." *JBC*, p. 525, adds that the *geographical* distance separating the churches was overcome through the circulation of epistles.
19. Metzger, *Canon* 6-7, has noted that when the apostolic writings began to be translated—into Syriac, Latin, and eventually into the Coptic dialects—in the second and third centuries, this was done for the purpose of using them in public worship. Certainly, as Christian writings began to be used in worship in the Christian communities, they also began to take on scripture-like status, even if they were not yet so acknowledged.
20. See *The New Testament in the Apostolic Fathers* (Oxford: The Clarendon Press, 1905). This study by the Oxford Society of Historical Theology is an old, but still very helpful, guide to these references. Helmut Koester's *Synoptische Uberlieferung bei den apostolischen Vätern* (Berlin: Akademie Verlag, 1957) is still one of the best discussions on the significance of these references, though his work is limited to the Gospels.
21. Von Campenhausen, *Formation*, p. 62, and Denis Farkasfalvy, "The Early Development of the New Testament Canon." In *The Formation of the New Testament Canon*, ed. Harold W. Attridge (New York: Paulist Press, 1983), p. 173n. 97. It is possible, but doubtful, that the τὰ βιβλία is a reference to the Gospels. See Koester's discussion of this in *Synoptische* 76 ff.
22. See Koester, Ibid., p. 68. These words may be a reference to the "commands of the Lord" handed down to the apostles as one finds in II Peter 3:2.
23. Kummel, *Introduction*, p. 340.
24. Ibid.
25. "Charters" (ἀρχείοις) in this quotation is generally considered to be a reference to the OT scriptures. Metzger, *Canon*, p. 48, translates this term perhaps more appropriately as "archives."
26. Metzger, *Canon*, pp. 43-49, has a helpful summary of Ignatius' familiarity with some of the NT literature, probably the Gospels of Matthew and John and several of the epistles of Paul. Although Ignatius did not call this literature scripture, the obvious parallels noted by Metzger show Ignatius' knowledge and acceptance of them as documents that express for him the proper Christian attitudes and conduct.
27. Since the Greek text for this passage is missing and was supplied in Latin, an argument could be made for a late dating of this reference, though that is generally considered unlikely.
28. Cyril C. Richardson, *ECF*, p. 50.
29. He is citing John 1:3 in this text. See R. M. Grant's translation of this letter in Stevenson, *ANE*, pp. 91-95, cited above.
30. Observe, for example, Ignatius, Ign. *Phld.* 5:1-2.
31. The "Demiurge" or "Craftsman" (Gk. δημιουργός) is Plato's term for the creator of the universe. Later in the second and third centuries C.E., the creator god was also referred to as "Ialdabaoth," a nonspiritual being, by some gnostics. See Bentley Layton, *Gnostic Scriptures*, pp. 12-16. Ptolemy, of the Valentinian school of gnosticism in the second century, claimed that the Demiurge was an angel, the parent of all animate things, who was the god of Israel and of *ordinary* Christians. Layton, *Gnostic Scriptures*, p. 279.
32. "Marcion." In *The Oxford Dictionary of the Christian Church*, eds. F. L. Cross and E. A. Livingstone (Oxford: Oxford University Press, 1974), pp. 870-71.
33. This passage is difficult to translate, but this appears to be what is intended.
34. Von Campenhausen, *Formation*, pp. 148 ff.

35. Ibid., p. 151.
36. We have no evidence that he specifically called his canon "scripture" or "canon," though it functioned that way later in his churches.
37. Tertullian wrote of this process of excising the Jewish elements out of Luke thusly: "Now, of the authors whom we possess, Marcion seems to have singled out Luke for his mutilating process" *(Adv. Marc.* 4:2, *ANF).*
38. *Adv. Marc.* 5:16-18. In the last of these chapters (18:1 ff.), Tertullian charges that Marcion had "interpolated" Paul's epistles. He goes on to clarify what Marcion did to Paul's epistles thusly: "As our heretic is so fond of his pruning knife, I do not wonder when syllables are expunged by his hand, seeing that entire pages are usually the matter on which he practices his effacing process" (5:18.1, *ANF).* (Tertullian goes on to list five examples of this "effacing process" from Ephesians, a book that Tertullian believed was written by Paul.
39. Tertullian noted that "Marcion expressly and openly used the knife, not the pen, since he made such an excision of the Scriptures as suited his own subject matter" *(Praes.* 38:7, *ANF).*
40. So far as we can presently determine, Marcion was the first to call one of the canonical Gospels a "Gospel." Raymond F. Collins, *Introduction,* p. 22, suggests the possibility that Marcion assumed that when Paul spoke of "his Gospel" he was referring to the Gospel of Luke. Marcion, he claims, evidently presumed that it was a written source that Paul had in mind, so he set out to restore it.
41. Although knowledge of a four-fold Gospel canon is unlikely at this early date (Papias, a contemporary of Marcion, only refers to Matthew and Mark), it is probable that Marcion knew of more than one Gospel. It is likely that he was at least aware of the Gospel of Matthew because of its great popularity in the second century. It is doubtful, however, that his was the first collection of Pauline epistles, even though he may well have been the first to have a closed canon of such epistles. In fact it makes more sense to assume that his collection was possible because churches well before him had made use of Paul's writings and had circulated them to other churches (see Col. 4:16, which should not be considered an isolated case). Ephesians was most likely intended to be an encyclical letter to all the faithful in Asia Minor since there is nothing in it to tie it to any one particular community (see the manuscript evidence of 1:1). Ephesians 4:20-22 indicates that the writer had not yet met the church at Ephesus. The epistle itself, which seems to reflect a post-Pauline era, may have been attached as an introduction to letters of Paul (so argues Edgar J. Goodspeed, *A History of Early Christian Literature* [Chicago: University of Chicago Press, 1983], p. 61) and circulated in Asia Minor (the birthplace of Marcion) and probably even to a wider audience by the end of the first century. Also, it is possible that Justin's neglect of Paul could have been a response to Marcion's sole use of Paul and to the Gnostics' frequent appeal to Paul, but certainly not his ignorance of such letters. Harry Y. Gamble, *The NT Canon,* pp. 43-46, has a brief but very helpful discussion of the use of Paul's writings in the second century Church. Although he gives several possible reasons for the lack of attention given to Paul by Justin and others—for example, the fact that Paul was appealed to by Gnostics and Marcion as well as the fact of Paul's apparent lack of relevance to many of the second century churches—he concludes nevertheless that Paul's writings were highly esteemed in most of the churches both before and after Justin, even though there is little direct appeal to Paul in the apologetic writings of the Church in that period. Gamble is probably right in assuming that Marcion took over an existing collection of Paul's writings (see *The NT Canon,* p. 41).
42. Von Campenhausen, *Formation,* p. 153, believes that Marcion created the Gospel-Apostle form that was later followed by the Church, but this conclusion is in no way required or likely. This order would easily commend itself to the Church at large owing to its recognition of two of the three major dimensions of authority already known within the Church (Law, Gospel, Apostle) well before the time of Marcion.

43. James Sanders, *Canon*, p. 37, maintains that the Church, in opposition to Marcion, insisted on multiple voices from both the OT and other Christian literature rather than limiting that voice to Paul and Luke. If this is the case, then Marcion would be responsible for spurring the Church into making a conscious and deliberate decision in this regard.

44. So claims Irenaeus *Adv. Haer.* 4:29-34 and Tertullian *Adv. Marc.* 4:2.

45. His list does not contain I and II Timothy or Titus.

46. Justin probably used only the Synoptics since the fourth Gospel does not appear to have made many inroads in the Western churches by this time, inspite of Irenaeus' four-fold Gospel canon shortly after Justin. What is more surprising is that Tatian, Justin's pupil, clearly preferred John's Gospel over the Synoptics in making his *Diatessaron*.

47. Von Campenhausen, *Formation*, p. 171.

48. Frend, *Rise*, pp. 212-17, calls this an "acute Hellenization of the Church."

49. E. C. Blackman, *Marcion and His Influence* (London: SPCK, 1948), p. 32.

50. It is not certain that he called these writings "scripture."

51. Contrary to the findings of L. G. Patterson, "Irenaeus," pp. 8-9.

52. See Galatians 3:15-22, in which Paul shows that historically faith preceded the Law and that the Law only had a temporary purpose in the economy of God. For a discussion of the problem the OT posed for Christian faith as well as Paul's solution to the problem—reading the scriptures correctly through faith in Christ—see von Campenhausen's helpful discussion in *Formation*, pp. 21 ff. James Sanders offers a helpful survey of the suggested solutions to the problem of understanding Paul's view of the Law in his *Sacred Story*, pp. 115-23. Although many suggest that "law" in Paul was basically *halachah*, or the legal prescriptive laws and regulations, Sanders stresses that it was also *haggadah*—story or mythos—as well. *Haggadah* answered who we are, and *halachah* answered what we are to do. Sanders suggests that Paul maintained a high regard for the Torah as *haggadah*, but argued that the legal regulations of the Torah did not apply. For Paul, according to Sanders, Christ had become the "New Torah" and superceded the Torah era, but did not eradicate the Torah that was "caught up in Christ in a new age." *Sacred Story*, p. 120.

53. Von Campenhausen, *Formation*, pp. 93-94.

54. See also 19:2, 5, 6; 20:1, 4; 21:1; 22:1, 11; 23:5; 92:3. Von Campenhausen, *Formation*, pp. 93-95, has a helpful discussion of this issue.

55. See L. G. Patterson, "Irenaeus," pp. 8-11, and B. M. Metzger, "Canon," p. 124. These "memoirs" are elsewhere described as "memoirs of all things concerning our Savior Jesus Christ" (*I Apol.* 33, 66, *ECF*).

56. That is, on the eucharist; see I *Apol.* 67.

57. On Justin's neglect of John, see Collins, *Introduction*, pp. 20-21.

58. Observe also I *Apol.* 28:1 in which Justin appeals to "our writings" (ἡμέτερα συγγράμματα) to clarify a point in his argument. Hennecke, *NT Apo.* pp. 31 ff., claims that these "writings" refer not only to the OT scriptures but also to Christian literature.

59. It should be noted again in passing that Justin did not make use of Paul's Epistles in his writings and, therefore, had little focus on the major themes of Paul's theology. It is not likely that he was unaware of these Epistles due to their popularity in the early Church but may have simply avoided Marcion's primary sources. It is also possible that he was unimpressed by Paul's focus on the cross, the atonement, the Holy Spirit, or even by Paul's lack of interest in philosophy and worse, perhaps, his apparent attacks against it (see I Cor. 1:18-31; Col. 2:8). Irenaeus overcame Justin's hesitation to use Paul and introduced his Epistles as an important part of his "New Testament."

60. Von Campenhausen, *Formation*, p. 182. See also Goodspeed, *A History*, p. 120 and Paterson, "Irenaeus," pp. 11 ff.

61. See note 1 of chapter 1 above for more examples.

62. For Irenaeus, the apostolic witness was the primary determining principle for the recognition of the authority of NT scriptures (*Adv. Haer.* 3.2.2). It should also be noted that Irenaeus did not limit that succession of the apostolic witness to the bishops at Rome (*Adv. Haer.* 3.3.2).

63. Koester, *Introduction*, vol. 2, p. 11.
64. That is not the intent of his concluding remarks in John 20:30, though the hyperbole in the later Johannine appendix in 21:25 may warrant that speculation.
65. Harry Gamble, *NT Canon*, pp. 24-25, also makes this argument and adds that Matthew and Luke must not have had a very high view of their sources (especially Mark), since they took such liberties in adding to and altering the sources they employed.

Chapter 5: Factors Limiting the Scope of the New Testament Canon

1. Kelly, *Doctrines*, pp. 82-83, lists two other creeds roughly contemporary with the last half of the second century.
2. Clement of Rome (ca. 95) speaks of Paul as inspired (I Clem. 47:3) and refers or alludes to his letters several times throughout his work.
3. Athenagoras, of course, is an exception to this, but his conclusions are not representative of most of the christologies of the second century. His trinitarian-type of formulation is, however, anticipatory of the fourth century when God and Christ are described in Greek philosophical categories, employing especially Platonic categories. However, Athenagoras does come close to the later position of the Church when he writes: "We speak of God, of his Son, his Word, and of the Holy Spirit; and we say that the Father, the Son, and the Spirit are united in power. For the Son is the intelligence, reason, and wisdom of the Father, and the Spirit is an effluence, as light from fire" (Athenagoras, *A Plea for the Christians*, p. 24, *ECF*). Regardless, Athenagoras' view of the Spirit is not representative of the views of the Nicene Fathers.
4. See further discussion of this in chap. 7, sect., I.
5. We will return to Constantine later in sect. V of this chapter when this argument will be supported.
6. Frend, *Rise*, p. 253.
7. *Ibid.*, pp. 254-55.
8. Collins, *Introduction*, p. 26.
9. So argues von Campenhausen, *Formation*, p. 232.
10. Eusebius, in his discussion of the "cataphrygian heresy" (Montanism), mentions several times that women were a significant part of the movement. See his frequent discussion of the women in the Montanist movement in *Hist. eccl.* 5.14-19.
11. Frend, *Rise*, p. 256.
12. W. Schneemelcher, "General Introduction." In *NT Apo* vol. 2, p. 685 n. 2.
13. Von Campenhausen, *Formation*, pp. 227-32.
14. *Elench.* 8.19.1, cited by von Campenhausen, *Ibid.*, pp. 229-30.
15. *Ibid.* Metzger, *Canon*, p. 106, also makes this observation, adding that it was with Marcion that the Church saw the need to expand its written corpus of authoritative writings and with the Montanists that they saw the need to limit their scope. This process of limitation, claims Metzger, was "the first step taken by the church toward the adoption of a closed canon of Scripture."
16. Von Campenhausen, *Formation*, p. 232. On pp. 232-42 von Campenhausen discusses the rather troubled history in the Church of the literature the Montanists appealed to most: the various apocalypses, the Gospel of John, and Hebrews.
17. See Layton, *Gnostic Scriptures*, pp. xv-xxvii. Layton has a very helpful introduction to the literature as a whole and also numerous annotations that help to clarify the meaning of the translated texts.
18. Book I of *Adv. Haer.* is painstakingly detailed both in the description and in the criticism of the Gnostic Christians.
19. Ptolemy's *Letter to Flora* is, of course, a major exception to this.
20. This brief description of a few of the characteristics of Gnosticism may only confuse the student who is unacquainted with the general outlines of Gnostic belief. Indeed, the

novice who tries to hold in his or her mind all the Ogdoads, Decads, Tetrads, and other Aeons and emmanations from the Pleroma, described in meticulous detail in Irenaeus, will probably not only become lost in the detail but worse, discouraged in the persuit as well. An excellent guide to the study of ancient Gnosticism is still Hans Jonas, *The Gnostic Religion* (Boston: Beacon Press, 1963). The more recently translated work of Kurt Rudolph, *Gnosis: The Nature and History of Gnosticism*, trans. and ed. Robert McLachlan Wilson (San Francisco: Harper, 1987) as well as the introductory chapter in Bentley Layton, *Gnostic Scriptures*, pp. xv-xxvii, and 5-21 are helpful. A brief but helpful survey of Gnostic beliefs is found in Thomas P. van Baaren, "Towards a Definition of Gnosticism." In *Le Origini dello Gnosticismo*, ed. U. Bianchi (Acts of Messina Colloquium, 1966; Leiden, 1967), pp. 178-80. Finally, an excellent, though brief, article by George MacRae helps us to understand why this form of Christianity was a "loser," why it failed to carry the day. See his "Why the Church Rejected Gnosticism." In *Self-Definition*, vol. 1, pp. 126-33.

21. Frend, *Rise*, pp. 452-61, has a very helpful discussion of this matter.
22. Ibid., pp. 457-58.
23. From *Acta Saturnini*, XVIII, col. 701. Cited by Frend, *Rise*, p. 462.
24. Kelly, *Doctrines*, pp. 410-12.
25. See, for example, Ramsey MacMullen, *Christianizing the Roman Empire* [A.D. 100-400), (New Haven: Yale University Press, 1984) 43 ff. MacMullen raises valid questions about the extent of Constantine's conversion by highlighting some of his brutality toward non-Christians and also his coercion of the Church.
26. Since we possess no surviving writings from Marcion, we cannot say that he specifically called his collection of Luke and Paul "scripture," but these writings appear to have functioned that way for him. *The Marcionite Prologues* to the epistles of Paul, including prologues to the Pastoral epistles that Marcion either rejected or did not know, *are most likely to have arisen in the Marcionite communities after the time of Marcion*, but not from him. See Metzger's helpful summary of the evaluation of these ancient prologues in *Canon*, pp. 94-97.

Chapter 6: Ancient Collections of Christian Scriptures

1. F. W. Grosheide, *Some Early Lists of the Books of the New Testament* (Leiden: E. J. Brill, 1948). Grosheide has compiled a helpful collection of twelve lists of early NT canonical books. All of his lists date from the fourth century C.E., including the lists presumably from Origen and the Muratorian Fragment. Alexander Souter, *The Text and Canon of the New Testament* (New York: Charles Scribner's Sons, 1917), see especially pp. 205-37, also has a helpful collection of such lists, but his discussion on pp. 160-204 is not clear. See also Grant, *Formation*, pp. 163-80; Farmer, "NT Canon," pp. 9-22; Kümmel, *Introduction*, pp. 340-55. Metzger, *Canon*, pp. 305-15, has put together several similar ancient lists that actually circulated as lists in the fourth century. His collection is quite valuable and needs to be studied in detail. The major point that such collections impress on the reader is that although there was a general concensus in the fourth-century Church on the broad parameters of the NT body of sacred writings, a fair amount of disagreement existed on about a third of the writings that finally made it into the NT canon.
2. Kümmel, *Introduction*, pp. 340-55.
3. Farmer, "NT Canon," pp. 9-22.
4. Again, Helmut Koester's *Snoptische* is still the best study on this subject.
5. The term *list* is not always the best to describe this collection since not all of the patristic authors mentioned below drew up a closed list of Christian scriptures—for example, Irenaeus, Clement, Tertullian, and Origen. See Albert C. Sundberg, "The Bible Canon and the Christian Doctrine of Inspiration." *Int* 29, no. 4, (1975):364-65. In this section

we will see references to Christian literature that was recognized as having normative value for the Church.

6. Raymond Brown insists that the patristic citations do, however, give evidence of the acceptance of this literature as authoritative in the life of the Church and as an indication of the beginnings of a Christian canon of scripture (Brown, "Canonicity." *JBC*, p. 530). The specific context of each citation, however, is important before a judgment can be made in this regard.

7. Kümmel, *Introduction*, p. 338.

8. Grant, *Formation*, pp. 121-24.

9. Ibid.

10. Aland, *Canon*, p. 12. See discussion of this below in sect. XI.

11. More complete lists than those in this study can be found in Souter, Grosheide, Kümmel, Farmer, and Metzger. A duplication of this information here would not add significantly to the point that the following examples will make: that a fair amount of diversity regarding the substance of the NT canon existed in the Church well into the fifth century.

12. Helmut Koester, *Introduction*, vol. 2, pp. 297-305.

13. Ibid., pp. 298.

14. The term *scripture* in reference to NT writings is probably anachronistic on Tertullian's part.

15. See the whole of *Praescript.* 32.

16. Metzger, "Canon," p. 124.

17. Notice, for example, 3.3.3; 3.11.8; 3.12.15; 3.14.1-15.1; 3.21.3-4, and so on.

18. See Edgar J. Goodspeed, "The Canon of the New Testament," vol. 1, pp. 64-65.

19. F. W. Beare, "Canon of the NT" vol. 1, p. 529.

20. Ibid., p. 528.

21. Metzger, "Canon," p. 124, and also Goodspeed, "Canon of NT," p. 133.

22. Metzger, "Canon," p. 124.

23. See Henry Chadwick, ed., *Alexandrian Christianity* (Philadelphia: Westminster Press, 1954), p. 21. Chadwick has shown the parallel here with what Paul said about the Law of Moses' being a *paidagogos* (Gal. 3:24) to bring one to Christ.

24. A. C. Sundberg, "The Making of the New Testament Canon." In *The Interpreter's One Volume Commentary of the Bible*, Charles M. Laymon, ed. (New York: Abingdon Press, 1971), pp. 1222-23.

25. Rufinus' translation of Origen's *Hom.* 7.1 on Joshua is clearly inferior and unreliable. Whenever he found difficult passages in Origen, he simply left them out of his translation, believing that they were interpolations by heretics.

26. A. C. Sundberg, Jr., "Canon Muratori: A Fourth-Century List." *HTR* 66:1 (January, 1973):36-37.

27. Everett Kalin, "Re-examining New Testament Canon History: The Canon of Origen." Unpublished paper read at the Society of Biblical Literature, 1984.

28. Ibid.

29. According to Eusebius, he introduces II and III John with the words "and it may be" (ἔστω δὲ).

30. Beare, "Canon of NT," p. 529, claims that Origen is the first writer to refer to James.

31. Metzger, "Canon," p. 125.

32. Kahlin, "Re-examining" has supplied this translation.

33. ἀνωμολόγηται (see *Hist. eccl.* 3.3.1), but also ἐνδιάθηκον (literally, "testamented" or "canonical"). See 3.3.6, where he uses ὁμολοωουμένοις ("recognized") and 5.8.1 where he speaks of "handed down scripture" (or "scripture that has been handed down [in the churches]", παραδόσεις γραφῇ). See also 6.14.1, where he speaks of "all the canonical scripture" (πασης τῆς ἐνδιαθήκον γραφῆς).

34. Hebrews was attributed to Paul (see 3.3.5), but not without question. See also 6.25.11-14.

35. In 3.3.1 he called this book "noncanonical" (οὐκ ἐνδιάθηκον).
36. Denis Farkasfalvy, "Early Development NT Canon," p. 161n 1.
37. Hennecke, *NT Apo*, vol. 1, pp. 43-45. An attempt has been made here to present a more readable translation for the sake of the less technical reader, though it is still in keeping with the original intent of the Latin text. For the scholar seeking a more literal translation, see Metzger, *Canon*, pp. 305-7. Metzger offers one of the best and most recent translations of the MF with many helpful notations. However, the above translation, though freer, is in keeping with the original purpose of the MF author.
38. See Grant, *Formation*, p. 301; Metzger, "Canon," p. 124; Beare, "NT Canon," p. 527; Edgar J. Goodspeed, *A History of Early Christian Literature* (Chicago: University of Chicago Press, 1983), p. 31; Hennecke, *NT Apo*, vol. 1, p. 42; von Campenhausen, *Formation*, p. 242 ff.; and others. The complete Latin text, both original and restored, is preserved in Theron, *Evidence*, pp. 106-12.
39. Von Campenhausen, *Formation*, pp. 244-45n 192.
40. Sundberg, "Canon Muratori," pp. 1-41.
41. Farkasfalvy, "Early Development," p. 161, dismisses Sundberg's article in a footnote without seriously considering Sundbergs's major arguments.
42. See the last lines of paragraph 5 of the fragment above.
43. A. C. Sundberg, "The Bible Canon and the Christian Doctrine of Inspiration." *Interpretation* 29, no. 4 (1975):362, has made a strong point that even if Canon Muratori were a second century document, it has no parallels until the fourth century and could not have played a significant role in the development of the Christian canon of scriptures that has been ascribed to it. The document appears to have come from the middle to late fourth century C.E., when the ambiguity about the acceptance of certain books expressed by Eusebius had already disappeared.
44. Sundberg, "Canon Muratori," pp. 8-11.
45. Notice in *Adv. Haer.* 3.3.3, quoted in chapt. 4, sect. V, that after Pius, the bishop of Rome, came Anicetus, followed by Soter, and then by Eleutherius, who was bishop of Rome in the time of Irenaeus (ca. 180 C.E.).
46. Everett Ferguson, "Canon Muratori: Date and Provenance." In *Studia Patristica*, Elizabeth Livingstone, ed. (Berlin: Akadamie Verlag, 1982) vol. 16, pp. 677-83.
47. Metzger, *Canon*, p. 193. Metzger is more convinced than I that the designation of Rome as *urbs Roma* indicates necessarily a Western origin of the fragment. But even if those terms are restricted to Roman use alone, one has to consider that the fragment itself is a seventh-century translation of a Greek list. If it were a Western document from the late second century, one would expect to see other parallels from the same time. The closest parallel, Irenaeus, is significantly dissimilar.
48. Even Metzger's analysis of the fragment's listing of the four canonical Gospels, which he sees rightly as evidence of their fixed status in the Church (there is no defense of the fact that these four and only these four Gospels are to be read in the churches), is an argument against a second century dating of the fragment. See *Canon*, p. 200. Irenaeus' strange way of arguing for these four and only these four Gospels at least suggests that not everyone in the second century was as convinced about the matter as he was. Also, Metzger's acknowledgement of Tatian's use of more than the four canonical Gospels in his *Diatessaron* (*Canon*, pp. 115-16) would seem to show that the contemporaries of Irenaeus did not all agree that they should be limited to the four canonical Gospels, at least not as rigidly as did Irenaeus. Even if some of Tatian's followers later inserted clauses from the Gospel of Hebrews and from *the Protevangelium of James* into the *Diatessaron*, as Metzger allows, (Ibid.), still one cannot find in Tatian the loyalty to the "inspired text" that one would find in Revelation 22:18-19. From the fragment of the *Diatessaron* that has survived and that Metzger has included in his section on Tatian (ibid., p. 115), it is clear that much of the context, especially from the Synoptic Gospels, is omitted. Could this not indicate that the full canonical and "inspired" status of the four canonical Gospels was not yet fully recognized by Tatian? No doubt he saw them as responsible and faithful documents, but clearly not as inviolable texts.

Although it can be argued that Irenaeus' canon was not universally accepted in his day, hense Irenaeus' defense, the same cannot be said about the MF, in which the acceptance of the four canonical Gospels is assumed without debate. The only question is what else is to be added.

49. The above is admittedly a rather loose adaptation of this section of Athanasius' difficult and cumbersome text in Schneemelcher, *NT Apo*, vol. 1, pp. 59-60, although it follows somewhat closely that of Souter, *Text and Canon*, pp. 215-16. The translation, though quite free in portions, nonetheless brings out Athanasius' original intent in the Greek.

50. Kümmel, *Introduction*, p. 350, also agrees with this claim. This conclusion depends, however, on how early one dates Amphilochius' writing. See sect. XI where his writing is put at the end of the fourth century. Some scholars have claimed that Eusebius was the first to use the term in relation to sacred literature by appealing to his discussion of Clement of Alexandria in *Hist. eccl.* 6.25.3. Eusebius' comments there about Clement are as follows: "in the first of his (Commentaries) on the Gospel according to Matthew, defending the canon of the Church (τὸν ἐκκλησιαστικὸν θυλάττων κανόνα) he gives his testimony that he knows only four Gospels" *(LCL)*. In this passage, however, Eusebius' use of the term κανόνα has nothing to do with a collection of writings, but rather the faith of the Church.

51. After listing his books, he concludes οὗτος ἀψευδέστατος κανὼν ἄν εἴη τῶν θεοπνεύστων γραφῶν. See the whole list in Grosheide, *Some Early Lists*, p. 20.

52. Ibid.

53. Koester, *Introduction*, vol. 2, p. 256.

54. D Contains the Epistle of Barnabas, the Shepherd of Hermas, the Acts of Paul, and the Revelation of Peter, but omits Hebrews.

55. Kirsopp Lake, ed. and trans., *The Apostolic Fathers*, LCL (Cambridge, Mass.: Harvard University Press, 1977), vol. 1, p. 339.

56. In defense of this Aland, *Canon*, p. 12, gives the example of Cassiodorus (ca. 550), who could not obtain a Western commentary of Hebrews and, therefore, had the one by Chrysostom translated from the Greek. He also cites the case of the Spanish synods around 600 who were still fighting against those who rejected Revelation.

57. See Sean P. Kealy, "An African Contribution," pp. 17 ff. Kealy notes that the Ethiopian canon contains some forty-six OT books and thirty-five NT books and claims that it was this canon of scriptures that was carried by the Christian missionaries to Ethiopia in 330 C.E. Metzger has listed the NT collection as follows: the four Gospels, Acts, the seven catholic epistles, fourteen epistles of Paul (Hebrews included), Revelation, *Sinodos* (four sections), I Clement, the book of the Covenant (two sections), and *Didascalia*. See Metzger, *Canon*, p. 227. When the canon was settled in the greater Church at a much later date, the Ethiopian community of Christians was isolated from the rest of the Christian world (because of the Islamic conquests especially in the seventh century) for almost nine centuries and did not know of the agreements in the rest of the churches. Hence, although they have a much larger canon, they may well represent a much older tradition in the Church than does the present biblical canon.

Chapter 7: The Criteria for a New Testament Canon: Another Look

1. G. W. H. Lampe, "The Early Church." In *Scripture and Tradition*, F. W. Dillistone, ed. (London: Lutterworth Press, 1955), p. 42.

2. Ibid.

3. Ibid., p. 43.

4. Oscar Cullmann, *The Early Church* (London: SCM Press, 1956), p. 91.

5. Funk, *Parables*, p. 182.

6. Funk has a helpful discussion of the success of the Church in seeking to ground its faith (traditions) in Jesus through a closed apostolic canon. Although he acknowledges that

the early Church aimed at supporting its traditions by an appeal to the apostolic root-age, he calls into question the outcome of its efforts. *Parables*, pp. 182-86.

7. For a discussion of this, see Raymond E. Brown, "Canonicity," p. 525.

8. Ernest Best, "Scripture, Tradition, and the Canon of the New Testament." *JRB* 61:2 (1979):279.

9. Von Campenhausen, *Formation*, p. 260, is undoubtedly correct in this matter.

10. Helmut Koester, "GNOMAI DIAPHOROI: The Origin and Nature of Diversification in the History of Early Christianity." In *Trajectories Through Early Christianity*, eds. James M. Robinson and Helmut Koester (Philadelphia: Fortress Press, 1971), p. 115.

11. See the many Gnostic documents presented in the name of an apostle in the *NHLE*, ed. James M. Robinson which claim either implicitly or explicitly the apostolic tradition—for example, the Acts of Peter and the Twelve Apostles in *NHLE*, p. 265. Note how the Apocryphon of John (paragraphs 2 and 32) claims to be a report of what the Savior revealed to the apostle John. Ibid., pp. 99, 115.

12. See especially the important collection of noncanonical sayings of Jesus in John Dominic Crossan, *Sayings Parallels: A Workbook for the Jesus Tradition* (Philadelphia: Fortress Press, 1986).

13. David Ewert, *From Ancient Tablets*, p. 131. See also Glenn W. Barker, William L. Lane, and J. Ramsey Michaels, *The New Testament Speaks* (New York: Harper, 1969), pp. 30-31. They ask, "Was that which was written a genuine witness to Christ and from Christ? . . . The church was confident that if a document were genuinely inspired it would conform to the truth which God had revealed through tested witnesses." See also Everett F. Harrison, *Introduction to the New Testament*, (Grand Rapids: Wm. B. Eerdman's, Co., 1977), pp. 11-12.

14. See, for example, the speeches in Acts where the death of Christ "for our sins" is no-where in view (2:14-39; 3:11-26; and so on), but found frequently in Paul, especially I Corinthians 15:3, as well as his focus on the cross in I Corinthians 1:17–2:2; Romans 3:23-25, Galatians 2:21, *passim*.

15. Best cites this and several other examples of problems of harmonization in the NT liter-ature in "Scripture," pp. 272 ff.

16. Kelsey, *Uses*, pp. 106-7. Unfortunately, Kelsey is not clear on what that "wholeness" is that ties the canon together.

17. Ibid., pp. 116-17n. 16.

18. Ernst Käsemann, *Essays on New Testament Themes* (London: SCM Press, 1968), p. 100.

19. Krister Stendahl, *Meanings* (Philadelphia: Fortress Press, 1984), p. 63.

20. Dunn, *Unity*, p. 377.

21. All of the Apostolic Fathers—Clement of Rome, Ignatius, Polycarp, Hermas, Barna-bas, and the Didachist—could *or* did agree to this, but so also could Marcion and the Montanists for that matter.

22. Von Campenhausen, *Formation*, p. 330, makes this careful observation.

23. Because of this Dunn, *Unity*, pp. 374-76, raises the question of the continuing validity of the canon but answers affirmatively because it not only canonizes the unity of Chris-tianity around the Lordship of Christ, but also "because it canonizes the diversity of Christianity."

24. Rolf Knierim, "The Task of Old Testament Theology." *Horizons in Biblical Theology* 6:1 (June, 1984):25.

25. Ibid., pp. 25-33.

26. James A. Sanders, *Canon*, p. 43, agrees here.

27. Ibid. p. 43 (italics his). Knierim lists eight such items that he contends are *not* the unifying factors of the OT. See his "The Task," pp. 31-33.

28. Koester, "Gnomai," p. 114. This has also been argued in Walter Bauer's earlier classical work *Orthodoxy and Heresy in Earliest Christianity* (Philadelphia: Fortress Press, 1979), see p. xxii.

29. Bauer, "NT Canon," pp. 231 ff.

30. See Robert Wilken, "Diversity and Unity in Early Christianity." *TSC* 1, no.2 (1981):107, and Gary T. Burke, "Walter Bauer and Celsus: The Shape of Late Second-Century Christianity." *TSC* 4, no. 1 (1984):1-7.
31. Frederik Wisse, "Use of Early Christian Literature." In *Nag Hammadi, Gnosticism, and Early Christianity*, ed. Charles W. Hedrick and Robert Hodgson, Jr. (Peabody Mass.: Hendrickson Publishers, 1986), p. 197.
32. Ibid., pp. 184-85. Wisse has a helpful discussion of what qualified as orthodoxy, as well as what did not, and why. He states that orthodoxy was that which was clear, rationally coherent, and conformed to the acceptable tradition of the Church. Heresy, on the other hand, was incoherent, confusing, and contradictory. This heresy, he argues, is rooted in the charismatic beginnings of Gentile Christianity (pp. 186-87).
33. Kelsey, *Uses*, p. 93n. 4.
34. See Knierim, "The Task," p. 25.
35. George W. MacRae, "Why the Church Rejected," pp. 126-33.
36. Cullmann, *Early Church*, p. 77.
37. Helmut Koester, "Apocryphal and Canonical Gospels." *HTR* 73 (1980): 108-10.
38. Ibid., pp. 123-29.
39. Ibid., p. 130. See also Koester, "GNOMAI" 118-19, 124-43.
40. Helmut Koester, "Gnostic Sayings and Controversy Traditions in John 8:12-59." In *Nag Hammadi, Gnosticism, and Early Christianity*, eds. Charles W. Hedrick and Robert Hodgson, Jr. (Peabody: Hendrickson Publishers, 1986), p. 98.
41. Ron Cameron, *Sayings Traditions in the Apocryphon of James* (HTS 34) (Philadelphia: Fortress Press, 1984), p. 131. Cameron has argued similarly, stressing that the authentic Jesus sayings in the extra-biblical literature are highly significant for our understanding of the Jesus story.
42. The criterion of antiquity by itself is awkward in principle because it suggests historical dating for dogmatic reasons. If a text agrees with one's theological bias, it is a temptation to argue its legitimacy based on some supposed and not always clear historical dating.
43. Best, "NT Canon," p. 281.
44. See previous discussion of this matter in chap. 1.
45. Metzger, *Canon*, p. 272.
46. Origen, *De Prin.*, preface 8, *ANF*.
47. Notice his "tryptich" of authority, but also how even belief itself was divinely inspired.
48. This apocalypse is possibly also alluded to in II Clement 11:2. The two names are mentioned in Numbers 11:26.
49. Gottlob Schrenk, "γραφή," pp. 756-57, cites other examples of early Christian writers, citing or quoting noncanonical literature as scripture, using traditional scriptural formulae.
50. This passage also makes clear what Theophilus means by inspiration. "But men of God carrying in them a holy spirit (πνευματόφοροι, "borne along by the spirit") and becoming prophets, being inspired and made wise by God, became God-taught, and holy and righteous." (2:9 in *ANF*).
51. A number of these examples are listed in Albert C. Sundberg, "The Bible Canon," pp. 365 ff. See also Everett R. Kalin, who gives a longer list of examples in his "The Inspired Community: A Glance at Canon History." *CTM* 42 (1971):541-49.
52. Cited by Everett T. Kalin in his unpublished Harvard thesis, "Argument from Inspiration in the Canonization of the New Testament," 1967, p. 170 from *Apologia hexaemeron* in Migne, *Patrologia Graeca* 44.61, but also in the wider context of 44.61-64.
53. *Vita Abercii*, p. 76. See Kalin, "The Inspired Community," pp. 170-71. Abercius Marcellus was bishop of Hieropolis in Phrygia of Asia Minor in the late second century. He died ca. 200 C.E.
54. Kalin gives several other examples of the ancient use of the term *inspired* (θεόπνευστος) to show that it is not exclusively used of sacred scripture. See "The Inspired Community," pp. 169-73.

55. See other illustrations of this in *Dial.*, pp. 87, 88. It is especially worth mentioning here that Justin believed that even the translators of the Septuagint were divinely inspired to do their work. This, he claims, was shown by the evidence from their work that not only agreed in meaning, but because their separate translations from the Hebrew, had even the same Greek words! See Justins' *Horatory Address to the Greeks*, in which he tells of King Ptolemy's approval of the translation of the *LXX*.

> And when he ascertained that the seventy men had not only given the same meaning, but had employed the same words, and had failed in agreement with one another not even to the extent of one word, but had written the same things, and concerning the same things, he was struck with amazement, and *believed that the translation had been written by divine power*, and perceived that the men were worthy of all honour, as beloved of God; and with many gifts ordered them to return to their own country. And having, as was natural, marvelled at the books, and concluded them to be divine, he consecrated them in that library. *(ANF)*

56. Eusebius, *Hist. eccl.* 5.14-19, is especially helpful here.
57. Everett R. Kalin, "The Inspired Community," p. 543. He concluded his study of Irenaeus, Origen, Eusebius, and other ancient Church Fathers by noting that only the work of the false prophets mentioned in the OT, the heathen oracles, and philosophy were noninspired. See also Kalin, "Argument from Inspiration," pp. 163, 168.
58. *Tosefta* (literally "supplements" or "additions") is believed by many to be an alternative to the Mishnah that sometimes preserves independent parallels to the Mishnah. See Koester, *Introduction*, vol. 1, p. 412.
59. Krister Stendahl, "The Apocalypse of John and the Epistles of Paul in the Muratorian Fragment." In *Current Issues in New Testament Interpretation: Essays in Honor of Otto A. Piper*, eds. W. Klassen and G. T. Snyder (New York: Harper, 1962), pp. 239-45.
60. Kalin, "The Inspired Community," p. 544.
61. Ibid., p. 545.
62. Ibid., p. 547. Von Campenhausen's discussion of prophetic literature among the Montanists—that literature born of or prompted by the Holy Spirit *(Formation,* pp. 215-50)—is relevant to this discussion and shows that there was no belief at the end of the second century that inspiration was confined to first-century literature. For these and other reasons, Dieter Georgi, *Opponents*, p. 430, insists that the concept of inspiration played almost no role in the later discussion of the biblical canon. He asserts unequivocally that "the customary idea that the Jewish as well as Christian concepts of canon grew out of the scriptures themselves, that is, by divine providence, the spirit's action, is nonsense." See also p. 441n. 184.
63. LaSor et al., *OT Survey*, p. 25.
64. This reference was supplied by Raymond E. Brown, *The Critical Meaning of the Bible* (New York: Paulist Press, 1981), p. 14.
65. He has also observed that by the word *canon* the early Church simply meant the list of books that were acknowledged as scripture. See Barr, *Scripture*, p. 48. Barr's understanding of the traditional relationship of inspiration to the biblical canon is similar to that explained by Paul J. Achtemeier, *The Inspiration of Scripture*, p. 119, who says that "God inspired the canonical books with no exception, and no noncanonical books are inspired, with no exception."
66. Barr, *Scripture*, p. 57.
67. The understanding of inspiration in Origen is clearly different from that in Clement of Rome and Ignatius, but also from *all* the Church Fathers who preceded him.
68. Take, for example, Clement of Alexandria, who cited the *Did.* as scripture *(Strom.* 1.100.4) and regarded I Clem., Barn., Hermas, the Preaching of Peter, and Apoc. Pet. as "inspired." See also Grant, "NT Canon," p. 302.
69. Kalin, "The Inspired Community," p. 548.
70. Koester, *Introduction*, vol. 2, p. 11. So also von Campenhausen, *Formation*, p. 261.
71. More specifically, it is likely that use in major churches, such as Rome, Antioch, Alexan-

dria, and so on, was the controlling criterion. This is different from Hans von Campenhausen's view (*Formation*, p. 261) that the primary determining factor in selecting which writings would be in the canon was "the usage and judgment of the *one true church*, spread throughout the world" (italics added). In that day as well as in our own, the smaller churches were strongly influenced by the larger ones.

72. F. F. Bruce, *Tradition*, p. 74.
73. Koester, *Introduction*, vol. 2, p. 11.
74. See, for example, Irenaeus' *limitation* of the gospel literature to the four evangelists in *Adv. Haer.* 3.11.8, 9, quoted in chap. 4, sect. V, and also Eusebius' "spurious" category for Christian literature, discussed in chap. 6, sect. VII.

Chapter 8: Final Reflections

1. For a helpful discussion of this see, Helmut Koester, "GNOMAI," pp. 117-18.
2. Bruce Shelley, *By What Authority?* (Grand Rapids: Wm. B. Eerdman's Co., 1965) 57.
3. The importance of the apostolic tradition in the early Church, or the apostolic eyewitness account of the words and event of Jesus, was established quite soon after the death of Jesus (see I Cor. 15:3-8; Acts 1:21-22) as well as later, after the death of the apostles. It was also taken up into the Church's witness both for inward community concern (I Clem. 42:1; II Pet. 3:2) and polemical argument against heresy (Justin, I Apol. 42:4; 50:12; Irenaeus, *Adv. Haer.* 3.3.1-3; Tertullian, *Praes.* 6). In the examples from Irenaeus and Tertullian, the guarantee of the accuracy of the Church's canon of faith is secured by apostolic succession, wherein the truthfulness of their understanding of the gospel was passed on through bishops.
4. *Orthodoxy* itself was only in its early formative stages at that time.
5. See *Appendix B*.
6. See the discussion of this chap. 2, sect. II.
7. There can be little doubt that scriptural canons had the effect of legitimizing only one branch of Christianity.
8. This, in spite of Irenaeus' overly optimistic and somewhat naive assertion that "The churches which have been planted in Germany do not believe or hand down anything different, nor do those in Spain, nor those in Gaul, nor those in the East, nor those in Egypt, nor those in Libya, nor those which have been established in the central regions of the world" (*Adv. Haer.* 3.10.2, ANF). And again, "The Catholic church possesses one and the same faith throughout the whole word, as we have already said" (3.10.3, ANF). See previous discussion on the criterion of "orthodoxy" in chap. 7, sect. II.
9. So argues Dunn, *Unity*, p. 377.
10. Although a Pauline corpus of writings probably was in circulation by the end of the first century, and most assuredly collections of the sayings of Jesus were in existence well before then—*Q*, Matthew and Luke, the Gospel of Thomas, and so on—still there was no need at that time for a fixed or closed list of such writings. This is evidence of a Church whose oral traditions were still serving it quite well some one hundred years after its beginnings. Apart from Irenaeus' gospel canon, probably no other canon of Christian literature existed before Eusebius. Even Origen's "list," as noted earlier, may have been an invention by Eusebius.
11. Shelly, *Authority*, pp. 57-58, suggests that the earlier Judaizing and Docetic heresies were not the *type* to call for a theory of apostolic authority as were the later Marcionite and Gnostic heresies. The "heretical" groups of the middle to late second century also appealed to an apostolic tradition as the foundation for their teachings. The Church, therefore, understandably appealed to an apostolic tradition, which it claimed was passed on through the churches by the apostles through the bishops, who inherited the leadership of the churches and teaching from the apostles.
12. Why else would so many creeds crop up in the Church after the relative acceptance of a canon unless the message of that canon was somewhat blurred or imprecise?

13. See Ephesians 6:5-8; Colossians 3:22-25. It is an established fact that the greater
    Church as a whole had very little conscience about this matter for the first six centuries
    of its history.
14. See Ephesians 5:22-23; Colossians 3:18; I Timothy 2:11-15 and I Peter 3:1-6.
15. Krister Stendahl, "Ancient Scripture in the Modern World." In *Scripture in the Jewish
    and Christians Traditions*, ed. Frederick E. Greenspahn (Nashville: Abingdon Press,
    1982), p. 205.
16. Ibid.
17. Ernest Best, "Scripture," pp. 271-77, also raises this question.
18. I have always had difficulty understanding those Christians who place the Bible first in
    their creeds instead of God! Nowhere do the biblical writers ever give us the impres-
    sion, nor yet the suggestion, that *they* have prior claim over God for our devotion. Even
    less could they argue that historically the Bible preceded God!

SELECT
BIBLIOGRAPHY*

Achtemeier, Paul J. *The Inspiration of Scripture*. Philadelphia: Westminster Press, 1980.

Ackroyd, Peter. "Original Text and Canonical Text." *USQR* 32, nos. 3-4 (1977):166-73.

Aland, Kurt. *The Problem of the New Testament Canon*. Oxford: A. R. Mowbray & Co., 1962.

Anderson, G. W. "Canonical and Non-Canonical." In *The Cambridge History of the Bible*. Edited by P. R. Ackroyd and C. F. Evans. Cambridge, England: Cambridge University Press, 1976.

Aune, David. *Prophecy in Early Christianity*. Grand Rapids: W. B. Eerdmans, Co., 1983.

Barr, James. *Holy Scripture: Canon, Authority, Criticsm*. Philadelphia: Westminster Press, 1983.

Beare, G. W. "Canon of the NT." In *IDB*, vol. 1. New York: Abingdon Press, 1979.

Beckwith, Roger. *The Old Testament Canon of the New Testament Church and Its Background in Early Judaism*. Grand Rapids: W. B. Eerdmans Co., 1985.

———"Canon of the Old Testament." In *The Illustrated Bible Dictionary*, eds. J. D. Douglas and Norman Hillyer (Wheaton, Ill.: Tyndale House, 1986, vol. 1, pp. 235-39.

Best, Ernest. "Scripture, Tradition, and the Canon of the New Testament." *BJRL* 61:2 (1979):258-89.

Beyer, Hermann Wolfgang. "*κανών*." In *TDNT*. Translated by Geoffry W. Bromiley. Grand Rapids: Wm. B. Eerdmans Co., 1965.

Brown, Raymond E. "Canonicity." In *JBC*. Englewood Cliffs, N.J.: Prentice-Hall, 1968.

Cameron, Ron. *Sayings Traditions in the Apocryphon of James* (HTS no. 34). Philadelphia: Fortress Press, 1984.

———. *The Other Gospels: Non-canonical Gospel Texts*. Philadelphia: Westminister Press, 1985.

von Campenhausen, Hans. *The Formation of the Christian Bible*. Translated by J. A. Baker. Philadelphia: Fortress Press, 1972.

Childs, Brevard S. *Introduction to the OT as Scripture*. Philadelphia: Fortress Press, 1985.

———. *The New Testament as Canon: An Introduction*. Philadelphia: Fortress Press, 1985.

---

*For full bibliographical information of some cited works, see the list of abbreviations, beginning on page 21.

————. *OT Theology in a Canonical Context*. Philadelphia: Fortress Press, 1986.

Collins, Raymond F. *Introduction to the New Testament*. Garden City, N.Y.: Doubleday, 1983.

Crossan, John Dominic. "The Cross that Spoke." *Forum* 3, no. 2 (1987):3-22.

Cullmann, Oscar. *The Early Church*. London: SCM Press, 1956.

Dungan, David L. "The New Testament Canon in Recent Study." *Int* 29, no. 4 (1975):339-51.

Dulles, Avery. "The Authority of Scripture: A Catholic Perspective." In *Scripture in the Jewish and Christian Traditions: Authority, Interpretation, Relevance*. Edited by Frederick E. Greenspahn. Nashville: Abingdon Press, 1982.

Dunn, James D. G. *Unity and Diversity in the New Testament*. Philadelphia: Westminster Press, 1977.

————. "Levels of Canonical Authority." *HBT* 4, no. 1 (1982):13-60.

Ewert, David. *From Ancient Tablets to Modern Translations*. Grand Rapids: Zondervan Publishing Co., 1983.

Farley, Edward. *Ecclesial Reflection*. Philadelphia: Fortress Press, 1982.

Farmer, William R. *Jesus and the Gospel*. Philadelphia: Fortress Press, 1982.

Farmer, William and Farkasfalvy, Denis. *The Formation of the New Testament Canon*. Edited by Harold W. Attridge. New York: Paulist Press, 1983.

Ferguson, Everett. "Canon Muratori: Date and Provenance." *Studia Patristica*. Edited by Elizabeth Livingstone. Berlin: Akamamie Verlag, 1982.

Fowler, Stephen. "The Canonical Approach of Brevard Childs." *ET* 96 (1985):173-75.

Freedman, David Noel. "Canon of the OT." In *IDBSup*. Edited by Keith Crim. Nashville: Abingdon Press, 1976.

Frend, W. H. C. *The Rise of Christianity*. Philadelphia: Fortress Press, 1984.

Froehlich, Karlfried. *Biblical Interpretation in the Early Church* (Sect). Philadelphia: Fortress Press, 1984.

Funk, Robert W. *Parables and Presence*. Philadelphia: Fortress Press, 1982.

Gamble, Harry Y. *The New Testament Canon: Its Making and Meaning* (GBS). Philadelphia: Fortress Press, 1985.

Georgi, Dieter. *The Opponents of Paul in Second Corinthians*. Philadelphia: Fortress Press, 1986.

Grant, Robert M. "Early Christians and Gnostics in the Graeco-Roman Society." In *The New Testament and Gnosis*, essays in honor of Robert McL. Wilson. Edited by A. H. B. Logan and A. J. M. Wedderburn. Edinburgh: T & T Clark, 1983.

————. *The Formation of the New Testament*. New York: Harper, 1965.

————. "From Tradition to Scripture and Back." In *Scripture and Tradition*. Edited by Joseph F. Kelley. Notre Dame: Fides Publishers, Inc., 1976.

————. "The New Testament Canon." In *CHB*, vol. 1. Cambridge, England: Cambridge University Press, 1976.

Grosheide, F. W. *Some Early Lists of the Books of the New Testament.* Leiden: E. J. Brill, 1948.

Hedrick, Charles W. and Hodgson, Robert, Jr., eds. *Nag Hammadi, Gnosticism, and Early Christianity.* Peabody, Mass.: Hendrickson Publishers, 1986.

Hennecke, Edgar. *New Testament Apocrypha.* Edited by Wilhelm Schneemelcher. Translated by R. McL. Wilson. 2 vols. Philadelphia: Westminster Press, 1963.

Jeffery, Arthur. "The Canon of the Old Testament." In *IB*, vol. 1. New York: Abingdon Press, 1952.

Jonas, Hans. *The Gnostic Religion.* Boston: Beacon Press, 1963.

Kalin, Everett R. "The Inspired Community: A Glance at Canon History." *CTM* 42 (1971):541-49.

Käsemann, Ernst. *Essays on New Testament Themes.* London: SCM Press, 1968.

Kealy, Sean P. "The Canon: An African Contribution." *BTB* 1 (1979):13-26.

Keck, Leander E. "Scripture and Canon." *QR* 3, no. 4 (1983): 8-26.

Kelly, J. N. D. *Early Christian Doctrines.* New York: Harper, 1978.

Kelly, Joseph F. *Why Is There a New Testament?* (BB) Wilmington, Del.: Michael Glazier, 1986.

Knierim, Rolf. "The Task of Old Testament Theology." *HBT* 6, no. 1 (1984):25-43.

Koester, Helmut. "Apocryphal and Canonical Gospels." *HTR* 73 (1980):105-30.

———. "GNOMAI DIAPHOROI: The Origin and Nature of Diversification in the History of Early Christianity." In *Trajectories through Early Christianity.* Edited by James M. Robinson and Helmut Koester. Philadelphia: Fortress Press, 1971.

———. "Gnostic Sayings and Controversy Traditions in John 8:12-59." In *Nag Hammadi, Gnosticism, and Early Christianity.* Edited by Charles W. Hedrick and Robert Hodgson, Jr. Peabody, Mass.: Hendrickson Publishers, 1986.

———. *Introduction to the New Testament.* 2 vols. Philadelphia: Fortress Press, 1982.

———. *Synoptische Überlieferung bei den apostolischen Vätern.* Berlin: Akademie Verlag, 1957.

Kugel, James L. and Greer, Rowan A. *Early Biblical Interpretation.* Edited by Wayne A. Meeks. Philadelphia: Westminster Press, 1986.

Kümmel, Werner Georg. *Introduction to the New Testament.* Translated by A. J. Mattill, Jr. New York: Abingdon Press, 1966.

Lampe, G. W. H. "The Early Church." In *Scripture and Tradition.* Edited by F. W. Dillistone. London: Lutterworth Press, 1955.

Layton, Bentley. *The Gnostic Scriptures.* Garden City, N.Y.: Doubleday, 1987.

Leaney, A. R. C. *The Jewish and Christian World.* Cambridge, England: Cambridge University Press, 1984.

Leiman, Sid Z. "Inspiration and Canonicity: Reflections on the Formation of the

Biblical Canon." In *Jewish and Christian Self-Definition*, vol. 2. Edited by
E. P. Sanders et al. Philadelphia: Fortress Press, 1981.

Lewis, Jack P. "What Do We Mean by Jabneh?" *JBR* 32 (1964):125-32.

Lighthouse, Jack N. "The Formation of the Biblical Canon in Judaism of Late
Antiquity: Prolegomenon to a General Resassessment." *SR* 8, no. 2
(1978):135-42.

Lohse, Eduard. *The Formation of the New Testament*. Translated by Eugene
Boring. Nashville: Abingdon Press, 1977.

Metzger, Bruce M. "Canon of the New Testament." In *Dictionary of the Bible*.
Edited by James Hastings. Edinburgh: T & T Clark, 1963.

———. *The Canon of the New Testament: Its Origin, Development, and Significance*. Oxford: Clarendon Press, 1987.

Moore, George F. "The Definition of the Jewish Canon and the Repudiation of
Christian Scriptures." In *The Canon and Masorah of the New Hebrew
Bible*. Edited by Sid Z. Leiman. New York: KTAV Publishing House, 1974.

Patterson, L. G. "Irenaeus and the Valentinians: The Emergence of a Christian
Scripture." Unpublished article obtained from the author.

Pfeiffer, R. H. "Canon of the OT," In *IDB*. Edited by George Arthur Buttrick,
vol. 1. New York: Abingdon Press, 1962.

Rudolph, Kurt. *Gnosis: The Nature and History of Gnosticism*. San Francisco:
Harper, 1987.

———. "'Gnosis' and 'Gnosticism': The Problems of Their Definition and Their
Relation to the Writings of the New Testament." In *The New Testament and
Gnosis. Essays in Honor of Robert McL. Wilson*. Edited by A. H. B. Logan
and A. J. M. Wedderburn. Edinburgh: T & T Clark, 1983.

Sanders, James A. *Canon and Community*. Philadelphia: Fortress Press, 1984.

———. *From Sacred Story to Sacred Text*. Philadelphia: Fortress Press, 1987.

———. "Text and Canon: Old Testament and New." Mélanges Dominique Barthelemy: *Etudes bibliques*. Edited by Pierre Casetti, Othmar Keel, and
Adrian Scheuber. Orbis Biblicus et Orientalis 38. Fribourg: Editions Universitaires; Göttingen: Vanderhoeck & Ruprecht, 1981.

———. *Torah and Canon*. Philadelphia: Fortress Press, 1972.

Schneemelcher, Wilhelm. "General Introduction." In *New Testament Apocrypha*. Edited by Wilhelm Schneemelcher. Translated by George Ogg. Philadelphia: Westminster Press, 1963.

Schrenk, Gottlob. "γραφή," *TDNT*. Edited by Gerhard Kittel. Translated by
Geoffrey W. Bromiley. vol. 1. Grand Rapids: Wm. B. Eerdmans Co., 1965.

Shires, Henry M. *Finding the Old Testament in the New*. Philadelphia: Westminster Press, 1974.

Silberman, Lou H. "The Making of the Old Testament Canon." In *The Interpreter's One Volume Commentary on the Bible*. Edited by Charles M. Laymon. New York: Abingdon Press, 1971.

Souter, Alexander. *The Text and Canon of the New Testament*. New York:
Charles Scribner's Sons, 1917.

Stendahl, Krister. "Ancient Scripture in the Modern World." In *Scripture in the Jewish and Christian Traditions: Authority, Interpretation, Relevance.* Edited by Frederick E. Greenspahn. Nashville: Abingdon Press, 1982.

———. *Meanings.* Philadelphia: Fortress Press, 1984.

———. "The Apocalypse of John and the Epistles of Paul in the Muratorian Fragment." In *Current Issues in New Testament Interpretation: Essays in Honor of Otto A. Piper.* Edited by W. Klassen and G. T. Snyder. New York: Harper, 1962.

Sundberg, Albert C., Jr. "The Bible Canon and the Christian Doctrine of Inspiration." *Int* 29, no. 4 (1975):352-71.

———. "Canon Muratori: A Fourth-Century List." *HTR* 66, no. 1 (1973):1-41.

———. "Canon of the NT." In *IDBSup.* Edited by Keith Crim. Nashville: Abingdon, 1976.

———. "The Making of the New Testament Canon." In *The Interpreter's One Volume Commentary on the Bible.* Edited by Charles M. Laymon. New York: Abingdon Press, 1971.

———. *The Old Testament of the Early Church.* Cambridge, Mass.: Harvard University Press, 1964.

Theron, Daniel J. *Evidence of Tradition.* Grand Rapids: Baker Book House, 1980.

Tucker, Gene M. "Prophetic Superscriptions and the Growth of a Canon." In *Canon and Authority: Essays in Old Testament Religion and Theology.* Edited by G. W. Coats and B. D. Long. Philadelphia: Fortress Press, 1977.

Wainwright, Geoffrey. "The New Testament as Canon." *SJT* 28 (1975):551-71.

Williams, R. R. *Authority in the Apostolic Age.* London: SCM Press, 1950.

Wisse, Frederik. "The Use of Early Christian Literature as Evidence for Inner Diversity and Conflict." In *Nag Hammadi, Gnosticism, and Early Christianity.* Edited by Charles W. Hedrick and Robert Hodgson, Jr. Peabody, Mass.: Hendrickson Publishers, 1986.